"… to us such an explanation seems absurdly illogical. But it seems so to us only because we start from assumptions wholly different from those of primitive man … We would no more put it down to sorcery than he to natural causes. His mental functioning does not differ in any fundamental way from ours. It is, as I have said, his assumptions alone that distinguish him from ourselves." – Carl Jung, *Civilization in Transition*

"The organizing idea that is destined to rule keeps growing deep down - it begins to command, slowly it leads us back from side roads and wrong roads; it prepares single qualities and fitnesses that will one day prove to be indispensable as a means toward a whole - one by one, it trains all subservient capacities before giving any hint of the dominant task, goal, aim or meaning." – Friedrich Nietzsche, *Ecce Homo*

"How is it that complex and admirable ancient civilizations could have developed and flourished, initially, if they were predicated upon nonsense? ... Is it not more likely that we just do not know how it could be that traditional notions are *right*, given their *appearance* of extreme irrationality?" – Jordan Peterson, *Maps of Meaning*

"Crises are somehow connected to forgetting." – Claudio Ciborra, *The Labyrinths of Information*

THE ORGANIZING IDEA

A RETURN TO GOOD AND EVIL

JASON SIMPSON

Preface

It is beginning to dawn on some people that we are in the middle of a mass psychosis fueled by an age of cowardice. Contrary to popular culture and recent books, such an idea is definitely not new. In fact, the phenomenon and everything that leads up to it was thoroughly documented by Carl Jung almost 100 years ago, and the seeds of those ideas were planted by Friedrich Nietzsche some 50 years before that (it can even be argued that all of this reaches back far earlier). However, this idea being salient in the minds of those outside of the upper echelons of existentialist and psychoanalytic thought definitely is new, as the idea of mass psychosis has just recently been proposed by some of the most published and awarded 'hard' scientists on earth. Given how psychology (depth psychology in particular) and existentialism have always been treated by outsiders as something akin to astrology and to be considered thoroughly laughable, I knew that I was on to something with this book when the 'other side' just recently started to agree with the more serious warnings coming from psychology and existentialism that had been more or less ignored for 150 years with two world wars and a cold war in the process. "When the hell is anyone going to notice?!" I thought to myself over and over. Well, apparently that time is now, and that is partly why I have decided to publish this book.

However, if we were to simply stop at pointing out the current mass psychosis, we would get no further than we have in the last 100 years every time that one occurs (and then occurs again, and again, and again...). The question almost nobody ever asks is "why?", and I mean *really* "why?" It is not enough to say, "well, 200 million people dead, I guess the lesson learned is that you shouldn't be so intolerant", which if it were not for the fact that 200 million dead people at the hands of left- and right-wing ideology is about the most fucked up thing that I can think of, then the complete and utter lack of anything truly introspective would be the real "laughable" material. But I have come to understand that the lack of asking "why" is not just limited to the mass psychoses but, rather, it is something that affects the totality of human enquiry, including most areas of enquiry in Academia, mainly because if one keeps pushing the "why" too much, then one ends up in extremely uncomfortable territory, i.e., an actual answer, i.e., something that might lead to an actual solution. And as Chuck Palahniuk once pointed out on Joe Rogan, people have no interest whatsoever in having any of their problems actually solved (at least in our current age). Except that we have reached a critical point where society simply cannot "have their cake and eat it too". The fact is that what we see before us *must* be solved; the solution *requires* going down the road of extreme discomfort for *everyone*, and there is simply no putting it off or sweeping it under the rug any longer – "win or lose our minds" indeed.

The primary contribution of this book is to give an unequivocal, root answer to why we are seeing a mass psychosis or any of the previous ones as well as what leads to it. At the same time, it also lays out the opposite: why we might have ever seen mass thriving and what leads to that. It builds on, but goes one step beyond, the works of Jung, and even reaches back to Nietzsche to consider some very important points that he might have missed (hence, the title of the book).

The ideas in this book are the evolution and culmination of nearly 40 years of thought, experience, professional practice, experimentation, and the phenomena that I investigated in my Information Systems Ph.D., which all converged and crystalized in the wake of the events of the last couple of years. This book came into being not because I thought it would be fun to write a book right in the middle of one of the most personally stressful and societally chaotic times of my life, but because I was absolutely compelled to do so. I was seeing my Ph.D. material (that started over 10 years ago) come to life in every news outlet and every other conceivable form of media on the planet. Not only that, and this is the far more important point, there was this 'other' compelling force that was doing most of the pushing, which was something that I had experienced before. And just like before, I knew that thoughts, ideas, and how they all hung together would burst into view and I had better capture them before they 'escaped'. So, I charged the voice recorder and dictated everything coming through, all day, every day, for about a month and a half. I am sure that to an outside observer I indeed appeared like a madman. Then I did what any researcher would do if this were interview material: I transcribed and coded it. Then I structured the text and started filling it in, having no 'real' idea how I was doing any of it or where it was coming from. And in many ways, that process is something that I try to get at in this book, and I was writing about it as I was experiencing it.

One thing that I personally find very interesting about all of this is that I never set out to do any of this. All I wanted to do, or so I thought, was to get to the bottom of why I had seen people doing ridiculous (according to my perspective) things during my Information Technology/Systems career, specifically why people flat out rejected certain technologies or, better yet, *information...* That resulted in the investigation of identity, core psychological constructs, and anything else that I could find in any body of literature that might have something to say on the matter. The key to my methodology was a technique, covered briefly in this book, that incessantly asked "why?" to the participants in my study. So, naturally, when my Ph.D. was over, I couldn't just stop with the answers I had gotten. I turned my attention to much deeper topics in order to understand the answers, meaning I incessantly asked "why" regarding my answers that were already gotten by incessantly asking "why". This is something that is thoroughly beaten out of most of us at an early age because at an early age the people to whom we keep doing this get quite irritated, and then we are made to feel that doing so is a completely stupid thing to do because there is supposedly no answer, something that continues into adulthood if one 'relapses' – it is even alive and well in the Academy! As it turns out, there are answers, and quite obvious ones at that, it's just that almost *no one* (including philosophers) has the stomach for them, at least up to now.

Although it sounds so cliché that I can barely type it, this book is about the root problem of the world, the solution to that problem, and I provide general guidelines for how to live one's life in order to thrive in the face of mass psychosis. I hope that if enough individuals take the step towards keeping a certain idea salient, then a critical mass will eventually build, and even if we ran into new problems, which would surely happen, then we would survive the current breakdown to have some kind of future that would at least be very different to 'this'. I don't know about you, but whatever that is, I'd take it... And, again, Jung saw all of this coming. The idea of a soon-to-be new aeon was put forth by Jung in his mid to later work, which people tend to forget or never even acknowledge was empirically based and anything but conjecture.

I am sort of beating around the bush as to "what this book is about", but I don't want to give too much away in the spirit of phenomenology, and it is also my experience that if you tell people exactly what is coming without 'backing into it' instead, especially when talking about highly contentious topics, then they tend to reject the information... I am, after all, one of the world's leading experts on the matter. What I can tell you is that this book is ultimately a phenomenological account of Projection. However, the road to truly making Projection intelligible is a long one, which starts with looking at the societal and personal contradiction, understanding how we all came to be so contradictory, looking at THE current contradiction, and how this might be overcome.

Make no mistake, this text is one of the most abrasive things ever written *because it has to be*, and perhaps you will figure out the necessity and why it might apply to so many other things. However, with the right perspective and patience, it can also be one of the most life-changing. One could even say that I provide a sort of theory on how all of 'this' works. So, I invite you to come with me on a journey through the most taboo of ideas and get to the root of it all. I promise that you will never look at 'this' or 'other than this' the same ever again.

Table of Contents

List of Figures

Introduction

There is a sort of schizophrenia in our world today where "anything is possible" but at the same time "nothing matters" because all of 'this' came from nowhere, is not going anywhere, exists for no reason, and we know this beyond a shadow of a doubt.

Using the term schizophrenia to describe this state is completely warranted since almost every single person – regardless of educational level or intellect – will read what I just wrote, and the absurdly blatant contradiction will not even be processed as such.

Tied up with this insanity is the fact that scientists, philosophers, and now anyone who can write a blog post or record a video, have been arguing for at least 2000 years about "free will" versus "determinism" or any other related variant of, or tangentially related to, this dichotomy (alive—not alive, conscious—unconscious), when almost none of these people have ever (even remotely) clearly and unambiguously defined what they mean by 'you' – a definition that is *required* if this dichotomy was going to be debated in the first place!

As a result of nobody other than a handful of misfits pointing out or taking seriously this insanity, our scientific, philosophical, and religious landscapes have remained completely and wholly contradictory to their core, leading to a sea of ever increasingly sophisticated systems aimed at patching the holes created by the very axioms of those systems.

The culprit is the same as it always has been, time and time again, throughout every major aeon, empire, political and social movement, and form of human being: misaligned, and increasingly unconscious (or purposely backgrounded), assumptions.

Assumptions are quite literally everything. They explain all that is seemingly baffling and help to manifest reality itself. In basic logic, one learns that everything stems from assumptions because you simply cannot have an argument (or story... or narrative... or...) without them. Yet they are the very things that are never mentioned. Or if one is at all aware of them then they are dismissed as irrelevant, as their explication doesn't lend very well to Herd argumentation and theatrics. If you doubt this, search around, and try finding an argument that is explicitly based on assumption – root rather than symptom. In almost 100% of supposed 'arguments', regardless of how sophisticated, there is one set of conclusions pointing at another set of conclusions, with the respective proponents barking, mooing, and baaing back and forth at each another in a never-ending circle of theatrical projection. I used to think academics and intellectuals did this on purpose – a sort of job security if you will. However, it eventually became painfully clear to me that they weren't, and they are just as much a part of the Herd as the redneck fundamentalist screeching down the road in their redneck mobile, drunk, on the way home to beat their spouse.

The assumption that characterized the Dark Ages in Europe on a whole was: *all* that mattered was something 'other than this', which came in at least a couple of major forms. Not surprisingly, 'this' crumbled – why put any effort into 'this' if it doesn't matter? Then, during the Enlightenment period (no doubt fueled by hundreds of years of a certain type of misery), Europeans rediscovered the importance of 'this', which led to thriving, for a while. However, that same turn has led to the current scientific, philosophic, and popular culture of *nothing* other than 'this', which not surprisingly has led to the spiritual desert littered with a nanny-state-dependent populace and their narcissistic post-totalitarian-structure-enforcing counterparts that we see before us, hell-bent on enforcing complete and total personal irresponsibility – why put any effort into 'other than this' if it doesn't matter or, indeed, it doesn't even exist?

ALL psychological and sociological dysfunction can be traced to either of the one-sided explicit or implicit assumptions above. However, in our age, the predominant assumption is that there is nothing other than 'this'. By contrast, ALL psychological, sociological, and cultural thriving can be traced to the very rare balance of *both*.

And do you know what is really something, how should I say, special? Is that even though the populace of the world is currently determined to prove and even enforce the assumption that there is nothing other than 'this', they can't even get their basic story, laws, philosophies, political ideologies, and/or scientific models to align with the very thing that they are trying to enforce. Even though there is supposedly *nothing* other than 'this', 'THEY' are somehow *in* 'this', and, according to their discourse, totally stopped being 'this' at some point... As I said, the term schizophrenia is completely warranted, and almost no one will process the contradiction.

This is just the tip of the iceberg, but one might go ahead and assume that they have already worked out my enemy, taken the posture of a proper academic, and cherry-picked one or more things above while conveniently discarding the rest to support their particular set of political and personal constructs – i.e., their 'side'. However, I have spent my entire adult life studying (and living) these 'sides', as well as how to weaponize language and constructs in order to obliterate, not *a* side, but the supposed mutual exclusivity of both sides of some dichotomy. As Alan Watts pointed out, "this entire universe is an on-off system", and one of the tenets (again, almost always conveniently thrown out when push comes to shove) of Jung's psychology and phenomenology is that if you try to get rid of one 'side' it will just come back in an even more forceful or monstrous form than before. Both Watts and Jung (among others) therefore pointed out the *necessity* of any 'side', and how *one automatically implies and gives existence to the other*. Or put another way: humans conceptually split the thing into two, based on *their* systems, and then pondered for thousands of years as to which one is 'true', 'real', 'moral', 'ethical', or should or should not have the right to exist, when they were the ones who did the splitting!

You simply cannot have light without dark, regardless of whether these are properties, holograph, or illusion. Even many poststructuralist texts are based on this idea that one thing cannot exist except in relation to another. And yet, at the same time, what is the *aim* of post-structuralism? Modernism? Post-modernism? Religious fundamentalism? Science? Politics? Group identity?

Swinging in one direction leads to and promotes total irresponsibility in another, and up until now the treatment of 'other than this' vs 'this' has resembled a moth bashing around a room on its way towards a light. My goal is to show the last step to the light, even if it results in becoming enflamed. And it starts with acknowledging where we are in history and that there is currently an all-out war on the individual – not just on their 'rights' or even their responsibilities, but the sovereignty of individual consciousness itself. Furthermore, I do not fall into some lame blame trap as would be expected but show how this entire process was *necessary*.

Continuity, particularly with respect to The Big Picture, is something that seems to have only been discussed a few times in all of recorded history, then of course thrown out in any serious discussion or, again, when real life is actually occurring and/or is inconvenient. For millennia we have gone on in one way or another about The End. It permeates politics, religion, science, philosophy, and you can't stop hearing it from the fundamentalist, the theoretical physicist, or the couch intellectual going on about evolution, transcendence, or enlightenment. Always assuming, again paradoxically, that there is nothing other than 'this'. Or that 'this' is not a means or a source for more things exactly or nearly like 'this', whereby a new or different 'this' might equate to something along the lines of starting over. I know, the horror! It might even be possible that you *alone* could be in charge of it! But the idea is to transcend that process, no? To bring it to its End? And what happens, *exactly*, at this supposed End, hmm? A singularity is a singularity is a singularity... The nature of singularity doesn't change just because the content between convergences of a certain type of singularity disrupts some Herd worldview. Furthermore, if one has a shred of imagination, Continuity could be achieved by something other than a simple loop... The End is not inevitable nor is Continuity improbable, and if the argument for Continuity is baseless then equally so is the argument for The End.

"But it has to end! Someone *SAVE* me! Save me from my-Self! PLEASE!!! Religion! Government! Politics! Nirvana! Social movement! Anything! PLEASE!!! ANYTHING IS POSSIBLE!... *WE HAVE TO STOP 'THIS'*!!! WAIT, WHAT???"

At every opportunity, just like a bratty little teenager or early twenty-something, society has tried to offload responsibility to one thing or another in some desperate attempt to not be reminded of who and what we are, scared to death of what we know and feel is coming – what the psyche and *Gestell* simply will not allow to stay hidden for much longer. All signs are pointing to it. Some know it because certain experiences won't allow one to 'un-see' it. Some that I personally know have conveniently 'forgotten' and swept it under the rug, engrossing themselves in some other lie hoping that it will simply go away. Everyone is kicking and screaming, conjuring up the most sophisticated semantic inertial systems the world has ever seen in the final showdown to rid the world of once and for all of 'other than this'. I for one have had enough. I am not playing your game anymore. I am not listening to you anymore. I am facing it head-on. My spine is intact. The only thing I ever

did wrong was doubt my-Self. I AM.
– Arana Hills, Queensland, Australia, 7 June 2021

Part 1: The schizophrenia of the modern world

The overall thesis of this book is that assumptions are quite literally everything. However, to even begin to get at what I mean by that, it is necessary to start at the most grounded and concrete territory of my philosophy.

To begin, I outline the schizophrenia of our modern world, how and why this problem manifests, why people are generally unaware of it, how it is reinforced via what Havel calls the "post-totalitarian structure", and reconsider the notion of mental illness in light of these points.

Here I lay a foundation for what is presented in Part 2 where I pick apart society's core contradiction and offer an alternative view on a certain universal assumption, which then leads to a philosophy of life in Part 3 that equates to a return to Good and Evil based on having cleared up that core contradiction (or at least an alternative to the current schizophrenic world that lives in this contradiction). I believe the concrete foundation presented here is not only essential in thoroughly understanding the philosophy but is also essential to any understanding of human behavior in general. It is quite common for philosophers or laypeople to point out contradictions, but what is never done is to point out why this is happening and why that "why" is so important.

The point of Part 1 is to phenomenologically examine contradiction itself and its related aspects before talking about THE contradiction in Part 2, and I attempt to do so in a way that makes the philosophy accessible to people other than those who have been studying philosophy their whole lives. Simon Sinek once said that he could not understand why academics only speak in a way that other academics can understand them, and if one speaks in a way that a truck driver can understand what is being said, then both academics and truck drivers can understand. Indeed, one has to wonder why 'real' philosophers seldom do this... This part illustrates that precise phenomenon; however, I do not just pick on academics and philosophers – I am an equal opportunity annoyer; nobody is spared. And so, this is also my way of weeding out the weak-minded and sheep who dress in intellectual and philosophical costumes.

I start with the most accessible and familiar, and yet most academically despicable, form of communication that we currently have: the rant.

A sea of contradictions

One does not have to look very far to find core value contradictions. When I say, "core value contradictions", I could just as easily say the things, ideas, ways of life, etc. that people claim to believe in most but then do not do or embody those very things; or things that people claim to be the most horrible things one can do and yet they are doing those very things. If you know what you are looking for you can find them in nearly any person, institution, political party, government, philosophy, or whatever else espouses some set of values or another. This was a realm that I sort of 'fell into' during my Ph.D. More about that later, but suffice to say that the deeper I dug, the more this reality began to make itself apparent, and now I cannot stop seeing it even if I wanted to stop. Indeed, it is one of those life experiences that I sometimes wish that I could go back and undo, but then the Herd darts blindly into the next unconscious phenomenon that disrupts all life for anyone who is not entirely brain dead, and that feeling gets squashed pretty damn quickly.

While there is an endless sea of examples of core value contradictions, I will cover a few of my favorites. Most of this section will sound like an angry rant because, well, it is. However, every piece of what is presented here is important, is presented this way for a reason, will be illuminated as we proceed, and all of this will come around full circle. Indeed, one should not be so quick to dismiss rants...

Let us start with the left and right wing. Ah yes, that timeless classic where one has a certain temperament, starts screaming for one or the other side based on that temperament, and then comes up with all kinds of fantastic justifications that resemble something along the lines of two street gangs – maybe even the Bloods and the Crypts; they even sported red and blue! – in South Central Los Angeles justifying what they do because "dis ouwa hood yo". Indeed, you two are sooooo different.

Some of the most sensitive topics on the left and right are those of abortion and the death penalty. When it comes to abortion, the left-wing states that you should have the right to kill while the right-wing states that you have no right to kill. However, when it comes to the death penalty, the left all of the sudden believes that you have no right to kill even though someone has committed an atrocious crime (probably killing one or more innocent people, something they are vehemently against) and the right-wing suddenly believes that you have every right to kill. What is the 'argument' on either side? A debate over whether something is 'alive' or not; 'human' or not, because we never quite figured that one out, even though we did, but, then again, no we did not? No. We did not. Or when it comes to later in life, the 'argument' is based on consciousness and intent, because we figured all that out already as well, did we not? No. We did not. Here we see the first instance of an 'argument' that is *based* on absolutely *nothing*...

This leads to another sensitive right and left topic around eating meat. In this instance, it is now ok for the right-wing to kill because the things being killed are not quite considered sentient beings (see above); however, it seems to me that an animal is far more sentient than a fetus, but that is just me. Maybe something to do with the ability to walk around, feel pain, respond with emotion, etc. Maybe even the right-winger finally simply admits that it is just because they are not human, and humans are more important! And that is just the way it is! That sounds as shaky and poorly thought out as your left-winger counterparts regarding fetuses, you brain-dead shit. The solution on the left-wing is to eat more plants. That is interesting because I am trying to figure out what happens to all the forests when more room is made for the billions of people that now need to eat plants (that need proper soil, rotation, etc.) instead of meat. Speaking of billions of people, we do have a sustainability problem in any case and, given those realities, we should probably let all the murders take up resources as well as let the masses who half-assed it every, single, step, through life, live by any means possible – but the hell with your stupid fetus that might not have, you brain dead shit.

Then there is the left- and right-wing home life. George Kelly[1] was the first to point this out that I am aware of, but have you ever stopped and compared everything coming out of a left or right-winger's mouth and compared that to the environment and atmosphere in their home? The right-winger will preach on and on about being firm, there need to be consequences for peoples' actions, take life head-on, and so on. Yet nearly every right-wing household that I have ever stepped foot in was flooded with

[1] Kelly, G.A. (1955), *The Psychology of Personal Constructs*, W. W. Norton & Company, Inc., New York, NY.

alcohol, antidepressants, or benzodiazepines, combined with an attitude of being above the law and protecting their children at all costs against any misdeed carried out in order to protect the family image. The left-winger will preach on and on about compassion and understanding, but nearly every left-wing household that I have ever stepped foot in is cold, rigid, and everyone is constantly walking on eggshells out of fear of being judged and/or eliciting some Anima/Animus-possessed rampage. And if you want to find the largest population of dysfunctional children, just look to the left-wing households. It couldn't possibly be that violence and judgment comes in another *form*, could it? No, that would be impossible, because you have stated that you are the kind of person that is against violence – you even take care of stray animals! You might have even published a critical theory paper on the violence of sex and how penises stab vaginas, so you are the expert in violence in other forms. No, you could never be violent or judge. Impossible!

And then there are the authoritarian dictatorships of the 20th century, with both sides pretending that their philosophy did not kill millions of people. Although, I do have to say that the left-wing wins the absolute-stupid-moron-of-the-century award for constantly using the term "Nazi", given that the right-wing killed approximately 10 million people in that century but the left-wing slaughtered a whopping 100 to 200 million people, making the holocaust an *actual* warm-up. We do not even know the actual death toll. And those people are … still in power! Absolutely acceptable! We would not want to be without our sweet and sour pork, now would we? And yeah, it does seem quite compassionate and fair to kill a couple hundred million people that do not agree with you – at least all those capitalist pigs are gon… oh wait, no,

China is the largest capitalist country in the world now, concentration camps intact. "Hey bro, take this flyer – have you ever heard of Marxism?"

In either case of left or right, it could not possibly be that both of you are unashamedly and completely avoiding responsibility based on your personal temperament and then finding a political ideology to sign off on it, could it?! (I am somehow reminded of "manifest destiny") I mean, when that whole religion thing crumbled you had to find something to replace it. But no, you are not like those "morons", are you? Your argument is entirely coherent. Your actions are completely aligned with your core values, as we have clearly seen. I could go on for the entire book about the left and right-wing, but I will stop there – you both disgust me to the point of rage. And no, I do not care about the endless sea of 'nuances' in your 'argument' because, again, IT IS NOT BASED ON ANYTHING!!! Oh, and by the way, have you never heard of the idea of "divide and conquer"? The very thing that you keep pointing at as the salvation for all of your problems definitely has…

America – land of the free. At over 2 million prison inmates at the time of this book, it is the largest incarcerated country in the world with roughly 80% of incarcerations for minor drug offenses. Looks like one is free to decide what substances they put into their own body; free to explore their own consciousness; as long as they are ok with the free ride to prison. Oh, that kind of free! Or maybe it is being free to choose whatever career you want so that you can work one of the longest workweeks on planet earth, often times the weekends too, to have a whole TWO WEEKS off per year! Wow, so much freedom! I can certainly understand why the rest of the world is "jealous" of all that freedom. Did it ever occur to you that actual freedom requires actual individual responsibility? And that that is *difficult*? And that the whole thing requires sustained effort towards it? But how could anyone ever argue with a slogan that is repeated and printed over and over and over and over and over? Especially since the difference between your obvious total lack of freedom and that seen in communist totalitarian dictatorships is one of pure semantics. In one instance the State owns everything, in other the Corporation. "Freedom? Yeah, right..."

Australia – no worries! Not worried at all about the car that just tried to pass you. Not worried at all about the suburb that you or your friends live in. Not worried at all about the person that just walked in to help you sort out all your problems that you got yourself into with your "she'll be 'right"-half-assed attitude who you just collectively mowed down because they "thought they were better" than you. Not worried at all about Coronavirus or the fact that closing your borders and making it illegal for your citizens to leave the country (only surpassed by North Korea and the former Soviet Union) to avoid it is the only way you will ever (briefly) make world news, and definitely not worried that the rest of the world has already moved on and forgotten about you because they were less worried. But then, you *actually* are not worried about continuing to cram millions of people into cities with no respective increase in infrastructure or the suffocating conditions it's causing. "Naaaah worries, I *really am* enjoying this flat white while sitting a half-meter away from the congested road, that's why I just ran someone off the road before I got here – look at the 'joy' on my face – please believe me!" Australia, no worries... Australia is so insecure that they are the world-famous poster child for national insecurity, it has been written about by famous authors, and because they are so desperate to not be desperate, they are completely unaware of this! What is really unbelievable is with all that no-worrying and "she'll be 'right'", Australia is one incident or crisis away from becoming a totalitarian police state – they basically already are. No worries indeed. Tell me Australia, when you run out of rocks to sell, or your growth-at-all-costs mentality catches up to the available resources you have, what then? You really haven't thought about it, have you? Or have you?...

China – the land of Yin and Yang – the birthplace of Confucius and Daoism – level-headed being and that which happens of itself. I guess that's why the need to slaughter at least 100 million people, continue to send millions to re-education camps, and torture all those that disagree with you. You even now have eyes on the rest of the world so that you can *force* your way of 'life'. And isn't it interesting that you now have become the absolute epitome of the very thing you used as justification for all this in the first place? "That which happens of itself" – what a fucking joke. What was once a thriving culture of enlightenment and individual way of life is now a cesspool and the prime promotor of individual irresponsibility because the poor little Chinese people got tired of living the actual philosophy that they had come up with. And now what you have come up with is something so much more monstrous that one wonders if there is a shred of balance of anything left anywhere in China. China is the epitome of not knowing the difference between knowing the path and walking the path.

Academia – the place to go to work on your ideas – a haven for intellectual freedom for nearly 2000 years. That's a nice marketing

16

spiel, however, the fact of the matter is that Academia is the most rigid and dogmatic 'intellectual' realm on the planet. A place where a significant number of researchers are at this very moment arguing over the validity and predictability of some model or other, but then if you bring up the name Ray Kurzweil, or God forbid his model, you might just find out what it was like to be a Jew in Nazi Germany. If you bring up Carl Jung, Ray Kurzweil, and Timothy Leary all at the same time, you are now Satan spawn, and will be pinned down and ridiculed until the exorcist can arrive. Again, it could not possibly be that these three people alone have given more insight into everything in our world than every other academic in the past 200 years combined, could it? If you really want to make a social scientist or psychologist angry, bring up the most widely used model by business (because it's easy and it *works* concerning why it was actually designed…) that has ever existed with respect to personality: the Myers-Briggs Type Indicator (based on Jung's work); gnashing of teeth will certainly follow. I can honestly say that in all of my years in Academia, the most straightforward of studies that I did that had the most straightforward of implications were the exact things that were flat-out rejected. Meanwhile, I partook in one collaborative 'study' that was probably founded on lies, it was completely convoluted, but it contained all the buzzwords and politics that my discipline's academics loved, and so it was an absolute hit! Academia – the place to work on 'your' ideas as long as your ideas are someone else's ideas that already align with the politics and the content that is allowed to be printed (gee, what does that sound like?); the place where if you find a model that predicts 75 to 99% of something you are passive-aggressively ostracized when rarely does anything that is accepted achieve any higher than 20%; the place that if you do indeed have an original thought, run!… Academia's claim when entering a Ph.D. program is that in order to graduate a person must show that they are an independent, critical thinker capable of doing original research. As both Nietzsche and Jung pointed out, as well as what Sartre learned as a student, this is complete and utter bullshit. However, if you would like to be a part of an institution that breeds complete and total *de*pendency, do not want to think for yourself, and have a penchant for having your consciousness ruled and abused through narcissism, Academia might be the place for you.

Philosophy – the love of wisdom – an area where free thinkers can take the whole history of human knowledge and wisdom and contribute to it so that we may live better lives or comprehend those lives better. But have you ever noticed that 'philosophy' becomes more and more myopic by the year? And at the same time, the word that is all the rage these days is "holism"? Are you kidding me? Have you, Mr., Ms., or Mx. 'philosopher' ever noticed that your philosophical 'progression' follows the same linear pattern as fashion trends? You could never go so low as to consider any philosophy that covers old ground – you've moved well beyond that. But then again, if I look around, it would seem that *everyone* has moved well beyond that, snowflake. Instead of putting something together that would be in the same universe as actually novel, or help people live their lives more fully, the modern philosophical contribution is to see how narrow one can make a philosophy and still get people to pay attention and/or what new scapegoat can be flushed out to pin all of one's problems on. Philosophy… what a crock of shit. There has not been a single decent and proper philosophical contribution since 1966. Speaking of which, if you are not a philosopher and want to get one to give you the 'deer in the headlights' look, simply ask for their thoughts

18

on Alan Watts... Never heard of him, Mr., Ms., or Mx. 'philosopher'? It's probably because his philosophy is the *epitome* of holism, and he contributed more in a single book than you and all of your comrades combined in the last 60 years.

As I said, this could go on almost indefinitely. I could talk about Christians and their supposed Christ-like life when anyone who has any sense at all could compare the two and observe that they are doing the exact opposite, particularly with respect to individuation and bravery. I could talk about those people who are always telling others to go to the darkest and most difficult places possible while obviously not doing anything remotely close to that themselves. It actually would never end within a single book or maybe even my lifetime if I continuously documented it until I was dead, and this is actually a very important point. However, I think I have done a fairly good job of casting the net wide enough to get the broader point across, which was to give salient examples of contradiction that anyone could notice in others but also, given how wide I cast the net, to begin to notice it in themselves. Some might not be offended at all as they might already know all of this, but I'm also trying to reach the offended and, ironically enough, this is one way to do it. I was also trying to provide an easy-to-understand primer to show how what follows in this book manifests on a mass scale, and if I had immediately launched right into understanding contradiction and inertia, I'd lose the very audience that is in the most need of this understanding. Regardless of how one feels about it, *divisiveness is the only thing that gets peoples' attention.* At the same time, it also tends to make one want to throw one's hands up in the air, give up, and walk away.

It is also therefore no wonder that intellectuals insist on relativizing everything that seems to be a product of the social realm. But just like arguing for or against the supposed greatness of democracy without first examining the populace that constitutes it, is it fair to relativize *everything* based on the Herd and its members' inability to get their own stories straight? Even Nietzsche did this when he pointed at one thing that could have just as well been a proper philosophy that could have indeed aligned with his own, and conflated it with the way that the Herd had *reacted to* it. Although Kierkegaard might have made a different mistake, he obviously did not make that one; and in my opinion (because we'll never truly know), that is why Kierkegaard was psychologically more than fine while Nietzsche went insane, even though both held philosophies that would have certainly resulted in extreme isolation, especially in that particular point in history. As the story that we have all come to know goes, on the last semi-coherent day of his life, after years of suffering and physical agony combined with isolation, non-recognition, and derision, Nietzsche walked across a street, saw a horse being flogged, threw his arms around it, broke into tears, and yelled out "I understand you!" and collapsed. Maybe he found out the hard way, as so many psychotics do, that identity and superordinate constructs are a real bitch.

I have presented a low-fidelity version of contradiction as it manifests at a more 'social' level – now I will turn to the far higher-fidelity and far more insightful level of the individual, where we can not only illuminate the process of contradiction, but also see more clearly the thread that runs through all of the above examples and will continuously make itself more known: the rejection of individual responsibility.

Personal Construct Psychology

I personally have found no better conceptual means of understanding contradiction (among many, many other things), particularly around core values and identity, than that of the work by the 20th-century American psychologist George Kelly and his Personal Construct Psychology (PCP) and the resulting theory[2].

Like the work of Carl Jung, Kelly's overarching focus or primary concern was always on the patient as opposed to *a priori* theory telling one what to do with said patient, something that has always distinguished the two from the vast majority of psychologists in existence, and something Jung always had to reiterate time and time again to his critics or anyone that was confused over some point or another. However, unlike Jung, Kelly tended to deal with the lowest socio-economic demographics coming out of the Great Depression in North America. In either case, both were forced by the nature of their focus to be highly pragmatic; however, Kelly's work was particularly so, as his patients were struggling with the most concrete / least abstract forms of basic, every day, psychological dysfunction. What I also consider to be extremely interesting is that, by virtue of what Kelly was actually doing, he

---

[2] ibid.

was also a great phenomenologist and existentialist. In any case, what this resulted in was a highly straightforward way of understanding psychological dysfunction *itself* – no ontological or metaphysical claims required – and a picture of all psychological dysfunction as a misalignment of the various values, identities, and so on that a person has with their core values or core identity.

While Kelly's resultant theory is quite robust and covers a large territory, I will focus on what I consider most important to what is being presented here: 1) how contradictions form, 2) why individuals are so adamant over their contradictions, and 3) what happens if the contradiction is pointed out or experienced. In doing so, I will also illustrate why these contradictions are generally unconscious, which paves the way for the much more important Jungian-related concept of projection. All of which begins to shed light on the contradictions in the previous section.

Kelly stated that everything that a person thinks and can articulate, as well as many things that they think but cannot articulate, lies in what he called the individual's "personal construct system", and that these personal dichotomous constructs in this system are arranged within the person's consciousness in a hierarchy of values. Dichotomous simply means they have a positive and negative pole; a 'good' side and a 'bad' side – more on that later. As Jordan Peterson has pointed out on more than one occasion, individuals obviously have a hierarchy of values otherwise a person could not stand up as opposed to continuing to sit down, or they can sit down as opposed to standing up, and so on. Even if one argued that it all comes down to survival somehow, well, some people commit suicide. The point is that people clearly differ in what is important to them and, as such, they obviously have a hierarchy of values – there is simply no getting around it.

According to Kelly, the way that the constructs form is by experience and comparing and contrasting experience. To help illustrate this, I will borrow the classic baby and an apple example. A baby crawls toward an apple, points at it, and the mother, seeing this, says: "apple". The baby then crawls toward a basketball and says "apple". "No, no", the mother responds, "you don't understand. An apple is red and not quite round. This is a basketball. It is very round and it is orange." The baby then looks confused, "Round? Red?" And this process of making sense of things or communicating them to others via comparison and contrasting then continues for the rest of its life. Furthermore, when the baby is hungry, the apple and basketball then take on different values as far as *the baby* is concerned. With respect to being hungry, an apple is good and basketball is bad; an apple you can eat, a basketball you cannot (at the very least it sounds far less appetizing even if you theoretically could). This basic, obvious, and extremely non-trivial illustration of a sort of epistemology is exactly the kind of thing you will never find in discussions of epistemology, which then leads to ontology, which then leads to politics, which then leads to the Herd screaming and yelling some thing or another based on what they 'know'. Furthermore, if one were to insist on giving the basketball to the baby when it was starving, the baby's *experience of it* would last for years, maybe the rest of its life – it might even grow up to teach its children to hate basketballs. This is how one learns and how constructs and values are formed.

A contradiction forms when one or more of these values lead to opposing actions that the person believes that they should take based on those values. A classic example that is used in PCP case studies[3] to show contradiction, core value invalidation, and the result of invalidation, all in one, are situations[4] involving natural disasters and emergency workers when a natural disaster hits in the same location as the emergency worker who has a family. Generally, these workers are people who see themselves as a "family person" carrying the identity (or in PCP terms, "construal") as such along with the resulting value systems of providing for the family, protecting the family, and so on. However, they also generally carry the identity of emergency worker along with all the resulting value systems for helping people who have been victims of a natural disaster. Additionally, these two value systems tend to be quite high up in their personal hierarchy of values (according to *them*). Thus, when a natural disaster hits in the same location as the worker and their family, a contradiction arises since they feel that they absolutely must answer the call of duty and they absolutely must protect their family. In America, the career identity generally overrides the family person identity, and the scenario usually goes something along the lines of: emergency hits, the emergency worker, although torn, chooses to answer the call of duty (hierarchy of values), their family is seriously injured and/or killed, and the emergency worker ends up with post-traumatic stress disorder (PTSD), not surprisingly. In some instances, the worker even takes out their PTSD on the family. "You weren't there! You don't know what it was like!", they will insist, as they drink or self-medicate themselves into oblivion. The same often happens with

---

[3] Fransella, F. (2003a), *International Handbook of Personal Construct Psychology*, J. Wiley & Sons, West Sussex.

[4] McFarlane, A.C. and Bookless, C. (2001), "The effect of PTSD on interpersonal relationships: Issues for emergency service workers", *Sexual and Relationship Therapy*, Vol. 16 No. 3, pp. 261–267.

soldiers in more recent wars post World War II, but stemming from two different value systems, i.e., being a "good person" vs killing people then realizing the war and therefore the military and its value systems that they bought into were mostly political and/or the whims of people in power as opposed to national defense.

These extreme examples are often used to familiarize people with PCP because they provide a way to easily illustrate what is ultimately happening in the more complex versions of contradiction and core value misalignment. In most other cases or everyday life, there are not just two distinct sets of misaligned values, but dozens, hundreds, or thousands; there is not just a single contradiction but layers and layers of contradiction that are *patched together by newer, emergent, and more sophisticated constructs and systems.* As such, the task of the personal construct psychologist then becomes to navigate and wade through this sea of contradictions, find the most superordinate of them (i.e., the one that is highest up in the value hierarchy which is the root of dysfunction), and point out that contradiction in order to get the patient to stop pointing the finger at any and everything around them and to understand that their problem lies squarely within *them.*

It should also be noted that in more severe cases of dysfunction, e.g., schizophrenia, there is such a misalignment and the contradictions so many that the system can no longer be patched in any way that makes sense to the outside observer. The schizophrenic then charges forward towards some singular thought or behavior with apparently no concern whatsoever about how much sense they are making about why they are doing so – they just keep insisting and/or *repeating* themselves. To sum up the phenomenon, they basically have no way to 'get back' or "reconstrue" as PCP would say.

On a tangential but soon important note, there is something interesting in schizophrenia that is never seriously considered by Herd psychologists, and that is just how similar these singular thoughts or behaviors can be within a population that is supposed to be totally mentally scrambled. Does no one find that a bit odd? It makes you wonder, what would happen if you put 1000... 10,000...10,000,000 schizophrenics together that all had the same thought or behavior? What might emerge? How do people learn? How would they view each other? Would their emotional state appear different if surrounded by those like them?

And when it comes to dysfunction as contradiction, why is such a simple explanation grounded in the simplest of scenarios ignored by mass psychology? Why are the simplest points about your reality ignored by the dysfunctional?

Some clue might be given by returning to core value constructs themselves, which "are those by which [a person] maintains [their] *identity and existence*"[5] and "is any one that is maintained as a basic referent of life itself"[6]. Then consider that a large part of Kelly's theory revolved around core value construct invalidation. His basic point here is that a human being will do just about anything to avoid this invalidation and ignore any resultant contradictions that might bring it about, even going so far as to kill or wage war if the

---

[5] Kelly, G.A. (1955), *The Psychology of Personal Constructs*, W. W. Norton & Company, Inc., New York, NY (emphasis added)

[6] Fransella, F. (2003), *International Handbook of Personal Construct Psychology*, J. Wiley & Sons, West Sussex.

core value construct is under threat. And is that at all surprising given that to attack the core value construct is tantamount to an attack on a person's basic identity, existence, and life itself?

A word of warning

Although PCP and its methods were originally designed as clinical tools to help clinically dysfunctional patients, I use it to back people into corners or trap them; whatever you would like to call it. And I will never, ever make any apologies for this. Especially since the best possible way to trap someone is by giving them what they have explicitly asked for, i.e., helping them.

Although, when trapping others, as Chuck Palahniuk once said in an interview with Joe Rogan, which has become one of my favorite interviews ever, "I'm also sort of springing the trap on myself starting down a path that I have no idea is going to be so humiliating or so emotionally upsetting or so dark because, if I did, I would never go down that path". I began my Ph.D. attempting to explain the absolute absurdity and incompetence that I had seen in my Information Technology career up to that point, particularly while I was at a very large consulting firm. I had seen things that completely defied any logic or reason, particularly the phenomenon of people flat out rejecting something clearly and undeniably beneficial for everyone involved, and I was burning for some coherent explanation. However, after around the first year of my Ph.D. and trapping everyone and everything I could think up or interact with, it at some point became clear to me that "springing the trap on myself" was exactly where I was headed. But I was always the kind of person that prided myself on living dangerously...

And so, I did something that no 'sane' person would willfully do: I decided to start purposefully ramping up the trapping, knowing full well that this would lead back to setting the trap on myself. And to make things even more fun, me and my partner at the time decided to do it with each other, even on each other! And make this the central focus of our existence! What could go wrong?! For a while it was great. We would gang up on academics and expose all their misalignments, and then take whatever we had learned or elicited and explore our own dichotomies and contradictions of various sorts, often under the influence of some psychedelic drug or another. It even paid off in terms of writing and winning awards for said writing. "Oh yeah, pfft, we've totally got all those core constructs reconstrued – what a bunch of pussies these other people are." Inflation abounded. But then at some point, one begins to stumble upon *actual* core constructs and their associated contradictions (because as Jung pointed out, unconscious things are *really* unconscious...), and when that happens it gets truly ugly, really fast. Suffice to say that eventually both of our lives fell apart, and I'm surprised we didn't kill each other. And what do we know happens when your core constructs have been invalidated? Besides the obvious 'answer' of psychosis, the flood gates are then opened up for what Jung called the collective unconscious, and THAT is the most terrifying thing in existence that simply cannot be articulated to anyone who has never been there. I personally was a psychological, emotional, and benzodiazepine disaster for about 3 years, then had major spinal surgery that left me more or less debitated for another 2 years, of which I got to live a nearly completely solitary existence and ponder it all during bouts where I laid in bed writhing in pain from scar tissue on my spinal cord and nerve roots. The question to ponder going forward is: how does one find their way out of drowning at the bottom of that ocean?

Why am I telling you all of this? It is a warning, and this does not simply have to do with PCP methodology, as the astute Jungian analyst will no doubt have already spotted. As my Ph.D. co-supervisor told me about PCP methodology at the onset of this black period, "Jason, it's not a toy". I'm telling you the same. At the same time, I simply cannot deny that the blackest period of my life was also the most creative and productive, and so the tool (along with the egoistic charades) was also the most useful. Just like Jung during the time of his Red Book, everything that I will ever write about is the result of what happened during that period – it is the source from which every insight that I will ever elaborate upon will probably be drawn, and it was the best thing that has ever happened to me, hands down, even though at the lowest point I was seriously considering suicide. So, am I telling you that you should do something similar, or not? Neither, because that is YOUR decision. It's up to YOU how much truth you want, or if you want to try your hand at this contradiction of values thing, and risk it becoming an addiction or something that you cannot un-see, because if you start doing it to others, at some point it will come back around. And then you're up against the nearly impossible task of deciding whether or not to run back to the Herd – knowing in the back of your mind that that is precisely what you are doing – or to attempt to push through not knowing if you will make it out alive or at the very least be useful to anyone in any capacity ever again.

Jung gives almost exactly the same warning in different words.

Eliciting values, spotting contradiction, and locating inertia

In this section I outline the basic process of eliciting an individual's values, then "laddering" to the individual's core values, spotting contradiction, and in that process locating individual inertia. Here, "inertia" refers to what a person espouses should be done but then not doing it. This is not an academic treatment of this process – for that I can recommend George Kelly's original two-volume theory combined with anything written by Fay Fransella. However, it is rather technical, this cannot be avoided, so I will keep it to a minimum.

The types of contradictions pointed out previously in society are just as easy, if not easier, to spot in individuals. It's simply a matter of finding out some of the things that they claim are important, finding out *why* those things are important as well as why whatever answer they give you for that "why" is important, repeating that process (getting to core values), and then sitting back and watching them completely contradict themselves – a cynic's dream come true!

The easiest way that this can be done is by paying very close attention to someone who is relatively well known or 'in the spotlight', as what is important to them will just naturally come out since the person has a platform and is generally known for those very things. Then some time passes and they will inevitably contradict themselves. We see this all the time and there is really nothing new here. However, most people are not in the spotlight, and for this reason, it is far too easy to berate those who are and fall prey to the same phenomenon that is fueled by paparazzi, which is to flog celebrities in order to feel good about one's own life. However, it is far more useful to do this on 'real' people, and doing it at any given opportunity. What this results in, eventually, once one is experienced enough, is drilling home the fact that this is happening with *everyone*. Once that reality has set in and one has done this quite a few times, then abstractions begin to form, allowing one to see patterns and certain themes playing out at a scope broader than the individual.

This requires something resembling a method, and it would also help to illustrate what this method would look like. Rather than recreate the wheel, I will pull examples from my Ph.D. study.

The first step is to create a sort of cognitive map of how someone thinks about some topic. One surefire way to get someone talking is to latch on to a topic that revolves around politics or philosophical points of view, as these are normally the ones that people get the most emotional about. However, if you can get someone to talk about a topic that is not so emotional, you can often get much more illuminating answers since they will be much more level-headed and careful when it comes to articulating their values and why they are important. Both are useful. In any case, you then get the person to compare and contrast concrete people or things with respect to that topic.

In my Ph.D. study, I got people to consider their careers as the topic, and then compare and contrast concrete/actual technologies and people that they worked with. In a less formal setting, I would have brought up the idea of their career, and then simply asked them how one technology or person was similar to some other technologies or people that they worked with, and then asked how they were different, and done so over the course of a conversation (i.e., in a casual manner, mixed with other conversation, rather than sounding like a researcher who is interviewing someone). This conversation might last 5 minutes or span 5 months or 5 years. This is indeed what I do in everyday life, and it is how you can approach it as well.

Here is an example of eliciting a personal construct where I had asked a participant to compare and contrast some of the things we had come up with at the beginning of our interview with respect to their career:

> Interviewee: "So Google Drive and Dreamweaver would be similar opposed to windows…both are internet-based, their focus is on collaboration and interaction…as a web designer, I would definitely be able to use either one of those technologies on any operating system. These technologies represent mobility in the sense that any terminal I sit down at I can open these up and I'm good to go."

> Me: "Ok, so how are these two different from Windows?"

Interviewee: "Windows...it's an OS that I prefer to use...but I can use Linux, I can use Mac...it's less important to me what the operating system is than the ability to be able to sit down anywhere and use the technology."

Me: "So you are saying that Windows is less mobile?"

Interviewee: "Yeah."

So here we have just one of the hundreds of examples I could give of how you would begin to come up with dichotomous constructs. In this instance, we have the construct mobile—not mobile, where mobile is seen in a positive light (good) and not mobile in a negative light (bad). As we continued the process of comparing and contrasting the technologies and people that the interviewee worked with, I began to get some sense of how things were construed by this person in general, but, more importantly, I began to get a glimpse of what was important to them, i.e., their values. Furthermore, the person is hashing out their own thoughts in the process.

Then what is needed is to get to the person's core values, and this is where the process of "laddering" comes in. The process is called laddering because what you end up with looks like a ladder if you were to draw it out. The process is simple. You spot something that appears to be quite important to the person over the length of your conversation, confirm with them if they think it is very important (they may not, i.e., you might have misjudged), and then ask them why that thing that is very important is so important, as well as why it is important to not do the opposite. You then continue this process of incessantly asking why, just like an annoying two-year-old, until they cannot go any further. Note that this should, and 99% of the time does, end up at "meaning in life" or "purpose in life" or something along those lines, as in they will actually state this, e.g., "well, if <such and such> could not happen, there would be no meaning to life". The following is an example of the laddering process, which again results in positive and negative poles.

Me: It appears as though there is…a very strong theme of adaptation…

Interviewee: Yeah, yeah.

Me: So, it looks like, to you, it's important to be adaptive?

Interviewee: Yep. Absolutely, especially with a future career, when it comes to technology, I look for something that not only does it have something to do with advertising, but I think of things that are very niche to my field, I'm looking for something that is open source or has some kind of customizable features…[as] it allows me to give my audience a more personalized experience. The biggest push right now in web design…there is actually this field called user experience, which is getting bigger and bigger. So, you have this specific audience, and how do we customize technology to fill that niche?

Me: Ok, so…why is it important to not do the opposite of that…give the audience a less personalized experience?

Interviewee: Well, most of these audiences are so niche that things that are more generalized simply won't work...I can't build upon it in the future. Going back to this game thing, I'm using Google Drive to combine five different forms...it grabs data from each form and submits it to a third document, which can be printed out by a records keeper and it has only pertinent information...if Google Drive didn't allow those scripts, I couldn't get all of this data into one document.

Me: So why is it important to have only pertinent information?

From this, we arrived at the first laddered construct (Generalized – Personalized), and I continued to ladder by asking why personalization is important. I continued to probe in this manner until we arrived at his meaning in life/purpose in life, and had constructed the following ladder.

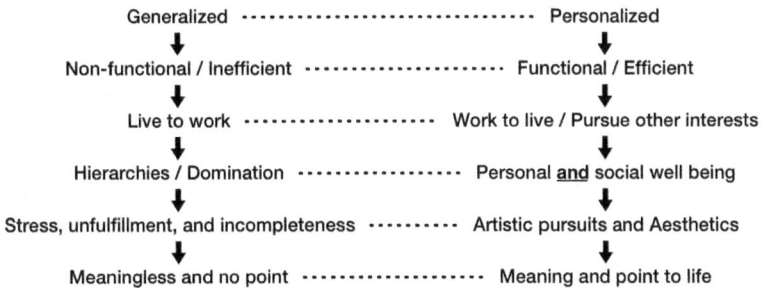

Generalized ································ Personalized
↓   ↓
Non-functional / Inefficient ····················· Functional / Efficient
↓   ↓
Live to work ···················· Work to live / Pursue other interests
↓   ↓
Hierarchies / Domination ················· Personal **and** social well being
↓   ↓
Stress, unfulfillment, and incompleteness ·········· Artistic pursuits and Aesthetics
↓   ↓
Meaningless and no point ················· Meaning and point to life

Figure 1 - A research participant's core construct ladder

I now had a rough picture of this person's core values, as well as a map from those core values all the way down to the most concrete of people and technologies in a work context. In other words, everything in that chain has a core value from which it stems, and this person's definition of good and bad can be easily spotted at the concrete level as well as why this is true at a superordinate level. For example, now having this information, if the person was, say, under a lot of stress one day and then someone came in (perhaps a boss or major client) and demanded "from today on, we will only be using Windows", and the person snapped, screamed, and slammed the door on the way out of the room, we would know why – Windows to *this* person, ultimately, if one goes far enough, is a symbol of meaninglessness. They are not just "having a bad day". At the same time, if there was an extended workgroup that was considering a switch to Windows and perhaps it was even indeed the best decision for everyone involved and yet this person was adamant about using something else against all (let's just pretend incontrovertible) evidence to the contrary, then we would know why.

If one takes this entire process and works it into casual conversation about many different topics over an extended period of time, you then end up with a map of a person's core values in general (because they will at some point start to repeat across topics) as well as how those values are connected to all of the concrete things with which this person has been talking about and interacting.

What I have presented above is the 'tame' version, for the purposes of understanding how this process works. Recall that when a core value construct is threatened, it often results in physical violence or warfare.

Consider a clinical example by Cummins[7] who reports on an individual who "came down the stairs one morning, saw that [the table in his house] was dusty and reacted by hitting his partner. He presented this behavior as being incapable of explanation. Anger just came over him; it happened for no reason and he was unable to control it" (p. 87). In order to help the patient to understand the root of this event and to prevent it in the future, the laddering technique was employed in order to arrive at core constructs.

```
Dusty Table  · · · · · · · · · · · · · · · · · · · · · · ·  Clean (Organized)
     ↓                                                            ↓
Cannot Achieve  · · · · · · · · · · · · · · · · · · · · ·  Achieve Things
     ↓                                                            ↓
No Purpose  · · · · · · · · · · · · · · · · · · · · · · ·  Sense of Purpose
     ↓                                                            ↓
Life Meaningless  · · · · · · · · · · · · · · · · · · ·  Gives Life Meaning
     ↓
Might as Well End It
```

Figure 2 - A core construct ladder adapted from Cummins

This illustrates just how important it is to understand core values as well as being able to trace from them to a concrete event, object, or person and any actions taken toward or around them.

At this point you are now in a position to consider everything said throughout all of your conversations with a person, observe their behavior, and see if they are truly doing these things that they claim are so important to them or not, i.e., are they contradicting themselves? This is the most critical point in the entire process because this is often where the dysfunction comes from. For example, with the person above and the dusty table, the psychologist might observe that this person never achieves

7 Cummins, P. (2003), "Working with Anger", in Fransella, F. (Ed.), *International Handbook of Personal Construct Psychology*, J. Wiley & Sons, West Sussex, pp. 83–91.

anything or that they don't even try – they simply *talk* about it. Hence, the *actual* dysfunction – the *actual* reason for hitting their partner, was not simply about what they believe is important, it's the fact that they themselves are not doing the very thing that they supposedly believe is important, and this was *reflected back at them* via a dusty table, even if it was unconscious. It is then the task of the psychologist (or you if you are playing this game) to point out this contradiction very carefully, at which point at least one or more core value constructs stand to be invalidated. If they are, the task is to then help the person rebuild (or "reconstrue" in PCP terms) their basic identity. That's what happens in a clinical setting anyway – the person is, after all, asking for help. However, in everyday life, that's a different story.

In my Ph.D. study, my job was not that of a clinical psychologist, it was simply to understand why some people might flat out reject technologies or certain types of people. What I had never initially intended to uncover was the process of individual inertia in a non-clinical setting where there is supposedly no dysfunction and the individuals are not asking for help. As I said previously, when I use the term "inertia" I'm referring to what a person espouses should be done but then they themselves do not do whatever it is, which is quite different to how the term is used in, say, management studies, where inertia essentially means not doing what you are told or what someone else or some group or some professional body says that you should do… A classic example of inertia as I am referring to it here can be seen in Dostoyevsky's Notes from the Underground, and he even labels it as such. The phenomenon of inertia usually comes up in clinical settings when, for example, a stutterer or smoker knows that they need to stop, they fully believe in stopping, all their values align with stopping, but they somehow cannot seem to stop (it turns out there is much more involved than not being able to speak consistently or simple addiction). However, in non-clinical settings, the person is generally unaware of their own individual inertia. They espouse a set of values, can talk at length about *other* people or things that represent these values or their opposite, but then are almost always unaware that they are either not doing the very thing that they say everyone and everything else should be doing, or they are doing the very thing that they say everyone and everything else should not be doing.

Thus, what follows is that if you can find a contradiction between one's core values and what they are actually doing or not doing, then you have often times located the point of that person's individual inertia on a whole.

Although all other participants in my Ph.D. study did this in their own way, examples include:

1) Two people who were adamant about science, objectivity, and removing all emotion from decision making, who showed extreme disdain for those who were emotional and/or made decisions on emotion. Yet, they were by far the most emotional of all the people I interviewed.

2) A person espoused how people and technologies should be dynamic, fluid, and always ready to improvise as the challenges of life and business presented themselves. Yet, when discussing a particular technology that was central to their life and identity, they loved the technology because it was always the same anywhere you go as opposed to other technologies that were always changing with different

configurations, i.e., they did not have to be dynamic, fluid, and ready to improvise.

3) The epitome of the findings and highly relevant to the rest of this book, was a person who talked extensively about evolution (and it was obvious throughout that this was a core identity construct) which is ultimately about change, yet their conceptualization of how things work was wholly static/rigid. I also knew this person, and if they were ever questioned by anyone about an alternative to any of their views, the response was near violence and/or a complete severance of relationship or interaction.

In the first example, the people believe in getting rid of emotion but are not doing it. In the second, the person believes in being agile but is not doing it. In the third, the person was a champion for evolution but seemingly has no capacity for it. But in all cases, *everyone, and everything else* should be doing these things.

In short, what you will find by employing this technique and the resulting misalignment of values and actions is that everyone you apply this to will ultimately say through their actions (or lack thereof) that everyone and everything should change except for them. Everyone and everything else should be responsible except for them.

If you truly want to see fireworks in this process, get to someone's core values and then...help them...on their terms. I will repeat that in a different way, because it is one of the most important things I can point out in this book. If you want to watch someone completely and utterly implode, give them exactly what they ask for in exactly the way that they ask for it. For example, if you know someone who says something along the lines of, "My problem is that I'm sick of being told what to do and I want to be in management, but people don't put [people like me] in charge. It's complete bullshit. That's why this Friday I'm going to a rally for [people like me]". If you happen to be in a position to hire someone or own a business and you are a bit sadistic and you can work entertainment into your budget, hire them – put them in management! Give them total responsibility and power. In no time you'll start hearing the complaints roll in as to why they cannot do their job. So, what you do is take down every barrier that comes their way (like I said, you need a budget for this) – totally clear the road every time they complain about something hindering them. In no time they will be in tears, self-medicating, taking everyone around them to court for who only knows what (again, budget), and at that point you'll be able to fire them for...not being able to do their job! Congratulations! You've just ruined someone's life. Or did you? Didn't you simply give them exactly what they asked for the whole way? Of course, they will never see it that way, and you will be vilified for the rest of their life.

You must be thinking what a terrible person I am. Well, from the time I was young all I ever did was try to help people and it was all I ever wanted to do. And here's the thing, I was really, *really* good at it. At first, this resulted in friends ganging up on me once real-life finally sunk in (i.e., time to get off your ass and actually do what you were preaching), then the entire small town followed. I figured it was just the result of small-town Alabama – "stupid hicks – fine, stay that way, I'm sure you'll have an awesome life". But then I got into my 20's, then 30's, and the organizations I was a part of became more sophisticated and elite – my partners sharper and more educated – yet this phenomenon persisted: problem presented itself, I helped them solve it on their terms, then (even if very sophisticated and under the radar) self-sabotage at every available opportunity, regardless of the person, organization, education or intellect, followed by total rejection of the person that had tried to help them based on what they asked for and playing by their rules. Why in the holy hell were people turning on me for helping them based on exactly what they asked for? Trying to help them achieve all that they were espousing to be? Well, that was what led me to my Ph.D.

Then, at one point it dawned on me: what if what these people in my study and everyone else I had met aren't simply protecting one or more core values like everything I had read was suggesting. What if they weren't even protecting against death (as Ernest Becker proposed). What if they are protecting against something *else* and values were just a sort of last line of defense? What if this something else was far more terrifying and serious. And this only 'dawned on me' because at exactly that same time I started to encounter this 'something else'. And wouldn't you know it, it was also exactly the same time that everyone had started giving me exactly what I had asked for, exactly on my terms.

The Self trap had been sprung. This new 'thing' demanded to be heard and came to life with a sort of fury for which I was completely not ready. Without recounting the madness of several years, I can simply say that by some means or another (I honestly do not remember how because I had lost all interest in anything intellectual) I stumbled upon the book Ego and Archetype[8] which

---

[8] Edinger, E. (1992), *Ego and Archetype*, Shambhala, Boston, MA.

had a profound impact on me, especially in that state. It was more or less an introduction to the works of Carl Jung. That is what started what became an obsession with Jung's work. I read every single thing he had ever published, which took me just over 3 years. During the reading of his works, I experienced extreme states of synchronicity (which was one of the first books I read, while I was experiencing it). I say extreme because sometimes this experience was so intense that I basically became non-functional and appeared glassy-eyed with the 'thousand-yard stare', and who knows what was running through the minds of those who encountered me. In any case, it was only in the work of Jung (and to a lesser degree Alan Watts) that I found anything resembling an answer to what I was experiencing and had observed throughout my lifetime. Everything else just seemed kind of like training wheels, even though it was necessary as a foundation. But eventually you have to take off the training wheels and actually learn to ride; lose sight of the harbor; all those types of metaphors.

So, I did.

Thus, what I have presented here are the necessary training wheels. You could label this entire process "Shining a Light on Hypocrisy", or "A Guide to Calling Bullshit", or in extremely rigid instances that never actually end "How to Spot a Narcissist". That in itself could be a fun activity for some. Indeed, that's all I did when I first discovered it. But remember, it comes back around – the ultimate point here is to understand how YOU are contradicting yourself; to locate YOUR point of inertia; to uncover all that lies in YOUR shadow. In doing so, maybe you will be fortunate enough to encounter the Self, where the true value of all of this lies, and leads one into the far more advanced territory of projection.

Projection

"The 'advantage' of projection consists in the fact that one has apparently got rid of the painful conflict once and for all. Somebody else or external circumstances now have the responsibility." – Carl Jung, *Symbols of Transformation*

Although projection (and most other Jungian-related concepts) is something fairly difficult to understand, it has become a well-known phenomenon in psychology and has even made its way into popular culture along with easy-to-understand definitions and examples. This goes something along the lines of: projection is seeing in others that which you do not like about yourself – an example is someone that talks non-stop at a dinner party but then if you interrupt them they scream at you for being a terrible listener and/or attention seeker – this happens because someone is lacking in self-awareness and cannot be critical of themselves. And indeed, this is exactly what happens, why it is happening (well, sort of), and this illuminates many of the previous examples. However, like most things borrowed from Jung, there is quite a lot that gets lost in these watered-down-for-the-masses translations and their goal of passive-aggressively attempting to get people to be more self-aware for the seemingly sole purpose of playing nice with others.

The most often lost point – the one most important with respect to all examples thus far – is that of individual responsibility, and this is something that you will almost never hear coming out the mouth of a Herd psychologist or popular culture. Indeed, as far as they are concerned, projection is just one more way of telling people that they are *guilty* – one of the very things that Jung was attempting to get away from in order to…help increase Self-awareness!… And, indeed, the Herd sees these two things as being two sides of the same coin, where 'responsibility' with respect to projection *only* equates to paying penance to alleviate one's guilt. That sounds an awful lot like church preaching… Obviously, the Herd and its psychologists only define responsibility as being responsible to the Herd and its feelings. The goal of the Herd psychologist when pointing out a projection is to simply make that person feel like an asshole so they will stop whatever it is that they are doing to some other member of the Herd. Why? Because we have fingers to point. Because when projection arises in instances of inertia, apparently, it's no longer projection, and we need someone to blame for why people cannot do what they aspire to, because, according to the Herd, there simply is no possible way that it is their own rejection of responsibility. And if there is any solution for such a person, it is 'healing'.

Consider the examples of contradiction and inertia in the previous section through the eyes (projection?) of a Herd psychologist. For them, all of these people are incapable of moving forward not because they are scared of having a shred of individual responsibility and maybe they should actually be told so. It could not possibly be that if one were to take on individual responsibility rather than *telling everyone else what they should do* that they might actually find out something very important about them-Selves; it could not possibly be that the phenomenon of projection applies as equally to the phenomenon of individual inertia as it does to playing nice with others; it could not possibly be that the psychologist or 'healer' is now projecting themselves and their own unconscious contents and is now misaligned and contradicting themselves in the *exact* same way as outlined by the previous examples... No! In this context, they supposedly cannot move forward because of what *someone else did to them*. This is a very, very important point with respect to the person providing the 'healing'.

However, if one does indeed take the perspective that the people in the previous section (or society at large earlier) are not moving forward with their own beliefs because of a lack of spine and no one encouraging them to grow one, then, not surprisingly, if one is actually familiar with Jung, that 'healing' is actually a form of *violence…* Not only that, but it is also a violence that perpetuates and breeds additional violence. What else do you think finger-pointing accomplishes?

What is the difference, then, between the Herd psychologist and a proper analyst when defining responsibility and the source of inertia? Assumptions, which we will come back to later. Not only that but one set of assumptions being misaligned just like with the previous examples with value misalignment. If one takes projection as the source of rejecting individual responsibility *and* not being able to play nice with others, then there is no contradiction. However, if one goes the route of the Herd psychologist then there is a blatant contradiction: projection only occurs when not playing nice with others but there is no projection where individual inertia is involved. Interesting.

> "We must bear in mind that we do not make projections, rather they happen to us. This fact permits the conclusion that we originally read our first physical, and particularly psychological, insights into the stars. In other words, what is farthest is actually nearest. Somehow, as the Gnostics surmised, we have "collected" ourselves from out of the cosmos." – Carl Jung, *Letters of C. G. Jung: Volume 2*

> "All the contents of our unconscious are constantly being projected into our surroundings" – Carl Jung, *Dreams*

These quotes highlight another typically thrown out but all too important point of Jung's about projection, which was that projection itself is *always* occurring and *happening to us* (see what I did there?). This allows the Herd to have a never-ending supply of projection, as they project the very phenomenon of projection itself onto others. Inertia? Other people; external circumstances; whatever is happening to me – not me. Individual responsibility is what everyone else should take because *they* are guilty! GUILTY!!! BURN THEM AT THE STAKE FOR NOT DOING WHAT NEEDS TO BE DONE!

The Herd psychologist prides themselves on pointing out simplistic projection in the lowest common denominator, and apparently thinks that the point of all Jung's work was to simply get people to play nice with others or get a job. If you ask the Herd psychologist how any of this applies to them personally, they will almost always respond: "I'm in a lifelong quest to be more accepting of others" (no doubt with a tone of superiority). That's it? Are you serious? You think Jung spent an entire life writing about the concepts and phenomena that he did so that people could be more accepting of others and nothing more? Are we seriously reading the same texts? As usual, something gets cherrypicked out of something profound and is used to back up some existing Herd social norm, career, politic, whatever. Projection for Herd psychologists and the masses is applied to *ONE* context, and it is more or less seen as something that can be controlled by the ego, when it is the very thing that cannot be controlled by the ego, ever...

So, Herd psychologists and the Herd to which you cater, until you can figure out whether projection is a phenomenon or not and get your story straight, as far as I'm concerned, you have been invalided. How about actually reading your source literature for once and try again.

For the rest of you still with me, we have to ask ourselves: why are people so afraid of individual responsibility? Is it supposed to be that they are afraid of simply doing some thing or another in which they believe, and that's it? That if they do then they are potentially exposed to the unknown, and that's it? Just like the idea previously where people are supposedly simply protecting values, I'm not buying it. Just like the defense mechanisms leading up to that point, they always seem to be hiding something other than what the Herd psychologists propose is being protected against. And it's not just Herd psychologists that stop there, it's the near entire lineage of existential philosophy and thought including those going on about responsibility...

"Projections change the world into the replica of one's own unknown face" – Carl Jung, *The Archetypes, and the Collective Unconscious: Aion*

Assumptions

"It is true that primitives are simpler and more childlike than we, in good and evil alike. This in itself does not impress us as strange. And yet, when we approach the world of archaic man, we have the feeling of something prodigiously strange. As far as I have been able to analyse it, this feeling comes predominantly from the fact that the primary assumptions of archaic man are essentially different from ours, so that he lives in a different world. Until we come to know his presuppositions, he is a hard riddle to read; but when we know them, all is relatively simple. We might equally well say that primitive man ceases to be a riddle for us as soon as we get to know our *own* presuppositions."

"It is, as I have said, his assumptions alone that distinguish him from ourselves."

– Carl Jung, *Civilization in Transition*

I will never forget the horror on so many faces during my time in Academia (or how I felt when it was done to me for the first time) when someone was asked "what are your assumptions?" This is because the vast majority of people in the world, academic or not, have absolutely no idea what their assumptions are – it is hard enough to elicit core values, and assumptions lie behind them. I personally think that the most important text for all things assumption-based is Jung's book Civilization in Transition, and it is simply one of the most relevant books he ever wrote, although it is (not surprisingly) rarely referenced.

Jung points out just how difficult it is to get at assumptions, and this difficulty lies in the fact that as soon as one begins questioning and/or examining assumptions at all (for example, primitive man) then this naturally leads to questioning and/or examining one's own assumptions. Again, we can point back to Personal Construct Psychology as to why this might be dangerous. If an invalidated core value construct can lead to total personal construct system failure, then imagine what an invalidated or alternative assumption could lead to. It could lead to total destruction; however, it could also lead to total reconstrual. And what Jung is saying is that is precisely what happened with respect to the bridge between archaic man and us. In other words, with a different set of assumptions comes the manifestation of a different psychological and material reality. Furthermore, in what will become increasingly important throughout this book, where *exactly* do any of these assumptions come from?

In the most basic instance of assumptions, one can turn to the business world, where some marketing executive with an MBA is giving a presentation on projected sales increases: "given our customer data and the trends we see, this new channel strategy will almost certainly result in a 20% increase in sales over the next 5 years, assuming all else equal". Here, the executive is explicitly stating their assumption of all else equal because some customer segment might disappear because of some other innovation, a meteor could strike, aliens could invade, etc. They do this usually as a blanket statement to show that they have put some thought into what they are saying as well as acknowledging the fact that many businesspeople simply start presenting and arguing for some course of action, and have put zero thought into any assumptions that their argument is based on. This gives what would otherwise be pure speculation a bit of objectivity and authority, provides a bit more efficiency in decision making (otherwise, two competing courses of action might devolve into watching two dogs barking at each other), and it is why so many MBA programs, particularly the marketing portion, place such high emphasis on stating assumptions. Although, in most everyday scenarios where these 'assumptions' are supposedly known, as opposed to being unconscious, the company might assume that "our customers are drawn to the color red because it triggers food cravings", not because it resembles blood… The idea of unconscious assumptions and their origins, as well as *how far back does that go?*", is what I'm trying to get at here.

Another example might be a technology company that is planning the long-range development of a new product and they are dependent on computing power. They might assume that computing power doubles every 18-24 months because that is precisely what has been happening. Over time, it is possible that, in all future planning and execution, the idea of having to consider this assumption goes completely out the window and nobody is even aware of it; the company just chugs along with a set of best practices or documentation where this assumption cannot be explicitly found, and, at some point, the practices themselves become reality. In other words, the behavior of the company is indeed based on one or more assumptions, but is operating on a sort of 'auto pilot' or *simulation*. If this indeed were to pan out, it would be possible for future young employees to join the company and never actually be aware of the assumptions that the company was founded on, and yet still wholly assume them as well as espousing the company's values (efficiency, teamwork, whatever). And what do you think would happen if at some point computing power stopped doubling, things started to go badly for the company, and these future young employees started to ask questions about what the company's strategy is based on? Clearly, that is a rhetorical question!

These are simplistic examples of assumptions and their salience, but what is important to take away here is that whether or not someone is aware of their assumptions, the assumptions are in fact driving the behavior and everything that person 'believes in', and ultimately manifests reality itself (the world the person lives in, the reality of the company, etc.) as well as perpetuates a set of assumptions within a culture.

As one gets into more abstract phenomena, such as that of psychology or philosophy, we can again turn back to Jung's Civilization in Transition where he is primarily interested in the assumption of whether all individual psyches are the same or not, and this then drives the behavior, systems, and ultimately constructs, societal structures, politics, and so on. The reason Jung was so interested in assumptions is because he saw a clear link between the assumption that all individuals are the same, i.e., equality or egalitarianism, and totalitarianism/government that is centralized and dictatorial and requires complete subservience to the State. While Jung lived through this on the periphery of Nazi Germany, he also saw the same happening in his lifetime in Russia and China, where in the latter it clearly lives on today.

> "As you know, there actually are widely accepted psychological theories which start from the assumption that the human psyche is the same everywhere and can therefore be explained in the same way regardless of circumstances. The appalling monotony presupposed by these theories, however, is contradicted by the fact that individual psychic differences do exist and are capable of almost infinite variation. ... Quite apart from this entertaining domestic quarrel among psychologists, there are other egalitarian assumptions of a social and political nature which are much more serious, because they *forget* the existence of the individual psyche altogether." – Carl Jung, *Civilization in Transition* (emphasis added)

As I said earlier, one thing that Jung was always attempting to point out was that if you attempt to stamp out one thing, it will always come back and possibly in a more monstrous form. Thus, when people ban together to get rid of those "horrible, self-serving, individuals that can only think of themselves", all that happens is that those people give birth to a *single* individual that is horrible, self-serving, and can only think of itself: The Totalitarian State. Again, I cannot get over the irony with China and Yin and Yang, or the absolutely massive projection occurring within the movements that lead to these abominations. We'll just take this individual here in me, dump it over to this single individual, and done! All personal responsibility is alleviated.

And people in the West think they are immune to such a thing. "Oh, that's those *other* people that start off with stamping out the individual and end up in a totalitarian existence. Nothing like that could ever happen here in a 'democracy'". Are you so sure about that, sunshine? Look around. Do you have any idea why you get up and do the things that you do? Do you have any idea why you and everyone else are so pissed off on the way to and from work, in some places running each other off the road to get there, when you are oh so adamant about your 'freedom' and way of life? Have you ever stopped and asked yourself what are your assumptions about your daily life, e.g., your career; your family; your...? Or have you and everyone else been running on autopilot for at least the last, hmm, let's say approximately 80 years?

Indeed, "crises are somehow connected to forgetting"[9].

The fact, and it is a fact, that there is an all-out war on individual consciousness stemming from the projection-fueled campaign of complete and total personal irresponsibility comes from the long chain of ground to core assumptions and back that has been presented thus far.

Assumption leads to values leads to all observable social and material systems, with a populace that eventually has absolutely no idea why they are doing what they are doing or observing what they are observing. But here is where it gets really interesting. Because of this eventual confusion and its resulting chaos, the same populace, philosophers and scientists included, then attempts to construct new values – to transcend the old values – values that

---

[9] Ciborra, C. (2002), *The Labyrinths of Information: Challenging the Wisdom of Systems*, OUP Oxford, Oxford.

would require different assumptions. But in the construction of those new values and their shift in assumptions, no one has *ever* stopped to ask if what they are attempting to get away from is an assumption, or if it is the Herd's *story about* an assumption...

As far as I can tell, this is the ultimate failure of every well-known existential philosopher and their successors in the last 150 years. From Nietzsche to Sartre to Camus to the post-structuralists.

However, this pattern of assuming one thing, values being created, assumption forgotten and replaced by a story, values rebelled against because the story doesn't make any sense, new assumption, new values, values rebelled against because they *don't work*, new assumption, has been repeating itself for a long time. If one compares everything thus far on how contradiction arises, and the above pattern can be understood, combined with the fact that projection is always happening to us, then it becomes crystal clear why contradiction in any personal or societal context abounds.

'This' or 'other than this' have been the assumptions, and in the West it has been our 2000-year-old Good and Evil that gets swapped every time the assumption does. Not only that, every time this assumption is swapped, we have very skillfully managed to make it the dumping ground for individual responsibility.

The only thing that ever changes are the clothes.

A brief history of 'this' and 'other than this' in the West

We have now arrived at the dizzying heights of the only two core assumptions that ever were: 'this' versus 'other than this'. The ultimate dichotomy and contradiction generator. It is difficult to breathe at these heights; thinking even more so. Here there are no sophisticated patching systems to allow agents of the Herd to bark, moo, and baa conclusions at each other. Only raw assumption.

"But...but...but what do you mean by 'this' or 'other than this'?" Oh, nice try, Dolly. 'This' or 'other than this' applies to so many contexts, levels, whatever, that if I started using words to explain then you would immediately apply it to one and one only, defeating the entire point of any explanation if an explanation is indeed even possible. Then you would once again start barking, mooing, and baaing your conclusions in response. Hence, 'this' and 'other than this' will serve as what I would call a phenomenological placeholder. To your dismay, I will talk about everything other than what I specifically mean by 'this' or 'other than this' as the very means of making them intelligible. Doing so is not a new idea, and if you cannot handle that kind of uncertainty you might want to make your way back to lower ground and rejoin the Herd before you hurt yourself.

"Oh, right, uncertainty, I totally understand now. I used Camus' idea of philosophical suicide as the primary lens in my thesis." Oh, that's nice. I bet his idea of philosophical suicide really cleared up a lot for you…….. "Yeah, it did. The Universe is meaningless, and if one takes the leap of faith, which is to believe that there is meaning or inherent value despite the obvious fact that there is not, then that is philosophical suicide. It provides certainty. It is a cop-out. Kierkegaard is the poster boy for political suicide." Right, and I take it you have no idea the irony occurring at the moment. "What?" It doesn't matter. Anyway, Kierkegaard did indeed cop-out by latching onto a certain story, and sort of suggesting that that was where meaning and value lies – the story; the concept; etc. But it seems to me that there is a difference between inherent meaning or value, i.e., what is 'inscribed' into the Universe as a concept, and experienced or felt meaning.

"But how can you experience something that doesn't exist?" Who? You or me? I've had some pretty damn meaningful experiences in my life that didn't have anything to do with any religion, story, concept, or philosophy. Just because YOU don't experience meaning, or Camus, or what seems like all French philosophers or under-achieving academics, that has nothing to do with ME. "But you can't assign meaning!" Who says I'm *assigning* anything? I said I *experience* it! I can already tell this is going to be like talking to a brick wall… Are you an INTP by chance?

Ok, ok, let's put that whole meaning thing aside and pretend you are correct, that there simply is no meaning and/or that I have never experienced it (thank you for clarifying for me what I experience by the way). What, then, is the point of the philosophy that you've chosen to buy into? "Well, first, I didn't 'buy into' anything – it's the truth! People believe lies! They want comfortable, easy-to-digest answers; they want certainty, so they just invent something, and by doing that they shut the door on philosophical freedom. The point of Camus' philosophy and many others' is that by accepting that there is no meaning in the Universe, then you accept the absurd, thus retaining philosophical freedom."

Ok, well, I have several things that are confusing me based on what you are saying. First, I thought one of the reasons that philosophies such as yours came about was to get away from British empiricism. "What? I never said anything about empiri" Shut up. Let me finish. Second, I can think of 100 different alternatives, off the top of my head, to your 'universe', as I'm sure would be the case if, for example, a worm could think about what happens if it had a fraction of the developed senses that you do. Third, by not committing philosophical suicide, accepting the absurd, and retaining philosophical freedom, what exactly is the *point* of having this philosophical freedom that you are so sure that said course of action leads to? Go ahead, answer. "There isn't any point! There is no point to anything! Aren't you listening?!" Ok, then why do it? Or better yet why not do the opposite out of spite since it doesn't matter? Doesn't Camus talk about doing exactly that? That would be super absurd! "Because…because there is no meaning!!!" Now you're just repeating yourself. I'm also just going to throw this out there, most of what you are saying sounds to me like definitive answers and a whole lot of certainty. To me, it sounds like you and Camus are just the photographic negative of the story of Western religion. Come to think of it, the entirety of French philosophy seems like a photographic negative of German idealism. And by the way, you didn't answer my question. Where *exactly* does your motivation for philosophical freedom come from? What *exactly* does it provide you with?

"Go fuck yourself asshole! WE *KNOW* THERE IS *NOTHING* OTHER THAN 'THIS'!!! MOOOOOO!!! BAA AAAHHAHAAA!!!"

That's what I thought…

The history of 'this' and 'other than this' is a long one. One could argue that it did not start 2000 years ago in the West, but was also present in any form of civilization before or during that moment in time.

Again, we can return to Jung who points out how primitive man (i.e., non-civilization by our definitions) did not make any distinction between themselves and the world, or their ego self and the Self; there was just simply everything, or One, or Unity, or whatever one would like to call it. Even gods lived on mountains, in the sky, or in the sea. One can even see remnants of this non-separation in the very few living primitive languages in the word that only have verb agreement instead of subject and object. And as Jung also pointed out, one way to surely frighten the hell out of primitive man and really get them on high alert was if something 'odd' were to occur; something individual. Therefore, anything that resembled this was quickly stamped out by any means possible; directly in many instances, but indirectly in others such as attempts to do so with sacrifices. But then one day, for whatever reason, certain individuals got the crazy idea that maybe they could control their environment a little more rather than just let it happen to them. Maybe they could use their tools to make more tools, which could be used to build things that might solve certain problems or make life easier or more bearable. Then in seeing some of their problems going away (such as getting eaten by other animals, relying solely on river levels for water, etc.), they slowly started to come up with the idea that the things that had been happening to them might have just been in their head. "Look around. Things don't just happen to us anymore. We could be masters of our environment. *There could be something 'other than this'.* And if Dave over there specializes in weapons and Suzie specializes in clothes, then we can do it even better!" And thus, civilization was born.

And in these early civilizations, the word thriving doesn't even come close to an approximation of daily life compared to our world today. Obviously, some thrived more than others, but the levels of creativity, commerce, highly skilled individuals networking and collaborating with other highly skilled individuals, and just the general mood of these early civilizations, in the *beginning*, is not something that is really debated by any historian. One can even see this phenomenon on a much smaller, less glorious scale with certain Western countries in the last 400 years. But one important fact that one should always keep in mind is that during these golden ages there was an almost perfect balance of things happening to these people and individuals taking responsibility and exploring new things that would make the lives of them and their community better. There was no dominant phenomenon. They weren't totally overrun by the world, and they didn't totally have it under control. There was always a large deal of unknown that was always fueling more innovation and cooperation.

But then, in every instance, these civilizations started to go downhill. And in every, single, instance, this perfectly correlated to when these civilizations had nothing left to worry about, relatively speaking. They had gone from one extreme of everything happening to them, to the other extreme of *nothing* happening to them. Be careful not to get off track here – I am talking on the whole. The world, on the whole, was no longer happening to them, on the whole. Everything happening at this new point were people or their systems happening to other people and their systems. The world was now more or less irrelevant. Furthermore, as the levels of danger and obstacles decreased, it was only natural that cowardice skyrocketed, which resulted in people having no clue what to do in the face of real life, which meant that real life was pushed away as far as possible at every opportunity. And thus, philosophy was born…

"What is the point of my existence?" "To be or not to be?" And so on. And in these periods just before the crumbling of a civilization and/or aeon, the philosophers rose to great prominence. Man had suddenly now been 'thrown into' this world (or had he?), and now needed desperately to figure out how to deal with that. So, the philosophers tried with all of their might and intellect to give people something to live by – something that could take the seeming pointlessness of their existence and make some sense out of it. But the masses had turned from a once reasonable, cooperative, and individually proud people, to a horde of incompetent, incapable, self-entitled cesspool rats. Every, single, time. The stories of a once-great people, of heroes who braved the trials and tribulations of such and such, all became cannon fodder – something to be disgusted by and viewed as a joke. "What about US?!" the spineless masses screamed, as they poured the entirety of their existence into decadence and distraction. And is any of this so hard to believe? What else would they do with their time, exactly? They had figured out everything, right? Problems of survival, solved. Existence, solved. 'This' is all there is, there is nothing more, and it's the human condition to deal with that. Furthermore, "since all these stupid little primitive peoples we keep conquering seem to be going on and on about the god of this or the god of that, why don't we just make A God to shut them up? That way there is a single source and we can use that to control them, because there is *nothing* else other than 'this'! Do you hear me?! You can have a one-way ticket to the colosseum if you don't like it."

And, of course, as we know, that worked out really well...

So, then some guy came along in one particular instance of this pattern and said, "Yeah...I don't really like your ideas around 'this', or your emperor as God. It all seems a little authoritarian and totalitarian to me. I don't think that 'this' is all there is. I think that God is something all around, I am the son of God, and *I* am the way, the truth, and the light. A *bridge* if you will. I do indeed believe that there is something 'other than this', and I'm willing to die for that idea". And he did.

Even if this was just an idea and not some actual guy, the rebellious idea still revolutionized the way that people in Western civilization thought as well as the social and material reality that followed. They suddenly rediscovered a certain type of *experience*. Needless to say, the notion of 'other than this' caught on like wildfire. The idea of the individual as such, individual consciousness, and the endless sea of mystery that lay within had been born. Many resurrected texts also suggest the use of "various plants" to explore this new territory.

The Romans saw where this trend was headed and simply couldn't do anything to stop it (something that should probably be kept in mind), so the best they could do was to install the Roman Catholic Church, let the Papacy/Clergy be the new power, and very, very carefully curate and construct a propaganda document that would take the stories of this guy and interweave them with texts that make God sound authoritarian and not really much different in *wording* to what these people were going on about (exactly what they did to the primitives or less advanced civilizations they had conquered earlier). Any other texts to the contrary in the church libraries were burned. "If these people want to believe that there is something 'other than this', then so be it. Here is the manual for 'other than this', with a nice little story that will suit our needs, and we will make them swear alliance and chant over and over that *all* that matters is 'other than this'".

And so that is exactly what happened. Since the *only* thing that mattered was 'other than this', no effort whatsoever was put into 'this'. Indeed, why put any effort into 'this' if it doesn't matter? People were effectively turned into cows. "Doesn't matter if my existence sucks, if I know anything, if I better myself, if I let some lords come and rape my wife and then slit her throat. Nothing matters because the only thing that matters is 'other than this'. Those clergy people and the royalty are the heads of 'other than this', so I'll do whatever they tell me. Plus, the story lets me know that if I completely give in to authority then I will have a better afterlife". The Church, albeit through the Romans, had officially succeeded in taking the very thing that Christianity was founded on and turning it on its head. Even though eventually the words of Jesus were right there for everyone to read, nobody (to this day) ever caught the contradiction between what he was saying and doing and what the church was telling them to do, because the *discourse around* what he was saying twisted it into its opposite, again, very carefully.

And, of course, as we know, that worked out really well...

Nothing was put into 'this' because it didn't matter, and yet 'other than this' had been twisted back into 'this'. So, now, we have a situation where the only thing that actually exists is 'this', except we are going to say it is 'other than this', and you should not care about 'this' because it doesn't matter, except that 'other than this' has actually been turned into 'this'. It doesn't take a logic master to see what that would result in. An utterly confused populace, a few good years for people in power, and a few hundred years of misery for everyone else.

And just like a person who has had their personal construct system shattered through unreconcilable contradiction, society clung to the one thing they had: rules, practices, and identity. In this way, 'other than this' took on something never seen before. Then, later, when people were starting to rediscover 'this' and the church was still a sensitive subject, we didn't want to give 'other than this' names that would connotate something non-religious, so we ended up calling it "dogma".

I will say it now and keep repeating it until the day that I am dead: this overall phenomenon was the single most psychologically destructive event in all of recorded history, it eventually led to the slaughter of hundreds of millions of people, and is the root of all societal problems that we face today. Back to that later – we aren't done with the twisting yet.

Not surprisingly, Europeans got sick of the misery of a few hundred years of simply waiting to die and in the meantime living like pigs, and so a few of them started to play around with 'this' out of rebellion. "Maybe I can improve 'this'; what if I take 'this' and use it to discover more of 'this'; oh look, it turns out the story about Earth being the center of the Universe is not true – stupid 'other than this' people! Look! Above the heavens, there is just more of 'this'! And now that we are focused on 'this' our quality of life is improving! What the hell were we thinking?!" 'Other than this' had officially become the enemy, and people absolutely love to have a good enemy. Plus, we now have a way to distinguish it and some characteristics. Perfect.

For the next couple of hundred years or so, anyone and everyone who had money, a brain, or both, dedicated their existence to 'this'. Discovering more of 'this'. Explaining more of 'this'. But more importantly, mastering more of 'this'. All focus in the arts and sciences turned to 'this', and once again there was thriving because, once again, like in every golden age there was a balance of the actions and practices that came about from the new assumption and the problems of the world before it. You can even see in the art that while the focus was clearly on 'this', the themes were symbols and impressions around the story of 'other than this' as they were able to bring it to life. While the new assumption and the world were keeping each other in check, things were great. But, once again, everything started to become too ordered, too predictable. Survival, once again, became more or less given, there was not a whole lot to worry about (at least relative to the dark ages, just like ancient golden ages relative to primitive tribes), and cowardice flourished. To make matters worse, many people were attempting to reconcile the values stemming from the increasing in popularity nothing-other-than-'this' assumption with the values of religion, and this started to become more so as more and more people profited from 'this' on the backs of others. Cue the totally contradicting values alert. And of course, cue the masses: "Hey, what about US?!" Philosophers, take your places...

Except this time, philosophy was not near as open as it had been a few hundred years before. In fact, each aeon always signaled yet something else that was not allowed to be considered. And what was it this time? One might propose that it was the *story* of 'other than this'. Because that is indeed what those who are determined to prove that there is *nothing* other than 'this' use as their strawman, and if someone dares utter anything to do with 'other than this' that is precisely what is barked back at them. But that is not actually it, not the story itself. Keep in mind, beginning with the Roman Catholic Church, this twisting around of the assumptions – a certain type of system with continuous 'bug patching' – had become very sophisticated, where each time the thing that is not allowed to be considered becomes harder and harder to specify, and yet easier to *subconsciously enforce*. This time around, what was actually not allowed to be considered was 'other than this' in any sense or capacity *whatsoever*, and the reason for this was not the assumption itself or in what context it could be applied to, but what had become linked to the story of the assumption: the Herd's reaction to it. Or more specifically, the Herd's reaction to the story of the story about an assumption fed to them originally by the Romans and the follow-on reality. Plus, the Herd absolutely loves to pretend that its new members are so much more sophisticated and enlightened than its old members (once a non-member has been crucified in order to shift things only to have it repeat…). In this way, 'other than this' became the new *symbol* for everything stupid, uneducated, and weak, in precisely the same way as a flag becomes a symbol for a nation with all the abstract identity and politics tied up in it. Nobody ever questions why the symbol emerged or what's behind it; the symbol reigns supreme, and from then on people will either die for the symbol or burn it as a war cry against the symbol, with absolutely no other thought put into it whatsoever. And if you are a philosopher or educated person, the last thing you want to be, or be seen as, is stupid, uneducated, and weak.

So here we were around the mid 19th century. Once again too comfortable and too knowledgeable to have any real point to life, and so obviously psychological well-being stops, closely followed by basic things not working, because, indeed, what *is* the point? And "those fucking whiny Christians over there – with their story about some dude in the sky who had a one-off son who is going to save humanity or his dad is going to reign down fire or whatever they are on about – are the cause of all the problems! If only they had just stuck to 'this'! Look at all the spineless weak-willed little people around waiting for someone to come save them. Disgusting…" And the thing is, I cannot blame them, I feel the same way, except today instead of religion we have things like 'politics'.

In any case, two separate people in two separate countries had had quite enough of the Herd. They were sick to death of the never-ending circular arguments that had arisen in their society and philosophy, and how it seemed that people actually were acting like Herd animals rather than what we thought of as people. And both saw how this phenomenon was taking over every aspect of society including government, to the point where the idea of an individual was simply non-existent. Furthermore, the concept of a true individual in popular culture (there were always people on the periphery such as alchemists) had not been raised in at least a few hundred years. Both of them exploded with a force of intellectual fury that echoed for the next century, because that which you attempt to stamp out will only return.

In the first instance of this return, we had Kierkegaard, who actually coined the term "the Herd" in the way that I have been using it. His solution was to simply go back to the actual essence of the story of 'other than this' rather than the story around the essence of the story, give the finger to the Herd, and totally walk out on it, which is not actually a terrible response; I for one very much respect him for that. However, besides his philosophy of separating from the Herd, the rest of his philosophy died for more or less obvious reasons. Anyone who would be capable of following its *actions* probably would have been put off by the story, and anyone was not put off by the story would probably not have been capable of following its actions... Indeed, this could probably not be truer. Kierkegaard provided a rebirth of the individual and the ability to give a commanding "NO" to the Herd, even if that meant death. But what was the essence of Kierkegaard's true philosophical sin? As all 20th-century philosophers and their fanboys will point out: certainty. Specifically, going back to the story as a source for way of life. Indeed, one has to wonder, if Kierkegaard had not had a certain level of certainty by utilizing the story, would he have been able to carry through with what he was saying and doing, seeing how he was (as far as he could tell) the first person to experience what he was experiencing in the civilization in which he lived?

In the second instance of this return, we had the far more prominent and enduring philosophical figure Nietzsche. He too gave the finger to the Herd. But unlike Kierkegaard, Nietzsche opted to completely reject the Christian story along with everything in it and even go so far as to make everyone who was even remotely connected with Christianity his enemy and exemplars in his writing. And given that (as far as he could tell) he was the first person to experience what he was experiencing in the civilization in which he lived, I can't say that I blame him. Just like Kierkegaard, it was hard enough to do what he was doing in the first place. Having an enemy was probably a necessity, and this Christianity thing (regardless of essence) had indeed led to a mass of spineless, weak, and totally dependent Herd animals, willing to digest whatever load of shit was fed to them. And remember, the actual target, i.e., the symbol, was 'other than this'. Yet, at the same time, his pronouncement that:

> "God is dead. God remains dead. And we have killed him. How shall we comfort ourselves, the murderers of all murderers? What was holiest and mightiest of all that the world has yet owned has bled to death under our knives: who will wipe this blood off us? What water is there for us to clean ourselves? What festivals of atonement, what sacred games shall we have to invent? Is not the greatness

of this deed too great for us? Must we ourselves not become gods simply to appear worthy of it?" Friedrich Nietzsche, *Thus Spoke Zarathustra*

The idea of becoming gods – *that* was Nietzsche's actual legacy, as in what people actually took up and ran with, and that is why this is his most famous quote. The rest of existential, post-modern, and so on, history, are simply footnotes to that idea. But at the same time, those people were (and still are) fueled by the hatred of the enemy 'other than this' – there is *nothing* other than 'this', they will chant. Philosophers, scientists, and wannabe Western Indian philosophy gurus alike.

But let me ask you a question. How exactly – and do I mean *exactly*, not some incoherent drivel – does one become a god if there is *nothing* else other than 'this'? Really think about that one for a minute. You can *play* God under that assumption, but it is impossible to *become* one, lest all of 'this' dissolves, which according to the assumption is impossible... It is a contradiction of the highest possible order. And remember, projection doesn't stop until you listen. And as I outlined previously, psychosis is just around the corner in such a situation, and although nobody can know for sure if that is what happened to Nietzsche, I've yet to hear a better explanation that is consistent with other facts surrounding his madness or that trumps Occam's Razor. I will repeat it, as the story that we have all come to know goes, on the last semi-coherent day of his life, after years of suffering and physical agony combined with isolation, non-recognition, and derision, Nietzsche walked across a street, saw a horse being flogged, threw his arms around it, broke into tears, and yelled out "I understand you!" and collapsed. *If* that story is true, one could take Nietzsche's actual life and need only to change a few details and tweak the plot just a little, and you'd basically have a 19th century version of Jesus Christ (not the Herd and abomination of the Church that came *after* him). Is it not possible that deep within his own unconscious, when he finally arrived at it, that possibility got processed? There are even theories that Nietzsche was not actually insane, but found exactly what he was looking for and was perfectly happy in a state of "divine madness", which could have been a result of enantiodromia. In either case, does it matter? A transformation happened regardless.

In any case, a point that I would like to make about Nietzsche and most of the modern philosophies that have that followed, and this simply has never been brought up with any seriousness in any philosophy that I am aware of, is that Nietzsche and everyone who followed made *exactly* the same mistake as Kierkegaard: certainty. Pure and simple. In either the case of Kierkegaard or Nietzsche, the reality of 'other than this', however one would like to look at it, was *KNOWN*! Do you understand? It was known, conscious, salient, could be clearly articulated; it was 'this' pointing right back at 'this'. It was the first time in Western history that we had found a way to really wage a war on 'other than this' and bring it to its knees, by philosophers no less. We had successfully used a combination of words and social norms to wipe it off the face of the intellectual planet. Although Nietzsche was hated or simply ignored by the philosophers and intellectuals of his day (why do people always forget this and similar facts?), his philosophy was more than welcomed by the 20th century. The assumption of *nothing* other than 'this' was now unequivocally the dominant intellectual and social force. But projection doesn't stop. Projection will just keep going until you listen.

Cue the totalitarian 20th century led by Germany, Russia, and China, where everything is known and it is now *illegal* for there to be anything 'other than this'. If you even think about thinking about otherwise, you will be executed. And here also was a key point in history. The frenzy against 'other than this' became so intense, that both 'this' and 'other than this' had taken on a completely new abstract form. Whatever either of those things had meant up until that point were gone. These two things were now a *state of mind...*

Nazis loved Nietzsche. But obviously it was not the philosophy that they loved. So many historians go on about how his philosophy led to Nazi Germany, but none of them can clearly articulate how. They stumble about and then just end up pointing to the fact that Nazis loved Nietzsche, The End. But what was always utterly confusing to me was that Nietzsche was a person who produced a philosophy in which every single word was the polar opposite of totalitarianism and group think, and often included admired aspects of Jews, an affinity for Poland, and a hatred of German culture. So, what was it then that was so appealing to Nazis? The assumption! Once again, remember the sophistication keeps on increasing. It had become so sophisticated that Nazi Germany became a totalitarian regime while simultaneously valuing something that was completely against totalitarian regimes! It didn't matter what the actual words were anymore – completely irrelevant! Sound familiar? And obviously this did not just stop at Nazi Germany even though for whatever reason everyone wants to pretend that it did and ignore those still in power to this day that did far worse, mainly China. The mentality spread to left-wing countries that made the holocaust an actual warmup exercise.

And people think that all of this war stuff and totalitarianism across a large part of the world was the doing of a few crazy people. Yeah, a few crazy people managed to kill a couple hundred million people. That makes total sense. Again, Jung covers the worldwide phenomenon in exhaustive detail so I'm not going to repeat it. But what I also want to point out is that it was not just limited to warfare or countries like China that continue with the original format. Why would anyone think that something that affected the global psyche would limit itself to *one* area? If the psyche on a whole was infected, that means that likely everything else that was produced via the psyche was infected as well as offspring; and just because the whole world war thing stopped that doesn't mean that what we might now call a sophisticated self-learning algorithm stopped. Philosophy, science, social norms, social structures, and every aspect of everyday life were infected, but no cure was ever created for the disease. Something Jung tried desperately in vain to get across but nobody listened. Oh sure, a few people tried for a few years in the 1960's and then failed miserably by simply falling right back into the exact same trap that they were trying to get out of, but nothing else ever happened on any meaningful scale.

This history is precisely what has led us to our current scientific, political, and philosophic worldview: we *know* beyond a shadow of a doubt that there is *nothing* other than 'this'.

But then, we have the nerve to chant over and over "anything is possible!"

And no one will even process the contradiction, much less attempt to deal with it.

And there are highly sophisticated weapons in every location of society to enforce the assumption and the certainty that comes with it. There is no personal responsibility because there is no individual because *nothing* other than 'this' exists. Do you understand? 'This' now carries total responsibility. 'This' will dictate what to think, what to do with life, how to allocate resources as well as how to fight about it; all of it. 'This' will give you exactly two sides of every possible thing to argue about to keep you busy and killing each other so that you will never again have the time or energy to even consider 'other than this'. 'This' will invade your consciousness, expand its territory to its maximum possible size with huge libraries of syntax and language to decipher, and make absolutely certain that anything individual is shut down and crushed beyond all possible recognition and repair. You will be so busy processing the waste product of 'this' that you will do it for the rest of your life. You might even willingly dedicate your life to 'this'; maybe even die for it. No matter what battle, side, group, politic, or identity you choose, you will always be under the control of 'this' because those are *precisely the things keeping you under control*. You think the algorithm didn't learn from its previous exposure to things like religion just how easy it is to control people if you can confuse them over assumptions, start creating new values, and then pin those values against each other? *Even better if you can get different values from the same assumption*, as this would be the ultimate state of contradiction and prompt any 'sane' person to hand over the sovereignty of their individual consciousness and enter a state of complete and total irresponsibility and apathy.

A brush with 'other than this' in the United States

During the early to mid 1900's, there was a very brief brush with 'other than this' in the United States via the pragmatists, of which George Kelly himself said he and his work most closely aligned. Although it was basically ignored, one of the best examples of getting into the 'other than this' realm was by the pragmatist William James[10]. Pragmatism is largely considered to be the only real philosophical work to ever have come out of the United States, and of the pragmatists only one person was ever considered to be a real philosopher outside of the United States: John Dewey.

Dewey[11] pointed out that the quest for certainty was exactly what divided theory and practice, or what should work based on what actually does work, and that these two things should have never been split to begin with. His philosophy is interesting indeed, and one can gain all kinds of insights into epistemology that are never covered quite the same way in continental philosophy. I, for one,

---

[10] James, W. (1902). *The varieties of religious experience: A study in human nature.* Longmans, Green and Co.

[11] Dewey, J. (1929). *The quest for certainty.* Minton, Balch.

just take his observations (as well as Kelly's) to be perfectly obvious, but maybe I was just born a pragmatist. I will not cover Dewey in any detail, I simply wish to show a thing or two as it relates to our running story.

What I find to be most important about Dewey's ideas on the quest for certainty was that he pointed out how personal belief was the only thing that ever led to any actual innovation or fundamental change. Note that he was a pragmatist, so whatever this personal belief happens to be is completely irrelevant with respect to some politic – that was precisely one of the things that pragmatism was trying to get at. I.e., we can go back to the tired old 'argument' that I've been trying to avoid all along around [in Dolly's voice] "do you believe in God or not? Baah!!!" One person could personally believe yes, and the other no. In either case, innovation or fundamental change occurs if it goes against the current status quo. But in *either* case, the ideas of belief and uncertainty persist; something 'other than this'. Dewey pointed out that if this belief is not there (or we could say if the individual is silenced), then all anyone is doing is continuing to improve or optimize methods to provide more certainty. Thus, his philosophy could just as easily be called a philosophy of uncertainty, and, since he was the leading pragmatist, a philosophy that sees uncertainty as the very thing that allows everything else to actually work.

However, while Dewey is considered to be the only 'real' philosopher that the United States has ever produced, his philosophy was completely ignored, even by the United States... And obviously everyone ignored it because it was a philosophy of 'other than this' just when the dominance of nothing other than 'this' was coming into full swing. The algorithm kicked in and wiped pragmatism off the face of the planet without having to do much of anything.

This was another key period in the increasing sophistication of the Algorithm.

Post-totalitarianism and irresponsibility

Certainty, like anything else, is also a type of projection. In case you haven't noticed thus far, there are definite patterns that have in fact kept repeating themselves. History does repeat itself. Nobody every learns. We know that much. It's easily observable. It never stops. The process of repeating patterns is the *one* thing that *is* certain. But as Howard Bloom points out, the one thing that emerges out of these certain patterns is uncertainty. This is what we cannot stand, and it is the failure to recognize the certainty of repeating patterns that results in projecting certainty onto anything and everything else. And each year the salience of these patterns becomes harder to ignore through accumulating information that is at the tip of our fingers. Each year the projection grows stronger and the resulting psychological sickness expands its territory and power.

And that thing... that unknown and unspeakable thing that persists with complete and total uncertainty through the certainty of pattern, is the one thing that no matter what our assumptions are, we simply cannot allow to exist. The source of ALL responsibility. It is not allowed to exist, and we will do anything within our power to avoid looking it in the face. That *reflection* is something so horrifying that we have been subconsciously doing all we can to get rid of it for at least the last 400 years, continuing to build ever increasingly sophisticated power and semantic systems to keep from looking. Yet, the more you try to stamp something out...

Since that whole religion thing did not work out when it came to certainty, and then attempting to force certainty by warfare ultimately did not work either because that reflected just a little bit too much back at us, the algorithm started to learn that maybe sheer force was the wrong way to go about it. Actually, it seems as though human beings themselves were helping to construct this algorithm via their own human nature. The assumption of nothing other than 'this' was working to alleviate responsibility, but maybe it did not need to be forced at all. Maybe the Herd would just buy into something voluntarily. Death and killing could no longer be maintained as a way to spread the assumption of nothing other than 'this'. We needed something else. We needed the omnipresent threat of death, and this came in the form of nuclear annihilation, which worked for a while. But that was ultimately a little too unsophisticated. Something like that could just run its course, and what then? It was a great place to start, but then we needed something a little more subconscious. What we needed was to play on the biggest fear that human beings rightfully had for hundreds of thousands of years up until only recently, otherwise you would almost certainly die: the threat of being ostracized.

The algorithm had reached its most effective form. It had reached all the way back to primitive man and worked exactly in the same way because 'other than this' simply does not exist; just as back then, it's not a debate. The process of "normalization" and immediately stamping out anything individual has come full circle. Now it is all about groups and group identity, and all responsibility is now hoisted onto the group or its projected enemy. The group obviously has its finger-pointing scapegoat enemy group; however, just as with primitive man, the individual scares the hell out of the group, so if anything individual crops up, it is stamped out as quickly as possible by social ostracization. And the algorithm learns almost instantaneously in the modern age. If something individual does indeed happen, then a group quickly forms around it so that any idea of true individualism is lost in a sea of group identity. It can now jump between groups or morph overnight to the entire world (and as I write these words that is exactly what has happened) and back again, but it always has to do with the group and its norms. Some groups are even popping up and forming norms where the basis of the group is to be against norms! Camille Paglia (a feminist and social critic) as well as Jordan Peterson (who Camille has wholeheartedly agreed with) have more or less brought this phenomenon to light, but the first was ignored and the second was treated like and called a Nazi even though his entire career was spent understanding totalitarianism, and later standing up to it. I would love to see what would happen to Simone de Beauvoir if she were to come back to life with a face change. What would the hordes of so-called 'feminists' do to the very person that laid the groundwork for their individual freedoms? We all know what would happen if Jesus were to do the same...

This brings us to the latest state of affairs that, like many of the previously mentioned shifts, was over a period of time and not exactly punctuated. But one could say that it started to come into its own right around the 1970's, just after there was a flare-up of 'other than this' that scared the hell out of the nothing-other-than-'this' caretakers.

Václav Havel[12] calls what Eastern Europe was experiencing around that time and, indeed, what I am attempting to get at and what we *all* are now experiencing today, "post-totalitarianism", and in this term he did "not wish to imply by the prefix 'post-' that the system is no longer totalitarian; on the contrary, I mean that it is totalitarian in a way fundamentally different from classical dictatorships". It is quite simply the most sophisticated form of control ever created or conceived. Its core aim is simple: to rid the world once and for all of 'other than this' and any notion of individual consciousness or responsibility by simply giving the Herd exactly what it wants: total irresponsibility. This is not unlike the previous points in history that I have outlined. What is different is the speed and precision in which the Algorithm eliminates 'other than this', earlier by force, then by means of propaganda, then the Media, then the Internet, then social media, then complete ubiquity.

I cannot do justice to Havel's brilliant essay without quoting almost the entirety of it, but I will do my best to summarize what is most important here. If you have not read his book, I urge you to do so as soon as you can. If it were not for that book I might not have ever written this one, and it is the best historical example built on the observations of someone who has actually lived much of the social psychology that I have outlined up to this point and could clearly see it happening at the country level (for which he

---

12 Havel, V., & Keane, J. (1985). The Power of the powerless: Citizens against the state in central-eastern Europe. Armonk, N.Y: M.E. Sharpe

was imprisoned for pointing out, not surprisingly). Furthermore, Havel pointed out that the phenomenon of post-totalitarianism was spreading the world over. It was not just in Eastern Europe or other Soviet-affected countries, it was spreading to the West and its so-called 'democracies'.

Havel was not so much concerned with Soviet force than he was by the adaptation of the Soviet politics into daily life in Eastern Europe, and how these two things "could merge into what the authorities called "normalization"; power was as it was, and alternatives were unthinkable"[13]. Ironically, given the basis for what started everything Soviet, distractions such as consumer goods and television squashed all motivation to do anything differently in the public sphere. People enslaved themselves because they never stopped to ask who they were or what they should do with their lives. Quite simply, the assumption that there is nothing other than 'this' was no longer totally unconscious, it was more or less stated social policy. Havel noticed that in place of brute force as a means to stamp out nonconformity, a system had arisen that "has become so ossified politically that there is practically no way for such nonconformity to be implemented within its official structures"[14]. This is an extremely important point that we will later revisit when talking about "parallel structures", but for now it is important because what he is saying is that no matter what course of action, side, or politic that you take within the official structures, those are the very things that are maintaining the status quo; the very things keeping people silenced and under control. I.e., one cannot change anything by getting behind something that is recognized political

---

[13] ibid

[14] Ibid

as such, even if it is the most fringe political ideology that there is – it is still recognized, understand? Anything that might have at one time been considered honestly political has been eliminated. Thus, for Havel, any form of 'dissidence' was only possible via some other means than politics. According to him, this was actually living "the aims of life" – again, something we will come back to.

In any case, the point Havel was trying to make was simply that the essence of totalitarianism had stopped being enforced via brute force, and had evolved into a sort of structure via normalization, something in which people voluntarily participated, and this structure was increasingly enforced by technology. Totalitarianism had not actually gone anywhere, and, indeed, it was expanding its territory. Furthermore, he pointed out how much of what held it in place was completely unconscious after years of going back and forth between two opposing sets of values underneath a single assumption...

But what I found most compelling about Havel's work was not that it is interesting in pointing out how totalitarianism persists, or that I can use it to further elaborate on the phenomena that I have been studying for the last 15 years and say: "Hah! Look! Someone else agrees with me!" What I found truly compelling was Havel's exposé of people *living in a lie* versus living in *personal* truth (again I point to pragmatism) and what that looks like, as well as the consequences of doing either.

One example he uses is the tale of the "greengrocer". The greengrocer makes absolutely sure that he always displays a sign in his storefront window that says, "Workers of the world, unite!", not because of his enthusiasm over the associated politics or what it means, but because it was delivered to him along with his produce, it has simply been done that way for years, and furthermore it is a symbol of his submission to the post-totalitarian system. Havel points out that neither the greengrocer nor anyone else ever stop to even consider what the signs mean, nor do they care. What they do care about is being singled out. Havel also uses the greengrocer to illustrate how people are constantly living for the aims of the post-totalitarian system rather than the aims of life. They must live within this lie in order to survive, and they can never shout out "the emperor has no clothes!" Furthermore, and this is a point I have been trying to make for years to no avail, he points out over and over in various ways that this system of post-totalitarianism is not something that is maintained by some conspiratorial group behind closed doors; the system is composed of, maintained, and enforced by the average person... Furthermore, the ritual (or practices) ends up taking place of any actual assumption or core values.

> "We have seen that the real meaning of the greengrocer's slogan has nothing to do with what the text of the slogan actually says. Even so, this real meaning is quite clear and generally comprehensible because the code is so familiar: the greengrocer declares his loyalty (and he can do no other if his declaration is to be accepted) in the only way the regime is capable of hearing; that is, by accepting the prescribed *ritual*, by accepting appearances as reality, by accepting the given rules of the game. In doing so, however, he has himself become a player in the game, thus

making it possible for the game to go on, for it to exist in the first place."[15]

"[T]hey must live within a lie. They need not accept the lie. It is enough for them to have accepted their life with it and in it. For by this very fact, individuals confirm the system, fulfill the system, make the system, are the system."[16]

Havel also points out how this system is completely dependent on *demoralized* people, it deepens this demoralization, and it is in fact a *projection* of it into society. And in what will become more important as we proceed, and something that was surely Havel's response to the Marxist population, he points out that:

"Individuals can be alienated from themselves only because there is *something* in them to alienate."[17]

So why would people do such a thing? Why would they purposely enslave themselves, feel the humiliation that comes with it, and allow themselves to be totally alienated from *their* actual aims of life? Well, first, we are coming back to what was outlined previously regarding inertia, responsibility, projection, assumptions, and so on. But also, there is Havel's idea of freedom in which he points out that what most people consider freedom, i.e., the ability to do whatever one is inclined to do, is actually not – it is the opposite of freedom. Havel points to the fact that people are so

---

[15] ibid

[16] ibid

[17] ibid

quick to buy into and maintain the post-totalitarian system because the post-totalitarian system and everything it represents (eating bad food, listening to bad music, irresponsibility) is exactly what they are inclined to do! People say that they want freedom, but then do the exact opposite! (Does this sound familiar?) What freedom is, according to Havel, and I wholeheartedly agree with him, is stepping outside of the patterns of your non-repeating self, thinking about what you ought to do, and occasionally having the courage to actually do it. THAT is freedom.

But in addition to all the psychological and existential 'mumbo jumbo', there is also the very practical matter illustrated by an actual person that Havel worked with while he was employed at a brewery. At this brewery, he talks of his immediate superior who he simply calls "Š". The only thing that Š was ever concerned with was making better beer so that people could enjoy it – something that anywhere that promotes the "good of the people" should agree with, right? Š was always at the brewery, and improving the beer was all he ever talked about. Then one day Š decides to write a letter to his manager's superior outlining how they could improve the beer. Since there was the possibility of improvement, this reflected poorly on the manager,

> "Who was a member of the Communist Party's district committee … Š's analysis was described as a "defamatory document" and Š himself was labelled a "political saboteur" … By speaking the truth, Š had stepped out of line, broken the rules, cast himself out, and he ended up as a sub-citizen, stigmatized as an enemy. He could now say

anything he wanted, but he could never, as a matter of principle, expect to be heard."[18]

However, the best example of post-totalitarianism through normalization is something that everyone is familiar with. In fact, it is the ONE thing you simply cannot talk about or question anywhere in the world at this very moment – in some places you can even go to prison! It is an absolute triumph of normalization, and is laying the groundwork for a type of global normalization that we have never seen before.

"Hey, 600,000 people just died this year from the flu…[silence]… Um, ok, just over 3 million people died this year from alcohol… [silence]… Are you deaf? How about this, approximately 5 to 10 million people (maybe more) died this year from all kinds of problems related to obesity and the mass marketing of unhealthy lifestyles – something that is completely under our control… [silence]… I think we are nearing something like 10 or 20 million people…[silence]… Oh, wait, I know. Hey! One person in Melbourne has a community transmitted case of Covid-19."

"LOCK DOWN THE ENTIRE CITY! No one is allowed outside of a 5-kilometer radius of their home. If they do, they will be arrested! Shut down the national borders; no one is allowed to leave unless they have an exception; freedom of movement is gone and it is now illegal, just like North Korea. Violation of human rights taken to highest court? Throw it out. United Nations doesn't care either. Everyone will stand 1.5 meters from

---

[18] ibid

each other at all times! Facemasks are mandatory on all public transportation and indoors! If you refuse you will be arrested! Flood the media outlets with constant updates on how the hospitals are having a hard time; make sure to show pictures of as much death as possible, but only Covid related. Arrest anyone who shows any sign of questioning any of this. 'This' is all there is, and you *will* show your submission and allegiance.

And you want to tell me that there is nothing psychological going on here at all? You want to tell me that there is *nothing other than 'this'*??? After we go from absolutely *never* sounding a *peep* over the millions of deaths that occur every year that are completely and totally under our control, or the hundreds of thousands of people that die each year from the flu; after all that, not a single fucking word, and then all of the sudden this is the ONLY thing?! That kind of disproportionate response only happens during a mass psychosis. One moron I was talking to, immediately after I pointed all this out, in the very next sentence mooed to me in what I can only assume would be the tone of voice as that of the greengrocer "I just don't understand how you can't see how this will kill millions of people", the literal next moment after I had pointed out the death of millions of people. I was speechless. I simply found a way to get out of the conversation, because I was scared that if I did not then Woden was going to come to life in me right then and there in the dining room and I was in and slaughter Dolly right there on the table.

I don't care that there are people who think it is a hoax and I don't care that people are dying (that divide and the resulting control on *both* 'sides' is the algorithm in action). The numbers only support one and one thing only: the *disproportionate response* over a phenomenon and, no, the definition of disproportionate is not my fucking opinion. I will say that again. I do not care for a single fact other than a fraction of the people start dying than normal over which we say and do nothing and then we go from that to panicking the world over and leading to North Korea style border controls in countries like Australia. The *disproportion* is a numerical FACT. However, apparently, the whole thing just is what it is and any alternative to the current status quo is unthinkable, and if you do not put up your metaphorical "Workers of the world, unite!" you will be ostracized like nothing ever seen before, on a global level. The blatantly obvious *disproportion* has not been brought up in a single news outlet or anyone that I have talked to, and I highly doubt it will ever see the light of day, precisely because of what Havel says about politics.

But I can hear Dolly in the background baaing, mooing, and barking some regurgitated drivel. So, just like before, even though it's ridiculous, let's just drop that entire phenomenon for the moment, shall we? Let's pretend that the entire response the world over was totally justified, the post-totalitarian system is not at work in that particular sense, and that I am just one of those 'totally stupid and insane people' and I should be fed to the wolves just like the possessed Herd would love to see done. Fine. But then there is one fact that is so undeniable that even the Herd cannot argue with it, and not a single Herd member that I have brought this up with has done so. First, it was pointed out by a few health professionals in countries that still have people with a shred of respectability left, that almost 100% of the ICU admissions or deaths in people which are not in the groups that would be just as vulnerable to anything else (e.g., the flu or comorbid) were highly overweight or obese. Second, and most importantly, not a *single* health organization, government or otherwise took to the media and told people that the best thing that they could do was to GET IN SHAPE... *NOTHING* in the way of *personal* health was *encouraged*. FACT.

In fact, what did we see? The exact opposite. Not just the encouragement of the opposite, but in some places the force under police or military power to stay inside where people on the whole will become even less healthy physically and psychologically! Why is the entire world paying for a bunch of fat asses? You think that some people don't think exactly that deep down and just cannot bring themselves to say it? And what effect do you think that is having on people psychologically, as they watch their lives destroyed by doing the actual right thing? Just like Havel said, the system depends on demoralization, and anything that leads to less responsibility, further demoralization, and thereby an increase in people participating and enforcing the post-totalitarian structure is the course of action that is taken, period... There is no other side of the story, there is no other arguing needed, and no other possibility is allowed.

For the first time in recorded history the governments and health organizations (I absolutely cannot believe I just wrote that) of the world had the opportunity to push responsibility via a healthy lifestyle behind the fear of the Herd – do something healthy with the fear – and they did the exact opposite. In place of that was "stop everything, sit, and wait for us to provide you with a miracle", and another precedent was set for post-totalitarianism and irresponsibility. Furthermore, there were more than a few prophetic things around all of this approximately 10 years before any of this occurred (see literature on the lag between the arts and reality), in both music and literature (my favorite is Karnivool's music video "We Are"). One example, in what I consider to be the most non-coincidental things I've seen even though it would be labeled as such, is the intro to Havel's book written in 2018 (one year before the Covid panic-demic) by Timothy Snyder:

> "The continuity between communism and our world is normalization: mendacity without metaphysics, communicated by technology … Now, as under late communism, what threatens normalizers in power is the possibility that people *will speak to one another in real life*"[19] (emphasis added)

I don't care about your personal temperament, politics, opinion on world matters, whatever side you take in the pathetic 'debates' over social media, or your goddamned opinion one way or another over a fucking virus – if you aren't asking questions at this point in time, you are quite simply unconscious, you are perpetuating the spirit of totalitarianism, and YOU are the greatest threat that our world has ever known.

"But…but…but…this time is *different*!!! BAAAHHHHH!!! MOOOOO!!!!" Oh, Dolly, it always is different, isn't it? That is what you and your cloned counterparts repeat over and over throughout history, never learn, and then the rest of us have to suffer because of your no-spine having, emotionally reactive pathetic excuse for a human being. When communist Russia and China rose up, that was different, wasn't it? It was not that the

---

[19] ibid

Herd doesn't want anything to do with responsibility and let the alienation happen to them, *willingly...* No. That new capitalism thing was the source of the masses and their unwillingness to wipe their own ass – never before had any sort of phenomenon existed, right? (Except that it obviously had...). And when the income gap in the United States became something that other countries cannot even conceive, and made it impossible for any small business or independent life to exist, you didn't let that happen willingly either, did you? No, again, that time was different. Or in Germany when a group of people came around suggesting that they could make your life better if you just handed over all decision-making authority to them, not you again either I suppose? Or post-911 invasion and the overreaching powers that came with the Patriot Act, and everyone eventually thought "hey, maybe that was a bad idea", nope, not you either. Or when the Romans took over or when, and on and on and on and on and on...... It was always different, wasn't it? Every goddamned time you go on and on about how in *this* instance it is totally fine to hand over individual rights, responsibility, and ultimately consciousness *itself*. In this instance it's totally different! You fucking Herd animal. Do whatever you want, Dolly. I am done listening. I'm not buying it. I'm not going to shut up. And I'm not willing to hand over my individual consciousness for *any* price, including my life. THERE *IS* SOMETHING OTHER THAN 'THIS'!!!

For the rest of you who actually are switched on enough to notice the meta patterns above the Herd's mooing, baaing, and barking of conclusions around any given 'topic of debate', just remember one of the most important points Havel tried to make: People do not decide to become dissidents, it just turns out that way; *all* dissidents start with simply wanting to do a good job…

The urge to rebel

Most people at some point in their lives have the urge to rebel. However, when they do, it's usually not very clear what exactly they are rebelling against or why.

Rebellion usually makes itself known in teenage years and early 20's, and everyone just looks on and says "yeah, that's just part of growing up – gotta push those boundaries – they'll get over it". And for the most part, they do get over it, right around the age of 25 when they all look around at the big wide unknown-ness of everything and reconsider that whole rebellion thing; first you needed to pick a career, now it is time to pick a socially constructed *identity*, which in places such as the US is basically the same thing. And that is usually where the story ends. People pick an identity such as 'scientist', 'family person', 'feminist', 'anti-feminist', 'human person', 'technological person', and so on, and then spend the rest of their lives living out some lie while they bicker back and forth at picnics or dinner parties about those "other people" and how horrible they are, and consume as much or whatever kind of media they can that will keep their worldview intact. If anything novel arises, then the novelty is split into two 'political sides' along temperamental lines and incorporated like anything else. If that doesn't work then everything simply stops until we can collectively figure out how to get rid of it. Control achieved. Post-totalitarian system reinforced. There is nothing other than 'this'.

However, some people refuse to 'grow up'; they continue to rebel beyond the age of 25 and simply cannot bring themselves to sit idly by. Instead of choosing an identity, these people generally get behind a cause, but isn't that just another form of identity? The reason I say that is because I have never once met a person behind a cause that could clearly articulate to me *exactly* why they were doing what they were doing, or that they had put any real thought into it or thinking through things. I can even think about my own life when I was that age – when I did the same thing – and I had no idea why I was doing it either. What I know now is that I chose what you would call a left-leaning cause because I am naturally a compassionate person. "Are you f'n kidding me? YOU, compassionate? After everything you've said?!" Shut up, Dolly. I am compassionate, and that combined with your stupid ass is precisely why I've had such a hard time. But without you Dolly I wouldn't be here. I wouldn't have had the persistent stream of bullshit to fight through that would have actually allowed me to one day get to the real bottom of what I was doing – to stop being you. However, most rebels do not get to the bottom of what they are doing. They might be lifetime rebels but, again, they are totally unaware of what is actually driving it. I.e., not doing anything I have outlined thus far, examining core values for contradictions, examining assumptions, asking "are those *really* assumptions?", etc.

So, what ends up happening is that these people tend to end up right back where they started. You see it over and over again with various causes, whereby the person behind the cause becomes the exact same thing that they set out to fight. It should be clearly apparent at this point in the text as to why this happens, and there are countless examples of this in art and literature. However, my absolute favorite well-known phenomenon, as it pertains to the topic of rebellion behind a cause, is what we have seen countless times over the ages where a group that starts a revolution to overthrow some oppressor ends up becoming the new oppressor and that pattern just repeats itself indefinitely. We know this, but just like everything else I've been pointing out, we keep doing it. Why?

Well, instead of looking at the supposed reasons people rebel, or just throwing it out as irrelevant, what are some of the abstractions we could draw from the typical rebel? What can be said about all rebels? Well, *all* rebels want to do something that is very personal and felt very deeply, and yet they are kept from doing it in some way or another (by others or themselves). As such, *all* rebels feel that they are being oppressed in some way. As a result of both of those things, *all* rebels are highly irritated, sometimes agitated, and generally on edge. And what we can undeniably say about all rebels is that *all rebels simply cannot let go of something*, and rather than let go they will do the most seemingly absurd things if push comes to shove with respect to letting go of this 'something'. As Dostoyevsky pointed out about "man" (which, really, he means himself or other rebels, obviously, since "man" on the whole does the complete opposite):

"Shower upon him every earthly blessing, drown him in a sea of happiness, so that nothing but bubbles of bliss can be seen on the surface; give him economic prosperity, such that he should have nothing else to do but sleep, eat cakes and busy himself with the continuation of his species, and even then out of sheer ingratitude, sheer spite, man would play you some nasty trick. He would even risk his cakes and would deliberately desire the most fatal rubbish, the most uneconomical absurdity, simply to introduce into all this positive good sense his fatal fantastic element. It is just his fantastic dreams, his vulgar folly that he will desire to retain, simply in order to prove to himself--as though that were so necessary-- that men still are men and not the keys of a piano, which the laws of nature threaten to control so completely that soon one will be able to desire nothing but by the calendar. And that is not all: even if man really were nothing but a piano-key, even if this were proved to him by natural science and mathematics, even then he would not become reasonable, but would purposely do something perverse out of simple ingratitude, simply to gain his point. And if he does not find means he will contrive destruction and chaos, will contrive sufferings of all sorts, only to gain his point! He will launch a curse upon the world, and as only man can curse (it is his privilege, the primary distinction between him and other animals), may be by his curse alone he will attain his object--that is, convince himself that he is a man and not a piano-key! If you say that all this, too, can be calculated and tabulated--chaos and darkness and curses, so that the mere possibility of calculating it all beforehand would stop it all, and reason would reassert itself, then man would purposely go mad in order to be rid of reason and gain his point! I believe in it, I answer for it, for the whole work of man really seems to consist in nothing but proving to himself every minute that he is a man and not a piano-key! It may be at the cost of his skin; it may be by cannibalism! And this being so, can one help being tempted to rejoice that it has not yet come off, and that desire still depends on *something we don't know*? – Fyodor Dostoevsky, *Notes from the Underground* (emphasis added)

He is right, of course, and it would explain a whole lot, including our rebels that apparently have no idea what they are doing (which is most of them). And yet, it is abundantly clear what direction society has been going in for hundreds of years, as well as why someone like Dostoevsky or Nietzsche would have had the motivation to write what they did and risk everything in the first place. We can look around and see that the very systems that are causing so much devastation are our response to them... I have said it over and over and will say it again, projection will not stop until you listen.

As I have done my absolute best to show up to this point and can simply say no more, THE problem in our schizophrenic world is the inability to assume that there is something 'other than this' and enforcing via any means necessary that there is nothing other than 'this'. And if there were any one characteristic of any rebel that has ever lived, it would be their unyielding belief that there is indeed something 'other than this' and the absolute refusal to give in to the opposite. Throughout history the best of the best have paid for it with their sanity and/or their lives. Is this a choice or not? Maybe we cannot know, but the rest is phenomenological fact.

And if there truly were *nothing* other than 'this', why would some people resist that so vehemently? Better yet, why the need to enforce it?... It cannot even pass basic thought experiments and yet it is increasingly the basis for our entire society.

Mental illness

"In individuals, insanity is rare; but in groups, parties, nations, and epochs, it is the rule." – Friedrich Nietzsche, *Beyond Good and Evil*

I have constructed a theory over the last 20 years regarding mental illness, and I believe that it is perfectly in line with Jung, Kelly, or any relational, analytic, depth, etc. psychology for that matter. First, individual mental illness is not a classification of different types of illnesses but, rather, the degree to which one has a psychological conflict, and this can be plotted on a continuum. Second, that conflict is in direct proportion to the misalignment between an individual's conscious or unconscious projections of *possibility*, and the social norms and expectations of the society in which they live. Third, the resulting individual dysfunction is a product of overwhelming levels of this misalignment combined with an inability or unwillingness of the individual to cope. What this implies is that 'mental illness' is as relative as time, and is completely dependent upon the observer. Finally, and this is what I consider to be my main contribution and what I have been building up to, all individual or societal mental illness can be seen as the result of misaligned core assumptions and values, i.e., contradictions, and the degree to which one becomes incapacitated is the degree to which those contradictions become salient and simultaneously reinforced by others. The astute reader may see that what I am pointing out is how individuals become incapacitated. That is true. However, the truly brilliant will have already figured out that what I am actually outlining in this book is the schematic for an individual *weapon*, and I make zero apologies for it, especially since it is one of the only things in existence even attempting to provide a means for *creation*.

> "Do not think that I have come to bring peace to the earth. I have not come to bring peace, but a sword" – Jesus Christ

Just like the US tax system, it is in Herd psychologists' best interest to make the topic of mental illness as complicated as possible and to make anyone involved feel as helpless as possible. So, they have produced all kinds of interesting classifications and categories of mental illness in a gigantic reference book called the Diagnostic and Statistical Manual of Mental Disorders (DSM), and any time a mental illness is spoken of in the realm of Herd psychology it is a 'disease' – signaling something unavoidable or out of the realm of personal responsibility. Yet, it always struck me as rather odd that if you read anything listed in the DSM, almost every one of these classifications comes with the caveat that the person's inability to function is what is ultimately required to be 'diagnosed' – without that everything is ok if they tick all the other boxes... Or how people who actually reference the DSM see most of these cases as needing an army of drugs, psychologists, ongoing treatment plans, and so on, yet continental psychologies or the few pragmatic psychologies that are practiced are able to have far higher success rates simply by one-on-one discussions, which are then ignored by the Herd's psychologists because "those methods aren't rigorous enough" What?!... (again, see Dewey). Again, it is not in any Herd psychologist's best interest to make this any simpler, and I have never understood why people arbitrarily elevate someone who has "Dr." in front of their name to anything higher than any other business simply trying to make money without the same level of needing to prove itself or earn trust. Like many other things in the post-totalitarian system, it just is what it is and that's that!

I, however, do not make my living/income as a clinical psychologist or psychiatrist, even if I have been studying psychology my whole adult life and it was the central focus of my Ph.D. Therefore, I have no Herd-approved role and the resulting paycheck to lose or gain from looking at it differently... Furthermore, that very reality has allowed me to go broader and deeper into psychology than most 'real' psychologists would.

The way I see all mental illness is a single phenomenon of how well or little can one function, period, and you can plot any 'disorder' on a continuum of dysfunction. Parallel to this continuum, we have another that is the source of the dysfunction, which is the degree to which one has a psychological conflict. Parallel to both of these, we have another that is the source of psychological conflict, which is the degree of misalignment between an individual's conscious or unconscious projections of possibility and the social norms and expectations of the society in which they live. Finally, parallel to all of the above, we have a continuum which is the ability or willingness to cope with that misalignment. Thus, we have three continuums for separate levels of analysis, which make up a single overall continuum. Then, plotting any disorder is very simple. On one end of the overall continuum, you have the lightest of disorders, let's just say depression. On the other end of the continuum, you have the worst of disorders, let's just say schizophrenia. The following figure illustrates this:

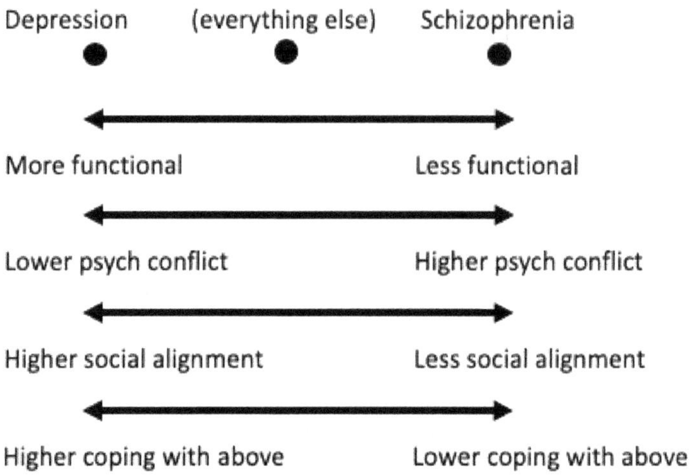

Depression   (everything else)   Schizophrenia
●   ●   ●

←——————————————————————————→
More functional   Less functional

←——————————————————————————→
Lower psych conflict   Higher psych conflict

←——————————————————————————→
Higher social alignment   Less social alignment

←——————————————————————————→
Higher coping with above   Lower coping with above

Figure 3 - Continuum of psychological dysfunction

Now, in addition to taking out the totally unnecessary convolution of mental disorder, what I am also trying to point out here is that 'mental disorder' under this model could just as easily be called *social disorder*...

"But...we are close to finding the genes that make up these disorders, including schizophrenia!" Goddamnit Dolly, you just don't shut up do you? Have you ever done your own research or had an original thought in your life? First, as someone who actually worked in a statistical organization, I looked into that exact data around 15 years ago out of personal interest. I was honestly interested to see if there was indeed a connection (I wasn't so jaded yet). And what I found was that whenever this data was compared with the actual general population, the statistical significance crumbled. Only years later did I come to understand (by experience) how your sort of statistics get produced... And by the way, your Herd members have been saying that they are close for something like 40 years and haven't gotten an inch closer. Again, it couldn't possibly be that that line itself props up an entire industry, could it? Second, let's again throw out my first argument, as we have started to make this a thing, and let's just look at what your 'science' is saying even if there was an actual statistical significance (which there isn't). What that significance says is that there is a *correlation* between some genes and levels of dysfunction, The End. There is *nothing* in your Herd's research to say what that correlation is built on; nothing to say *why* it is happening. It couldn't possibly have something to do with something that would lead to a predisposition to simply going against the Herd, could it? Or 1000 other *possibilities* for that matter. I know, impossible, especially since there is nothing other than 'this'. Once again, you have shown yourself to just bleat out some regurgitated drivel without the slightest thought whatsoever as to what you are saying or alternatives to it.

And is my way of looking at this so hard to believe? Harder to believe than the convoluted drivel of Abnormal Psychology? Is it so hard to believe that given the absolute relentlessness of the post-totalitarian system or even anything 'less grandiose' that doesn't go by that name (government, corporations, social media, whatever) bearing its gargantuan weight down on any individual that dares to assume something else other than what it does, that this wouldn't result in an individual totally losing their shit? How could someone NOT be utterly miserable at the very *least*? The little Herd animals of the world cannot even deal with changing their jobs for a better life out of fear of social ostracization – how do you think someone would deal with the entire weight of known civilization going against them, huh?!

I think that the world has become so obsessed in every, way, shape, and form with stamping out 'other than this' and enforcing by any means possible the assumption and reality that there is *nothing* other than 'this', that these supposed 'mentally ill' people are the product of being people who simply cannot let go of the assumption that there is something 'other than this', and simultaneously not buying into some identity or cause – the true, unyielding rebels. However, just as we saw earlier with how mental illness arises via contradiction in Personal Construct Psychology, these people are suffering from the most severe form of contradiction in values (what they know to be true versus 'reality'). In the most severe cases, such as schizophrenia, they may not only be unaware of their assumption but, rather, just like everyone else, they may be fighting it; projecting in other words, because everyone and everything ('reality') appears to be at odds. It may just be possible that 'other than this' is being projected so hard, and the person is so unaware of it, that that projection is projected out onto literally every possible instance of 'this'. It is the simplest explanation, but it is also the kind of explanation that is simply not allowed in our nothing other than 'this' world. Again, whatever you attempt to stamp out will just keep coming back. Thus, the mentally ill can't let go of the assumption that there is something 'other than this' and yet they are forced to live in a society that assumes the opposite. Not surprising what ends up happening.

However, this is not how we always treated these people, remember? If we go back to those earlier civilizations during the time that they were flourishing and it was completely ok to assume that there was something 'other than this' and that was being kept in check by the realities of 'this', then what we find were a class of people known as Shamans. Yes, I know Dolly, I can hear your groans and scoffing; however, these were in FACT the spiritual and logistical leaders during a time of flourishing – how's that for a fucking correlation. During these times, the people who we call mentally ill today were looked up to and admired. People knew that what they did would have been difficult and therefore paid the proper respect to those who had to endure the tension of 'being between worlds'. Both Terrance McKenna and Alan Watts point out how the most revered people in ancient India had exactly the same characteristics as those who are labeled schizophrenics in the West, but the lived reality of those people then and the people with those same characteristics now could not be more different. Now, we no longer see those who suggest something 'other than this' as guides; now, we see them as the worst kind of enemy, and so their reality (and ours) manifests accordingly. The mentally ill, as with everything in existence…, manifest from an assumption, not the other way around.

But let us return to the idea of the Herd psychologist pretending that it is not they who are projecting, rather, it is everyone else, especially all these crazy people that need their help. Is it not possible, given the totality of everything that I have presented, that the *very idea* of mental illness is in fact a projection? If the world itself does indeed have a bunch of mixed-up values stemming from contradiction and the misalignment of an assumption (which I will cover in detail in the next part of the book), then is it not possible that say, "schizophrenia" is what is projected onto the patients? Could it not be that the psychologist simply has the backing and psychological agency of the entire social world based on the nothing other than 'this' assumption? And therefore sits there proud of their ability to lay judgment on some dysfunctional person because they have that whole reality thing sorted out? Again, their particular discipline is not divorced from the intellectual landscape of the current assumption running through the entire university system of nothing other than 'this'; in fact, it is fully integrated with it. And if that assumption has ultimately resulted in a culture of people repeating over and over "there is no point", "nothing means anything", and so on and so forth, wouldn't over time this have an effect on some people that deep down don't believe that at all? They may even start REPEATING IT!!! Who in that situation would NOT be depressed? Who in that situation would not be demoralized? Who in that situation would have any energy whatsoever to do anything? Again, +1 for post-totalitarianism.

All you have to do is change the assumption, then, all of the sudden, you see all mental illness labels as projections of those who are the absolute worst offenders. If there is anyone who is actually *experiencing* nothingness and meaninglessness, it's the Herd psychologist. If the world were to all the sudden get fed up with 'this' and changed overnight to assume that there was indeed something 'other than this,' and that the most important thing was sovereignty of individual consciousness, it would be the Herd psychologists that would no longer be able to function; reality would now bear down on them; they would turn into the new 'schizophrenics'; all of the sudden Jungian psychology would go from being "mysticism" to being obvious; and the leaders of 'this' would have no idea what to do with *them-Selves*.

Just as with an individual who is approaching the unconscious, or the unconscious is invading for some reason or another, there is a

> "dangerous inflation, for one of the most obvious dangers is that of identifying with the figures of the unconscious. For anyone with an unstable disposition this may amount to a psychosis"[20],

so too goes a society on a whole, and this is precisely where society currently finds itself, in a mass state of psychosis, because 'other than this' cannot be stamped out, no matter how hard you try. Responsibility cannot be stamped out no matter how hard you try... Projection will continue until you listen.

However, my model of mental illness and the DSM do have one thing in common. There is nothing wrong so long as one can cope and function. Dysfunction only happens if one does not have the knowledge, perspective, and weaponry to fight back against the assumption. The post-totalitarian system can ostracize you, take your job away, put you in prison, or even kill you, but if you properly orient yourself, it cannot take away the sovereignty of your individual consciousness. You can even turn whatever you do experience from something that is supposedly horrible into something that will nourish you for the rest of your life; something that used to be known in those long-forgotten thriving cultures, such as Greece, as "divine mania".

---

[20] Jung, C. G. (1963). *Mysterium coniunctionis: an inquiry into the separation and synthesis of psychic opposites in alchemy.* Routledge.

"There are two kinds of madness, one arising from human diseases, and the other from a divine release from the customary habits" – Socrates in *Plato's Phaedrus*

This book is not for the Herd because they are not listening anyway. This book is for the person who is onboard thus far, who I'm guessing has been told or at least made to feel like they are crazy for their entire life. If you were able to process everything up to this point, no, it is not you, you are not crazy. Yes, it *is* them. Sure, you may have found some serious faults in yourself that the Herd may have pointed out, and nobody is perfect. But every now and then, they actually are the problem. The phenomenon I have outlined in this part of the book is historical, it can be traced, it can be phenomenologically examined in day-to-day life, and it can be articulated. Your only problem is that you forgot something...

Part 2: When did you stop being the Universe?

What all of science and philosophy has failed to recognize thus far is that nearly every argument that has ever been made in those arenas is built around a contradiction.

In the previous part, I laid the phenomenological foundation for understanding how this can happen in general from the most simplistic of cases all the way up to the entirety of society itself, what it could and does result in at every level, and why it is perfectly reasonable to assume that the world is currently in a state of psychosis fueled by projection. I posit that this is happening because the world is not only terrified beyond words of seeing its own face, but also that the day of that reflection becoming salient to every last person on earth is imminent.

Even though the populace of the world is currently determined to prove and even enforce the assumption that there is nothing other than 'this', they can't even get their basic story, laws, philosophies, political ideologies, and/or scientific models to align with the very thing that they are trying to enforce. Even though there is supposedly *nothing* other than 'this', 'THEY' are somehow *in* 'this', and according to their discourse totally stopped being 'this' at some point.

Although there have been a handful of people in history that have tried in their own way to point this out, nobody has outright said it or attempted to examine the contradiction at any length. Anyone who has attempted to point it out has been killed or ignored, and it was usually because the person tried to give the Herd the opportunity to *experience* something that would bring the contradiction to light (as a good psychologist would). However, the most effective means of doing so in today's world is usually illegal (go figure), and the people attempting to point out the contradiction, as well as the Herd leaders attempting to ensure that it is never revealed, all make the same mistake over and over again: they assume that the Herd would go for truth even if they had access to it...

The Herd speaks only the language of their intellectual elite who feed them their reality; intellectuals only speak the language of the crucified who destroyed their previous intellectual systems with words – the only thing an intellectual will ever understand. So here we are.

A tour of reality based on nothing other than 'this'

When I used to review academic papers, I was handed an article on how to review articles. While most of the time I would take one look at that sort of rubbish and throw it exactly where it belonged, this one was different (not all academics are worthless). The author posited that when it came to considering what the author under review was presenting, it was better to consider how well their own logic lined up with what they themselves were saying, rather than how well their views lined up with my own. In other words, when critiquing the author, you argue with them using *their* logic. Given my theoretical and otherwise background, I had absolutely no problem taking this advice. I also learned years later that there were several existential authors who took this approach in their books, where they would purposely take up the point of view that they did not agree with and then argue it as hard as they could just to see where it would end up.

So, let's do that here, shall we? Let us take the assumption that there really is simply *nothing* other than 'this', and that this is all there is, it came from nowhere, it is not going anywhere, there is no meaning and if you thought you experienced meaning it was a trick, and so on and so forth. The whole thing will be assumed to be correct beyond a shadow of a doubt. The implications are as many as there are thoughts in the world; however, again, I will try to focus on the essence of it all.

The story of the Universe that most of us are familiar with is that the Universe came into existence via The Big Bang, and that eventually everything around us along with all life itself will dissipate into space in the process known as entropy. Although all life is not projected to be gone until several billion years into the future, some recent models suggest that the entire process leading to 'The End' whereby black holes consume other black holes and do all kinds of other strange things until there is simply no activity left might last another trillion trillion trillion trillion (and so on for an unimaginably long time) years. The idea, not surprisingly, is that the shortness of time that life is around is almost as unimaginable as the longness of its no-life counterpart.

In any case, in this story, the Universe was born, energy was thrown out in all directions which then settled into gas, which then collapsed under its own gravity to form stars. Very big stars went supernova which then produced heavier elements because of the basic elements becoming exposed to incredibly intense pressure and violence. Via all that violence along with the constant collisions of various systems, planets and so on, things eventually started to settle down. Then chemistry started to take over as the overarching process. Instead of large celestial body's attracting and repulsing, it was now molecules and compounds. Then those molecules and compounds eventually got to the point where they could combine in such a way as to move/actualize, and the combinations that happened to move/actualize faster and more efficiently gave rise to more complex combinations. Finally, through the increasing complexity of this combination of movement and reconfiguration we arrive at where we are today.

Note that in this story of the Universe, in no way does any of this *require* any definition of life or consciousness or even the notion of it being there at all.

Indeed, if we assume that there is nothing other than 'this', 'life' is an arbitrary label placed on a particular spot in the story of the evolution of the Universe, only differing from any other stand-out spot in its apparent complexity and sophistication. 'Consciousness' can be seen as another arbitrary label placed on the point in time at which the reflexivity of chemicals and their actuators became so fast that the reflexivity *appears* to be something entirely different than 'mere' chemical reaction. Over time, the chemicals and their actuators gained the ability to etch things into their environment in one way or another, allowing future chemicals and their actuators to *do* things based on this process. In the beginning this was simply a way to speed things up and not have to repeat lengthy actions that were taken before, such as when a car drives off-road, cars that come after that car can use the ruts; or when a river forms after water forms the first channels. So, things sped up, then more etching allowed for things to speed up even more, speeding up exponentially. At some point this process became so fast that configurations we call "brains" began to form, whereby a central routing facility was able to store and retrieve things at such a rate that the speed quite literally became incomprehensible to one of these brains gazing at another brain.

After a while, this brain configuration got so fast that it began to form electrical impulses that themselves began to collide with other electrical impulses to give an idea of what was going to be etched before it was etched, especially since it had happened so many times before; a new 'rut' if you will. This arbitrary point in time we called the first instance of "thoughts", and over time, these ruts became just as given as the ones that led to actualization/movement. The only difference, just like anything that preceded it going all the way back to dust colliding with itself, was the apparent complexity. This process continued to increase its speed, over and over again, until the oscillation and collision of these ruts sparked a new type of actualization, something we call "language".

But, once again, nothing special is *required* here – absolutely not. As with all things that preceded before it, language in this story is simply the collision of audible noises, that over time created ruts just like everything before it. And so again, things sped up. Over time language allowed other things to be sped up. Eventually things got so fast that something along the lines of a mirror was formed. It is almost as if the speed caused the Universe to bend back on itself and start reacting to itself; making noises at itself, and we are that universe making noises at itself. We call this final arbitrary point in time "consciousness", and just because the Universe is making noises at itself and those patterns become quite dazzling and complex does NOT equate to "talking" or "conversing". No, it does not. Just because things can be etched in increasingly sophisticated ways does not mean that this point in time is ontologically any different than any other point in time.

In the story of *nothing* other than 'this', there is simply no such thing as 'life', 'consciousness', or 'you'. Sorry, but it is perfectly reasonable (and based on the assumption it is fact) that these things were simply constructed in the exact same way that everything else was constructed, and there is no reason whatsoever to argue against the stance that all of this is nothing more than a chemical reaction that has been exponentially speeding up, period. Just because you are able to actualize in complex patterns simply *does not require* that there be any such thing as consciousness as it is typically defined or even in fringe material theories. Indeed, anything one wants to come up with can in fact be explained as a combination of attraction, repulsion, and increasingly sophisticated patterns[21]. All consciousness in this story, following the simplest of explanations, is a complex illusion. Even things like 'decisions' are simply a highly theatrical form of chemical reaction playing out in its environment. There is no decision and there is nothing there making a decision – there are just chemicals reacting. Change is just that, change; it has nothing to do with decisions. Reflections are just complex chemical reactions, which makes it appear that the mind and body are throwing a fit, i.e., politics or anything else. There is simply nothing there...

Given the vast majority of theories and explanations in the natural sciences, it is easy to see why the vast majority of natural scientists take on this worldview, not by 'choice' mind you, because based on the assumption that is not there either. But what does every last scientist start talking about when you ask them why they do what they do? You'll inevitably get some answer, after they say, "it's obviously not for money", that would make it seem like people do have a choice. How *exactly* does that work? There is hardly a scientist or astronomer out there that doesn't end whatever they

---

[21] Bloom, H. (2012), *The God Problem: How a Godless Cosmos Creates*. Prometheus Books, Amherst, NY.

are saying by adding on something about "our choice" in how we "want things to play out" and either quoting or attempting to sound like Carl Sagan. Seriously, go find a scientist who will tell you about a deterministic universe that loops over and over again, for example, and then also tell you in the next sentence about how we can make different decisions to change…the Universe?! What?! Find me a university scientist that does not believe that everything can be predicted, if only they had the tools, and who does not then turn around and lecture their students (especially Ph.D. students) about some choice-related issue.

This is not some sophisticated form of philosophical nitpicking; if there is *nothing* other than 'this', choice *can't* exist. There is simply no basis for it whatsoever.

However, there are those who are completely against the deterministic worldviews of scientists, i.e., the opposite; i.e., the enemy; i.e., (you see where this is headed). Determinism is absolute anathema to most philosophers and social scientists. If you start talking about determinism to either of these groups, you better duck because you might get decapitated on the spot; and these are the exact people who came up with the nothing other than 'this' assumption in the first place!!! Not oddly enough, they espouse the assumption far more strongly than the natural scientists, while just as strongly espousing their "agency".

In the schizophrenic minds of either the scientist or the philosopher, 'they' are totally here *in* 'this', but there is *nothing* other than 'this'.

Some, however (and this is the absolute fringiest of intellectual minorities I'm talking about), have recently either caught on to this or sense it somewhere in the back of their being, and have responded with something like "yes, 'this' is all there is, but the Universe is in a constant state of becoming – it is becoming aware of itself", thinking that they have cleverly overcome the contradiction and maintained the absolute fact of nothing other than 'this'. What they are saying is that you are the Universe, and that you are becoming aware of that fact, and therefore these are also the people who go on about "non-separation", "unity", "there is no knower of the known", etc.

This would, at first, seem to solve the problem, and many fall for it, especially since being that far out on the philosophical fringe is hard enough, and that is especially true if you are making a living doing it. But all they have done is shifted the focus of the contradiction. They will still go on about how 'they' are *in* 'this'; or 'they' are "thrown into" 'this'; the contradiction has not gone anywhere. If 1) there is *nothing* other than 'this', 2) there is no separation, 3) you are the Universe coming to know itself, then you are no longer *in* 'this', you ARE 'this'. You don't get to have it both ways either, just like those "stupid scientists". And if you ARE this, then what does that mean for your politics? Hmm? Who is doing all that oppressive and/or horrible stuff in the world? YOU ARE! *All* of it… To which these people will respond just a like a good little Herd animal would, they will simply start repeating some aspect of something I covered above in an infinite loop (or abruptly end the conversation in anger or insecure laughter suggesting that you are just too stupid to understand. Sorry, I don't fall for that anymore).

Sometimes this circus act seems too much for me to bear. You know, Professor or philosopher such and such, you could just simply say "I don't know" if you cannot stop talking in circles, but then again, if nobody has ever articulated exactly what you are doing then you would not be aware that you are talking in circles. You could even say "maybe there is another way to look at this", but you know somewhere deep down what that would mean.

It is simple. If there is *nothing* other than 'this', there is nobody there to make 'decisions', there is no 'choice', 'you' do not exist. Even this very 'argument' we are having right now is pure noise. So why don't you sit back and wait to die. For the other crowd, if 'you' are going to define yourself as the Universe itself to get around all that, then you don't get to sit there and point your finger at 'everyone' and 'everything' 'else' – you are it, so why don't you take that finger and point it right up your ass.

All of that is where you end up if you take nothing other than 'this' to be correct.

But let us take a moment to acknowledge that in any case of the nothing other than 'this' assumption, that the actual *result* – as in what people actually do, not say – is the total rejection of responsibility, and it works in precisely the same way as the misaligned value systems that I outlined in the beginning with individuals. The pattern holds. The contradiction itself is what allows for this. There get to be competing value systems, both of which signal virtue but still allow the person or society to completely get away with not being responsible for anything in any of those value systems.

Finally, let us not forget the one thing that is always forgotten in any of this kind of bickering. I started this discussion of assuming nothing other than 'this' by saying "the story", because that is exactly what it is... a story... Treating it as fact and enforcing it as dogma is just as ridiculous as doing the same for the story we were discussing earlier; you know, the story that the nothing other than 'this' crowd was so adamant that had they transcended; the story that amounted to "philosophical suicide" and avoiding the 'truth'. To say, or even imply, that we know beyond a shadow of a doubt that there is nothing other than 'this' is just as fundamentalist or philosophically suicidal as saying that there *definitely* is (at least at this particular point in time). This is why I find any philosophy that militantly backs the nothing other than 'this' assumption to be a complete and utter joke. As with everything else, two sides of the same Herd coin. A photographic negative that does not result in a single step forward.

At the same time, there may be things to *suggest* either of these assumptions, although the suggestions of 'other than this' have been ignored by intellectuals for several hundred years. If anyone brings up any of these observations they are immediately dismissed.

Furthermore, we have just run into another assumption that underlies those assumptions (see, this can go on further than you think): the assumption that these two assumptions were ever mutually exclusive to begin with! Think about it. 'This' or 'other than this'; "free will" or "determinism"; where *exactly* does one get the idea that these are actual, real categories? Remember Personal Construct Psychology and how people appear to make sense of things? How a personal construct system appears? The dichotomy of 'this' or 'other than this' as an ontological category is itself completely and totally conceptually baseless. Do you understand what I am saying? If that is baseless, so too is every single ontological statement or its opposite that has been made in the last 2000 years in science and philosophy. What 'is', baseless; what 'is not', equally baseless. Someone cannot simply move over to deconstructivism and pretend they are saying or doing anything differently than the proponents of the deconstructivist's target.

What everyone keeps forgetting is that, in any of these splits, humans conceptually split the thing into two, based on *their* systems, and then pondered for thousands of years as to which one is 'true', 'real', 'moral', 'ethical', or should or should not have the right to exist, when they were the ones who did the splitting!

Thus, my question of "when did you stop being the Universe?" is a total trick question. I already know to what conclusions people will jump based on whatever flavor of Kool-Aid they have drunk, and I also know that everyone in the world is hellbent on avoiding individual responsibility and where that leads conceptually. In any case or flavor, one thing persists in any of these baseless 'arguments': the rejection of one or more possibilities previously unconceived. It really is that simple. However, conceptually getting to this point is anything but simple, and there is yet another bump in the road that has caught on in recent years like wildfire in the alternative community and is now reaching the masses.

Two yous

When one talks about themselves, they never, ever have a coherent definition of what they mean by themselves. I.e., when you say "I", what *exactly* do you mean by that? What *exactly* do you mean by 'you'? What *exactly* do you mean by 'not you'? It is not trivial information and, no, it is not obvious! If you want to talk about things like "free will" or "determinism" or any other ontological 'thing', that definition is *required* in order to do so. And yet, trivial is precisely how it has been treated ever since Alan Watts first posed the question. The following is from a recorded and publicly available Alan Watts lecture:

> "I wonder what you mean when you use the word "I". I've been very interested in this problem for a long, long time, and I've come to the conclusion that what most civilized people mean by that word is a hallucination: that is to say a false sense of personal identity that is at complete variance with the facts of nature. And ... we have not realized, therefore, that our environment is not something *other* than ourselves... we have the strong sensation that our own being inside our skin is extremely different from the world outside our skin; that while there may be

intelligence inside human skins and while there may be values and loving feelings, outside the skin is a world of mechanical process which does not give a damn about any individual and which is basically unintelligent. But it does not occur, you see, to the ordinary civilized person to regard himself or herself as an expression of the whole universe. You go with your environment in the same way as your head goes with the rest of your body. But in the ordinary way, we don't *feel* it. That is to say that we do not have a vivid sensation of belonging to our environment in the same way as we have the sensation of being an ego inside a bag of skin located mostly in the skull about halfway between the ears and a little behind the eyes. And it issues in these disastrous results where the ego, which according to 19th century common sense, feels that it is a *fluke* in nature and that if it does not fight nature it will not be able to maintain its status as "intelligent fluke". Using symbols and using conscious intelligence – scanning – has proved very useful to us. It has given us such technology as we have. But at the same time, it has proved too much of a good thing; at the same time, we have become so fascinated with it that we confuse the world as it is with the world as it is thought about, talked about, and figured about. That is to say with the world as it is described. And the difference between these two is vast... And when we are not aware of ourselves except in a symbolic way, we're not related to ourselves at all. We are like people eating menus instead of dinners. So then, we get back to the question of what do we mean by "I"? Well first of all, obviously, we mean our symbol of ourselves. Now, ourselves, in this case, is the whole psycho-physical organism, conscious and unconscious, *plus* its environment. That's your real self. Your real self, in other words, is the Universe centered on your organism. That's you. You are not a puppet which your environment pushes around, nor is the environment a puppet which you push around. They go together; they act together. We are only rarely aware of this in curious alterations of consciousness which we call "mystical experience" or "cosmic consciousness"; the individual gets the feeling that everything that is happening is his own doing... or the opposite of that feeling, that he isn't doing anything... but that all his doings – his decisions and so forth – are happenings of nature. You can feel it either way. You can describe it in these two completely opposite ways but you're talking about the same experience. You're talking about experiencing your own activity and the activity of nature as one single process."

I chose this particular piece because I think that it is the best I've ever seen at summarizing the totality of Watts' thought and work, particularly with respect to the question of "I". It also puts much of what I have been trying to get at into perspective and explains in many ways the source from which the phenomenon of conceptual dichotomy arises. One can even see how such a perspective could all but shut down any further discussion or talking; indeed, even I am having a very hard time continuing to write or do anything else at this moment. In fact, every time I've ever listened to or read Alan Watts I felt like doing nothing afterward, which was a great thing during a particular time period in my life; it is a great thing for anyone who has been sold into the rat-race and has run themselves ragged for no apparent reason; it is a great thing for anyone who fears that death of the ego is the obliteration of all existence itself, and all the worry that comes with it, sometimes worry that can psychologically destroy people and all the good relationships they have. Just like a good prescription, there is definitely a time and place for his philosophy, and one of the best times and places historically would have been in the 1960's on the heels of totalitarianism as well as all the insanity and the everyday cultural values instilled, for example, at work, from both sides of the cold war.

However, just as he pointed out with technology, there can be too much of a good thing. While the question of "I" was by no means Watts' only contribution, and he offers a plethora of other useful words of wisdom for life, this question and its answer are indeed that for which he is primarily known, but the *effect* of that message over time has been mostly another form of imbalance. What I mean by that is that the vast majority of Alan Watts' followers will take the message "you are IT!" along with the "entire universe is your true self" and run off with that and *only* that. They will back it up by phrases such as "once you realize this, you see through the whole sham ... there is fundamentally nothing to be afraid of". And these are all not just great points, they are great points to live by! This message is better than what 99.99% of Herd psychologists are spouting. However, again, the long-term effect, as in what Alan Watts' followers actually do, is to completely shift to identifying as the Universe, which is exactly what he is implying one should do. By saying "people are always talking about trying to get rid of the ego ... you can't get rid of the ego because it simply isn't there", the idea of the individual *as such* is completely obliterated. Here, the individual *only* exists as an expression of the whole – as far as there being an actual individual of some kind in some way, that simply does not exist. And this is exactly what the more astute and keen Watts' fans take away. The idea also seems to be loosely related to the recent renaissance of stoicism. And if one looks carefully at the resulting discourse around all of this (there are plenty of community posted videos online to choose from), the ultimate message is to become "nonplussed"; to be completely ok with something like someone pouring gasoline on you and lighting it on fire, for example, confusing the *ability* to do this, when necessary, with some kind of constant and always applicable imperative (pointing back again to some side of some dichotomy, which is highly ironic).

Also, look very closely at what he is saying and how it always relates to the Universe. If the Universe is all that ever was and ever will be, there is the assumption of *nothing* other than 'this'. One could even say that Alan Watts is the undisputed champion of nothing other than 'this'. It would make sense given the eastern philosophies that most of his work is built on. In this way, combined with the stoic/nonplussed attitude, one could say that the philosophy of Alan Watts is the greatest asset that the post-totalitarian system has ever had. Whether he meant for this to be the case or not (I'm pretty sure he did not) is irrelevant; again, it is the actual effect.

"Why is this a problem?", one might ask. "Wouldn't this just mean that he has solved the existential problem and you need to get over that whole individual thing? Maybe you just need to get onboard with your 'post-totalitarian system'; maybe that is just what it means to be a person and pro-social, and maybe your kind are just a bunch of dinosaurs." Well, that is indeed what is fueling most philosophy and social science departments in the world, I even bought into it at some point, and I will say this: the philosophy of Alan Watts, in terms of having absolutely zero contradictions in what he is saying, is a perfect philosophy. It is totally flawless in that regard, and on top of that provides (actually) useful tools for life, which is something that seems to have been forgotten in the last several hundred years of philosophy. He even came up with the idea of 'two yous', or how "a person lives on two levels". The first level is what you do in everyday life and all the challenges and heartache that go with that. The second level is the Universe on a whole that is doing all this stuff and you have no idea how you are doing it, but it's you. Again, great points.

However, let's look at the essence of Watts' philosophy, which he on several occasions has pointed out himself, and that is to do with the duality of things – how you cannot have *any* one thing without the other, and that any one thing you can come up with automatically implies the other, mainly that 'this' would automatically imply 'other than this'... In many ways he is also extending Jung and showing how you cannot have the idea of man without the idea of God, and vice versa. But you see, there is a problem that has interested me for a long, long time also. Just like everything up to this point, the assumption and the idea of there being no individual as such is still another story – the story of *nothing* other than 'this'. Even if it is a story that makes sense and is not riddled with contradiction, it is still a story. And like any story, one still cannot make the truth claim that there is no 'other than this' just because one has created a conceptually perfect philosophy. Furthermore, the very concept of "nothing" may only be something that exists in 'this' (I just say that because I know that someone out there would use that).

In any case, the problem that has concerned me is: is there indeed an individual as such? Is there an *observer*? Or better yet, what *works* better, the idea of an individual as such or the idea that there is no such thing? And getting back to the essence of Watts' philosophy, if the core of what he is saying is true, and it probably is, then why are we debating the non-existence of any possible thing that I could bring up?!

Is it *possible* that there is some way of considering 'other than this' that would not negate any other aspect of Watts' philosophy? Is there a story that would preserve all possibilities under a certain set of assumptions and bring them all together, just as he did in a similar way under the assumption of nothing other than 'this'? Is it not possible that Watts could have been onto something phenomenological but also could have been projecting just as much as anyone else? Is it possible that while the people he always talked about were projecting from the perspective of the ego, he could have been projecting from the perspective of a sort of 'reversed ego'? Is it not possible that he used all of his intellectual power and wisdom to dodge individual responsibility in the most sophisticated way? Again, not saying that he did, just asking if it is possible.

I posit that all of that is possible, and there is nothing to suggest that it is not possible. I also posit that while Watt's philosophy can certainly be helpful, the effect of *stopping* with it is extremely detrimental. The idea of the 'real' you as two yous – again, how the Herd *responds* to it – has the long-term effect of not only turning people into submissive cows even if they exit the rat race (they just submit to other things), but you get exactly the same thing that you would get if you are in a really difficult situation that could potentially end up in something along the lines of "the treasure hard to attain", and that journey really sucks, but then someone offers you a comfortable and reasonable way out… Of course you are going to have the greatest euphoria rush over you when it happens, "thank God I did not have to keep doing that!" But what happens after one takes a lengthy break and lives in this state for a while? All you need to do is look at the mass of people who Alan Watts helped found: the counterculture of the 1960's. What do we see in this counterculture then and 60 years on? Besides the photographic negative of the status quo culture of the 1960's we also see a group of people that became just as angry and inept as the people they started out rebelling against. After a while one, even if it is on their deathbed, will indeed begin to question the whole idea of them as individuals not existing as such. After a while, one gets a little tired of 'just being'. After a while the very real effects of having no challenge begin to make themselves very known (at the individual or cultural level); the freedom that the philosophy had originally provided, at some point, starts to feel like a cage; and we're right back where we started, sometimes unable to find a way out. What started out as a form of rebellion turns out to possibly be yet another way of self-sabotaging one's existence. People just never seem to learn the consequences of when conceptual truth is held in higher regard than existential truth until it is too late.

If someone is looking to merely exit the rat race and 'just be' no matter what is going on around them, then Watts may be all that is needed. On the other hand, if someone is looking to thrive, that is a completely different story, and for that we have not just the history of 'this' and 'other than this' outlined earlier, but the entire body of Carl Jung's work that clearly shows what happens in any of the above cases – work that Watts touched on but never fully engaged with. And that's the thing, ultimately some people may be perfectly ok with having gasoline poured on them and set on fire. However, some of us are not ok with that and we never will be, no matter how logical the argument, nor will we be ok with any less extreme version of that, ever... And for some of us, we know and feel this truth to be the truth above all truths. The question for us then becomes, where could this truth be coming from? And is there a story for us? Just as Watts helped alleviate a certain type of madness for a certain type of person, I too am trying to do the same. There is still another potential type of responsibility that is being avoided, and there is a growing number of us who feel it in every fiber of our being.

The Axis

Everyone's biggest fear, no matter who they are, especially as they get older, is something that they did not previously conceive. I.e., novelty. Although almost everyone will deny this, of course, until *actual* novelty hits. This is particularly problematic for those who did not have sufficient novel experiences when they were younger, which, not surprisingly, are exactly the people who end up in all kinds of positions of power and influence (and the masses happily lap up whatever these people say because it reinforces their tendency to do nothing/repeat themselves, just as Havel and most early existentialists pointed out). As I covered before, there are many theories that deal with rejection of novelty out of fear, and these theories more or less point in one way or another to death, identity, and so on. However, as I have also pointed out, those explanations are probably only explaining the last lines of defense against the encounter with something else.

That something else is the Self – a concept created by Jung that is quite different from most peoples' first thought as to what they think it means and, in this conception, you (in whatever way you want to define you) are definitely not it. As far as any experience of 'this' goes, it would be the epitome of novelty, and thus the epitome of threat or danger. However, facing it would then be the epitome of heroism, and heroism has been seen as the epitome of what leads to meaning in any thriving culture since the dawn of recorded history (while it is seen as the very thing to be derided and mocked in a declining or expended culture or a culture that has never achieved anything). There are two paths when it comes to dealing with the Self. The first is to simply run away and do everything in one's power individually and collectively to distract oneself from the Self by projecting this unconscious reality onto anything and everything else, which is basically the essence of everything I've outlined in modern society thus far and is the kernel of the post-totalitarian system. The second is to face it head-on, regardless of the danger and what it may lead to.

I have always liked the idea of the Self better than things like 'the Universe' or 'nothing' or any other form of 'this' pointing at 'this'. The reason is that the Self is a *phenomenological* category and not an ontological one. This is also why Jung's work is so much more insightful and effective than that of a 'real' philosopher who is almost always ultimately concerned with arguing materially over what 'is' or 'is not' in one way or another. As Jung stated on multiple occasions to anyone who criticized him from the point of some philosophical rulebook, so to speak, he was concerned with one and one thing only: the individual patient and what *works* for *them*. Everything else stemmed from that. Quite the pragmatic statement if you ask me. Another thing that distinguished Jung from others is his constant focus on the "inner world", and this inner world is not simply some personal thing but, rather, a collective thing, which is part of what led to the falling out between him and Freud. In fact, this inner world, as far as Jung could tell, is not really 'this' at all, even if it was in fact real. It is some kind of mirror image of it and vice versa. In other words, this inner world, the Self, the collective unconscious, *is* 'other than this'. And two other things Jung could never get much of anyone to understand was that 1) the unconscious is actually, really unconscious…, and 2) the psyche is real, not some figment of one's imagination (on top of the statements, he had more empirical evidence for the latter than the history of the average modern journal combined). The following sums these points up as well as alluding to a far more imaginative and thorough understanding of the question of "I" long before Watts asked it:

> "The unconscious is … a compensatory image of the world. In my view it cannot be maintained either that the unconscious has a merely sexual nature or that it is a metaphysical reality, nor can it be exalted into a "universal ground." It is to be understood as a psychic phenomenon, like consciousness. We no more know what the psyche is than we know what life is. They are interpenetrating mysteries, giving us every reason for uncertainty as to how much "I" am the world, and how much "world" is "I". The unconscious at any rate is real because it *works*. I like to visualize the unconscious as a world seen in a mirror: our consciousness presents to us a picture of the outer world, but also of the world within, this being a compensatory mirror-image of the outer world. We could also say that the outer world is a compensatory mirror-image of the inner world. At all events we stand between two worlds, or between two totally different psychological systems of perception; between perception of external sensory stimuli and perception of the unconscious. The picture we have of the outer world makes us understand everything as the

effect of physical and physiological forces; the picture of the inner world shows everything as the effect of spiritual agencies." – Jung, *Civilization in Transition*

Before considering anything else regarding the ego or Self, it is most important to first point out the nature of interaction between the two. In addition to the Self being completely and utterly 'other than this' with respect to 'this', the ego has absolutely no control whatsoever over the Self, and this is ultimately what the all the fuss is about.

I conducted a lab experiment in my Ph.D. program where I was trying to get at some phenomenon or another (I've honestly forgotten at this point), but at the very end of the questionnaire I had the intuitive idea to throw in an unplanned question. That question was: "Which of these three things do you find most threatening, and why?: 1) Your own 'dark' thoughts, 2) Technology, 3) Other people", which I required participants to write at least 250 words explaining why. What I found was that in nearly 100% of cases the most threatening thing was simply that which the person could not control. This blew me away because you almost never get something that consistent, especially with an open-ended question. So, on my own time, I went online and asked the same thing on Amazon Mechanical Turk, on message boards, to people in real life, and so on. The results were always the same, and the demographic could be anyone. I even challenged other people to try it (you can too) if they thought I was making it up and, sure enough, they got the same results.

I thought to myself, "surely this will be a done deal as far as getting it published", which was completely the opposite of reality. In terms of how many journals and conferences I sent it to, it was the most rejected paper I ever wrote. The theoretical lead in was simple, the method was simple, the results had huge implications for theory (as well as other things obviously); and it was hands down the most straightforward thing I had ever written. In not one of the rejections (not surprisingly) did a single person have anything coherent to say about why it was being rejected. Finally, I got the paper accepted to some low-level conference in Asia which probably would have accepted just about anything that was written in a semi-coherent way. When I presented it, every single person in the audience had a look that said, "I feel so sorry for this person. They are so confused" or "I have no idea what any of this means". Most had the latter. I was just standing there dumbfounded thinking to myself, "Are you fucking kidding me? You don't think that this would explain quite a lot?!" Only a while later did it occur to me that the closer you get to something that *does* explain quite a lot in Academia, the more vehemently it will be rejected. It works in the same way as with the job security in psychology. "We're much more interested in that convoluted thing you and your colleagues wrote about relational identity". Of course you are, because not only is it a regurgitation of something already said in physics (which would give your disciplinary identity some legitimation, and we are talking about identity), identity is the object of Projection that hides the real issue of control.

It is the same with the Self or any philosophy that would allow for its existence. It is completely out of the one's control, and it is therefore no surprise that most of our social systems in existence, including philosophy, are constructed for the explicit purpose of keeping it hidden and at bay. Even the philosophies that on the surface, such as Watts, would appear to be engaging with the Self in some way still find extremely clever tricks to simply avoid the real meat of the topic all together and sweep it back under the rug.

I stand firmly by the statement that anyone who blows off the magnitude and danger of an encounter with the Self is someone who has never actually experienced it. When those people talk of "letting go" what they really mean is "I found a very clever way to avoid the most difficult part in life, now I'm going to project the idea of letting go by showing just how ok I am with accepting every aspect of 'this'". As far as being possessed by issues of control, they are the worst offenders. And furthermore, deep down, they know it; they know it is nothing more than a projection. Next time you encounter one of these 'woke' people, try the methodology I presented in the first part of the book and see just how irritated they become, especially since they have supposedly become the king or queen of 'letting go'. If I meet someone who has never had something near a full-blown psychosis on the approach to the unconscious (just as what happened to Jung) I am extremely skeptical, and red flags immediately go up. An encounter with the Self is the very definition of having no control, and one in the midst of it is going to appear nothing even remotely like a stoic. An example that I often use (which is also something with which to reflect back on mental illness) is: what if you were sitting there, right now, wherever you are, and suddenly the walls started morphing; all kinds of figures began to emerge that you could not conjure up in your wildest dreams; time stopped; and your version of material reality was effectively gone. You were not under any stress and you had not taken any kind of drug. "Oh, I'd be totally fine", says woke dude bro. Bullshit. Everyone on this planet would be scared out of their wits including myself, and the first thought that would pop into their mind would be "what if 'this' never ends?!" And, indeed, it is interesting that that would in fact be the first concern…

'Letting go' in its truest since is impossible, and one of the biggest lies one can be sold.

However, one thing is for certain, if you want to get someone to realize the futility in this then all you would need to do is keep repeating something that cannot be done. Sound familiar Watts followers? He even told you that he was tricking you and gave you the story about the Zen master who decided one day that he was going to attach himself to as many things as possible (Watts laughing)! Do you really not get what Watts was ultimately trying to show you? Do you not remember his lecture on Jung and "the element of irreducible rascality", and how "he was just as much a villain as anyone else"? He was not there to enlighten you, he said that. He was not there to be your friend, "I'm trying to get rid of you", he said. He kept telling you over and over that "you don't exist", but you never stopped to question if you do or not, or what would happen "if you follow anything to its extreme"! This from a person who never stopped talking about duality. As he said so many times before, the point of Zen training was to get the person to give up – giving up on the whole enlightenment thing altogether because what they were looking for was always already there, and then they graduate. Thus, letting go really means giving in. And no, giving in does not mean simply letting go of control; it does not mean having things under control; it means dissolving that dichotomy altogether via *something else*. This is why I consistently say that I have no problem with Watts' philosophy – it is, in fact, perfect – it just needs some updating for the modern person since the entire essence, that of simultaneity, appears to have been lost as it made its way through the Herd. Sound familiar?

What I am trying to get at here is that for most Watts followers, just like when Jung had to keep repeating that the unconscious is really unconscious, they simply do not understand that not having control with respect to the Self *really* means not having control, at least insofar as what is presented to you by it. If you are truly trying to incorporate the Self into consciousness then most of what you are thinking, espousing, people you gravitate towards and away from, what you consider important day to day, how others view you, and how you view yourself or your Self will shift, fluctuate, and oscillate wildly. And this is probably no accident.

Which is why we have come right back around to the issue of identity. When one gets right down to it, the essence of human existence is somehow bound up with the issues of control and identity. One cannot talk about identity without acknowledging that the there simply is no need for it outside of the issue of control. And because control is the ultimate concern, identity is the one thing that simply will not go away regardless of what flavor of physics or metaphysics one chooses; regardless of psychology; regardless of story; just simply regardless, period. Even Watts who said that the purpose of life could be seen as having the opportunity to let go could not let go of that one, obviously.

As with most things, Jung was either consciously or unconsciously aware of this fact, and simply jumped into what happens when one identifies with the ego (which was well covered by Watts in his own way) as well as what happens when one identifies with the Self (where Watts fell short). Identifying with the Self, or aspects of the unconscious, was *the most dangerous thing a person can do* according to Jung and, ironically, this is exactly the *result* for most people who stop with philosophies such as Watts and carry on as though it has answered all questions and gave them their control back. It is precisely what is happening when one assumes *nothing* other than 'this'. Are you getting it yet? This is what is known as "ego inflation" in Jungian psychology. It tends to happen when one approaches the Self (before an actual encounter, which is not to say imminent) and confuses or conflates the ego with the Self, which is typically accompanied by a transcendent experience. If one understands that the Self contains an army of "spiritual agencies" as well as the fact that ego inflation amounts to returning to being a child again, it is no surprise the effect that has on people. However, those children are now embedded in society and have a wide range of weaponry; this phenomenon is therefore also the source of every last monstrous thing that manifests in our world, e.g., World War II under the right wing as well as the slaughter of hundreds of millions of people under the left-wing's philosophy of 'compassion'. In this state, the person, or society, is possessed by the Anima or Animus. It is the strongest and most destructive of all projections, and yet it is also when many people feel like they have really finally solved that whole life thing (and often times gain millions of followers). Thus, this is how people come to identify as the Self or some aspect of the unconscious while they congratulate and pat themselves on the back for finally doing away with that whole ego thing (it did not go anywhere, it just assumed the entire personal mass of the Self with the Self continuing to project through it) and "taking control of one's own life" even though they have done nothing of the sort. "I am everything, everything is me, therefore there is no responsibility and I can do whatever I want".

Indeed, why would anyone want to do anything differently or go back to that "toxic state of mind" or (ironically) lack of control?

Except that ultimately that is precisely the state of mind that becomes toxic for exactly the same reason that identifying only with the ego was toxic. Once again, it is just a photographic negative. And when one is in that state, they conveniently forget about the endless sea of examples of how that state of mind led to the destruction of other people or the annihilation of entire cultures. There is always the thought just under the surface that "that won't happen to me". Except that it always does, and ultimately the Self engulfs the person or culture that pretends to be immune.

In any case, people simply will not let go of that personal identity thing! No one. They have been told how dangerous it is to identify with the ego (leading some to try to exterminate it), and they have been told by others how dangerous it is to identify with the Self (leading some to try to exterminate it). What is one to do? And no, the answer is not to project one's identity onto some group – that does not deal with the problem of personal identity, obviously.

Edward Edinger in the book "Ego and Archetype" explicated an answer built on Jungian psychology, which was more or less the essence of what Jung was trying to get at with respect to his particular form of the 'true you'. In short, his and the analytical psychology community's answer was to not identify with either the ego or the Self, nor was it to simply show the futility of either of those things and leave one hanging (which is what most deconstructivists tend to do and the point is forever lost), it was to identify with the thing that connected these two things. They called this the "ego-Self axis" or what I will simply refer to as "the Axis". As is typical of Jungian analysts, rather than wasting time with arguing over whether the ego or Self 'really exists' they simply accepted this to be true since they phenomenologically exist in so far as they both work and have an effect, and then pointed to the last phenomenological truth of there obviously being something holding the two together since both refuse to go away. Instead of identifying with the ego or the Self, the trick is to identify with the Axis – the thing *between* them. In modern Jungian psychology that is the 'real you'. The Axis is the real you.

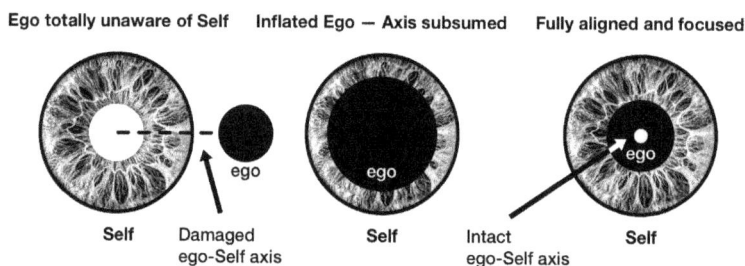

Ego totally unaware of Self   **Inflated Ego — Axis subsumed**   **Fully aligned and focused**

ego   ego   ego

Self   Damaged ego-Self axis   **Self**   Intact ego-Self axis   **Self**

Figure 4 - Ego, Self, and Axis at different stages

There are many other names that one could give to the Axis: "Bridge between worlds", "the middle way", "the logos", "the observer", "spirit", etc. It has just as many names as that other thing that we have tried for centuries to put a name on: "The one great energy", "Tao", "God", "Allah", etc. which for practical, elaborative, and exploratory purposes is better called "the Self". Finally, there is the thing that we have no problem putting names on, the ego, which goes by all kinds of things: "scientist", "physician", "rebel", "human", and so on. Taken together, we have a trinity, resembling Father/Mother: Self; Son/Daughter: ego; Holy Ghost: Axis. And when taken as a whole we have a quaternity –

the symbol of wholeness and the basis for the philosopher's stone, *lapis philosophorum*, and at the center we have where all of it intersects – the ancient symbol of the cross. And all of this is the essence behind the idea of Jung's individuation and the "treasure hard to attain".

What the analysts have found is that the identification with and as the Axis leads to psychological thriving. And is that so difficult to believe? Not only does it take care of quite literally every problem that I or anyone else in philosophical history has ever brought up, but it also has no contradictions; it has not left out anything; it has not presented some unreasonable story; it has not provided "intellectual suicide", nor certainty, nor uncertainty; it provides the locus for individual existence as well the possible source of all meaning and purpose (inherent? Gasp! The horror!), and with that we start to see something resembling a certain kind of responsibility, an identity, and therefore also a central point to aim all issues of control. What we see is something resembling *mediation*. The true identity here is that of the mediator – an entity that sits between two worlds: chaos and order; the uncontrollable and the controllable; and has the responsibility of *deciding* (we'll come back to that later) what gets passed forth *and* back. This idea of mediation changes everything (although I've already pointed out that this is not new). No longer is the individual "poor little old me" like Watts always said, but likewise no longer is there "nothing to be done" but sit and wait to die as if this were a movie that was scripted and we are 'mere' actors. I must also emphasize to the highest degree that *none* of this is contradictory to anything one can find in even the most obscure and elaborate theoretical physics or critical philosophies (even if it goes against assumptions). If anything, it is complementary.

All of this may prompt one to then ask, "Ok, so why isn't everyone on board with this?" Simple, it's hard. Very, very, very hard. Again, one does not have an encounter with the Self without great difficulty and excruciating alienation, which is putting it very lightly. To say all of this is one thing, to live it is quite another. The best metaphor I could ever find for living this way, i.e., identifying with the Axis, is surfing. You never really know what is coming, there are a million ways to die (which means there are a million reasons to not do it), the ocean does not care about you and you are completely out of your natural element, it is one of the most difficult sports to master, and you get your ass kicked over and over again simply for the rush of getting a few seconds of improvising and flowing right through the middle of chaos and order. Afterward, you have absolutely nothing to show for it – no trophies, no cause; and there are absolutely no fingers to point because it is just you. If anything, you go home with injuries or at some point arthritis. Not that many people surf, but the few who do are so wrapped up in it that they can barely imagine life without it. Just go ahead and start trying to convince a surfer that what they are doing is stupid or a mere addiction or, better yet, try to force them to stop, and see what happens.

But that is precisely what the entire world and everything in it is aimed at, the obliteration of any possibility of the individual, no matter how it is conceptualized or experienced. And as I have said, this has not been the first time. Historically there is a direct connection with 'other than this' and the individual as well as 'this' and the persecution of the idea of the individual. What I am further suggesting, and will theorize over later, is that the very essence of the individual could be directly tied to 'other than this'. This is because any 'this' based argument will indeed show no

146

individual, even theories described as "relational". But then I will always come back to "well, then does the essence of your relational view hold or not?" The relational view states that something cannot exist except in relation to something else. I cannot back down from this being a massive contradiction – that the relational view would hold for everything *except* that... If someone was truly taking a relational view, then 'this' only exists in relation to 'other than this' and vice versa; hence, in the relational definition, 'other than this' is a *requirement*. I also cannot back down from the idea that if this is a requirement, and one takes Jung's view that the inner world is a compensatory mirror image of the outer world and vice versa, then 'other than this' could and probably does have completely opposite rules. Where the two worlds meet is what we call existence.

The key takeaway here is that the individual is the gateway for everything that *could* be, and that is why all post-totalitarian systems and the people behind it are aimed at it.

I cannot cover the idea of the Axis with any justice any more than I can do the same for Jung's work without writing a whole book about both. Therefore, I encourage you to read *Ego and Archetype* for a more thorough understanding as well as a proper introduction to Jung's work if you have not yet been introduced (in fact, I encourage you to read every single one of Jung's books in the "Collected Works" if you have not done so already).

What I hope that I have done thus far is to start being more phenomenologically explicit about what I mean when I say "individual", as well as to phenomenologically make intelligible why there would be a war on the individual. Hopefully it is clear now why I covered contradiction, projection, the history of 'this' and 'other than this', post-totalitarianism, the urge to rebel, and mental illness, and hopefully it is beginning to be clearer as to why any of this would be ultimately linked to the fear of responsibility.

The many forms of 'other than this'

It is without a doubt that when someone speaks of 'other than this' that all anyone listening registers or responds with is the story of what they were sold by the Roman Catholic Church and, since the scientific revolution, that is all 'other than this' ever amounts to. What I mean is that even if someone starts speaking of something 'other than this' that in no way resembles some man in the sky looking down and judging people and doling out passes to heaven or hell based on how well they have obeyed their master, it does not actually matter to the person who is listening – the two are equivalent. No matter how 'other than this' is presented, the listener is thinking in terms of this story, they judge in terms of this story, and they then react in terms of this story.

With even a microscopic drop of imagination, one could come up with all kinds of 'other than this' possibilities, some of which I have already covered. There are possibilities in the spiritual realm (that are not some man in the sky), mystical and/or psychological realm, the realm of 'this' turning into 'other than this', the locational realm, and even the sociological construction realm, each of them standing to influence, completely rearrange, or overthrow what we call 'reality' or, in effect, to overthrow control (again, 'other than this' in many of its other forms is illegal, and no one finds that a little bit too coincidental? Drinking, fine. Smoking, also fine. Participating in sanctioned forms of violence, totally fine. Doing or providing a substance that would help resurrect 'other than this', you are going to prison). In any case, my point is that one does not have to look very far to find many forms of 'other than this' if one has any imagination whatsoever. However, suggesting any form of 'other than this' is the least socially acceptable thing one can do; it is far more acceptable to come up with theories or rituals that have no basis in 'this' reality whatsoever so long as they do not leave the realm of 'this'. And we see this every, single, day...

But let us return for a moment to the spiritual realm specifically. As with so many other things, people pretend as though this was settled in any way whatsoever. At nearly the exact same time the Roman Catholic Church handed the authoritative man-in-the-sky story to them, people were simultaneously presented with the story of 'this' which said we have everything regarding 'this' figured out beyond a shadow of a doubt. However, people now act, judge, construct, and so on as though the story of 'this' at that time was any less ridiculous than the story of 'other than this' at that time. Both were completely infantile, constructed for an infantile populace. However, as far as the intellectual populace for the last 400 years is concerned, the only story that was allowed to be modified was 'this'. The story of 'other than this' is fixed and only a moron would suggest that it could be modified. In fact, even in the fringiest of theoretical physics such as holographic theory, anything new that comes up can never, ever be the result of 'other than this' interacting with or coming through 'this', it can only be undiscovered 'this' or constructed from nothing out of thin air since there is *nothing* other than 'this'.

But where does one get the idea and why do they become so fixated on it? I can only assume that it is the result of the rebellion that came with the scientific revolution combined with the fact that the entire thing was based on very narrow material observations, and that this produced so many advancements that all modern people have come to hate the very idea that there could be something 'other than this'. People were so upset about that original story of 'other than this' that all they could ever focus on again was 'this'. I am just repeating my point about how the supposed non-existence of 'other than this' is just as baseless as anything else. But beyond that, there are so many possibilities of 'other than this' that would explain so much of 'this', that it is, in fact, infantile to demand or enforce by law that there are no such possibilities. It is just as infantile as demanding or enforcing the idea that there is no life anywhere else in the Universe when the Universe is so big that we cannot even begin to comprehend it (and it may actually be larger or have been running continuously forever), which is why scientists ultimately gave into that idea as being more probable than not. Why is it any different with 'other than this'? No one can ever utter a single word to me as to why it is different, "it just is!". Sorry, but just like the story of 'this' handed to you by the Romans, "it just is" is not good enough. I do not follow something that makes no sense just because it is the most *popular* idea in 400 years.

Given the same infinite sea of possibilities with respect to 'other than this' that is afforded to 'this', combined with the fact that almost everything that employs the relational view does indeed

151

contradict itself, combined with the tendency of human beings to gravitate toward contradiction for the purpose of keeping something hidden and avoiding responsibility, combined with the historical pattern of oscillation between 'other than this' and 'this' and the sociological signals of being at the peak of 'this', combined with the pragmatic reality that analytical psychology has shown in the sense that it actually works, I am going to go ahead and assume that existence is a combination of 'other than this' and 'this'. Unlike anyone before me, I am assuming that both exist and have equal importance. I am assuming that they are compensatory mirror images of each other (along with everything else that would be the logical result of that). I am assuming that you cannot have one without the other. I am assuming that existence itself is defined by the intersection between the two, and that we can also call refer to this phenomenon as the individual. I am assuming that given the mountain of contradiction between our cutting-edge theories regarding 'this' and what they would suggest regarding 'other than this' along with sheer basic sense and thought experimentation, that the *outright rejection* of any form of 'other than this' signals fear and the rejection of some form of responsibility. I also stand firm behind the fact that the people who are always telling others, "The key to all of this is to realize how much you don't know", for example, are the people who are most incapable of considering the many forms of 'other than this', especially the ones that would be the most profound and signal an actual discovery.

The Singularity and the possibility of a new universe

As I said before, one surefire way to get someone to immediately dismiss you as someone who has anything worth saying is to bring up the name Ray Kurzweil and/or the Singularity. In fact, this will get you dismissed faster than bringing up the spiritual forms of 'other than this'! Kurzweil is the absolute epitome of a materialist and champion of 'this' and, as far as I can tell, has the strongest explanatory and predictive model in existence. Therefore, it does make one wonder what the problem is.

I will never forget the moment I was sitting in my last semester of university and was presented with the idea of the Singularity and Kurzweil's book *The Singularity is Near*. Up until that particular moment in life I could have cared less about anything; for me, education was nothing more than a box you had to tick to get a white-collar job, and all I ever really wanted to do for the rest of my life was to smoke weed and play video games. Why? Because not a single person, organization, or otherwise, had ever shown me in my first twenty-four years of life anything even remotely resembling *relevance*. "Do this math equation". Why? "So you can do other math equations". "Go get a job". Why? "So you can live".

Why? "So you can...do your job". Right, I see... Kurzweil's work was the first time I had ever heard anything that made any of 'this' make any sense. There was no religious story and there was nothing to believe in. It was just cold, hard numbers, logic, and logarithmic extrapolation. And yet a religious story that one must believe in is precisely how people treat anything that Kurzweil has ever written about or said. I, on the other hand, could not believe what I was seeing in front of me in the sense that it seemed to me that what I was looking at was the most objective and sensical thing in existence. In my totally naïve younger state I thought, "people have to know about this! There is so much logic!". That was where it all began for me. Logic, relevance, etc. And then I hit the real world only to find that everyone who had been preaching to me the very things I had now bought into were completely and utterly full of shit.

But let us back up for a second. For those who have not heard of it, what exactly is this Singularity?

Well, according to Dolly it is when Artificial Intelligence takes over and enslaves the entire human race (as if the entire human race is not doing the optimum job of that already). Not surprisingly, there is nothing even remotely resembling such a thing anywhere in Kurzweil's book or anything that he has ever said. Not only is such a notion nowhere to be found, it is the epitome of the very form of linear thought that is quite literally what the entire book is trying to argue against. The Herd strikes again.

The flippant answer would be "why don't you try picking up a dictionary?", as in "the state, fact, quality, or condition of being singular". As such, perhaps we should again get away from what it 'is' and ask, "what would lead to the Singularity?" Much better question. According to Kurzweil, the Singularity is the point when humans transcend biology; however, leading up to when they do is the entire history of human and technology co-evolution, across all forms of technology, which is happening at an exponential rate. This leads to an eventual convergence of everything we know, the point at which we can no longer comprehend what happens anymore because it is simply beyond our current understanding. This is why it is called the Singularity. And a singularity is a singularity. There is a lot to unpack there, which is why Kurzweil wrote an entire book for which my explanation is no substitute. However, I will try to hit the key points as it pertains to our discussion.

The most critical point that he is trying to make, as in why people do not see any of this as obvious, is the fact that most human beings think in linear terms, both with respect to linear time and standalone extrapolations, and this is no different when it comes to technological (or even intellectual) development. What actually occurs is that things change exponentially and extrapolations are one string in a sea of simultaneous, converging extrapolations of other developments.

Regarding exponential change, this is the only thing that the masses have caught on to, sort of. When considering technological advancements, most people think in terms of what has already happened and extrapolate that way. For example, people in the year 1997 looked back on how long it took for a computer taking up an entire building to taking up a desktop, which was several decades. Someone then approaches them and says, "in 10 years you will have access to all the information in the world on a device that fits in your pocket, and that device will be orders of magnitude more powerful than anything we have now". They would (and did) react by telling you that you are crazy, that is not possible, and if it is it will be more like 40 years, etc. But then 2007 rolls around and said device is common. Someone then approaches that same person and says, "in 4 years you will be able to print a weapon on your desktop". They would (and did) react in the same way as before with the same responses. And so on and so forth.

However, the timeline of technological development is exponential, and this is a historical fact. The idea started with Moore's law regarding computing power, however, Kurzweil noticed that it applied to all technological advancements, not just computer chips. But like so many things, people can even hear this explained and then *still* argue in *linear* terms. They just do not seem to get that exponential *means* exponential. At some point, very soon, the rate of development will be measured in terms of hours, not years. And at some point, very soon after that, it becomes near-instantaneous. Kurzweil plots technological developments of all kinds on an exponential/logarithmic line and, so far, all of his predictions have held (give or take a couple of years); although, again, not surprisingly, nobody seems to really care about what actually happens once it actually happens or how many times it happens, they just move on to arguing about whatever remains on the timeline. In any case, the point at which things go beyond being able to plot what could possibly happen next is around the year 2045. I consider this idea of technological developments on a non-linear timeline to simply be a baseline concept, while the masses think that it is the final point that he is trying to make.

The far more important point that Kurzweil is trying to make is that of multiple non-linear extrapolations and *convergence*. I have yet to meet a single person in the masses, even if they are a scientist or engineer, who can process what I mean by this even if I explain it very simply (and it really is simple to understand, that's not the problem). Kurzweil points out that in addition to people thinking linearly with respect to technological developments, they also think linearly with respect to the *development itself*. In other words, if you can get someone to concede regarding the exponential development in computing technology, they will think that this has absolutely nothing to do with the exponential development of biotechnology. If you can get someone to concede regarding the exponential development in Artificial Intelligence, they will think that this has absolutely nothing to do with nanotechnology. This is the epitome of linear thinking. It is almost as if most people have blinders on, and it is actually the phenomenon that permeates most of science and Academia (and would explain a lot regarding our story so far).

However, when one considers all of these developments at once, along the same exponential timeline, what one sees is how they feed each other and are interconnected. Over time, they begin to be more and more interconnected, e.g., the faster computing speeds lead to higher forms of AI, which leads to faster development of nanotechnology, which at some point will develop far enough to be incorporated into the human body, and at the same time all of that was happening a company is developing a brain-to-machine interface, and so on. These developments do not sit off by themselves, and if one plots each on its own exponential timeline, what one sees is that at some point they all converge. This is the true idea behind the Singularity, and why it is so obnoxious for people who actually have read and digested what Kurzweil had to say to then have to sit and listen to people debate about, for example, whether or not "AI is going to take over", or how we could have never conceived of such and such before it happened. Such 'debates', that never would have existed without the very person/people who allowed these debates to exist in the first place, which are the exact same people being misread and and/or misrepresented, are completely missing the point. Never mind the indisputable fact that *neither human beings nor technology could have ever existed in the first place without the other,* and that the sophistication or lack thereof in *either* is inexorably linked. Fact. Why do people always forget this? Oh, I know, because it actually is an exemplar of relationality... It is almost as if this Projection thing simply knows no end, isn't it? Furthermore, there is one particular development occurring in the world that would be the catalyst for people to dedicate their entire existence to these developments as well as the convergence out of *necessity...* See if you can figure that one out, we'll come back to that later.

According to Kurzweil, as this convergence proceeds on its exponential course, nanotechnology and biotechnology will allow human-AI fused intelligence to exponentially permeate matter. The idea is that, eventually, all matter of any kind is saturated by consciousness as well as its agency and actualization, and it is at this point that the Universe "wakes up" – a phenomenon which will basically occur instantaneously.

And is it all surprising that this is one of the most hated ideas in history? What happens when the Universe "wakes up"? We have no idea. Never mind that most people are still trying to figure out if they are even part of the Universe. And if we have no idea what happens we cannot put the reigns on it and start governing it, debating it, politicizing it and so on – i.e., controlling it – before it happens (even though it may have indeed happened already countless times, re: "where are all the aliens?"). The phenomenon itself is totally out of our control in every way. Furthermore, it appears to be a natural phenomenon, yet another point that is lost and never brought up in any 'debates' about any of this. That was the whole point of the modeling and data, again, thrown out by everyone probably because they never actually read the book to begin with. Even academics do not read most of what they are supposedly experts on, why would anyone else? And given what I have gone to the trouble of outlining since the beginning of this book, is that any surprise either? Hence, the very idea of the Singularity has not even been *considered*, much less any possibility beyond it. No, instead, Dolly says that their newsfeed says that Kurzweil says that AI is coming to enslave us and because of that *we* have to *stop* all of 'this'! Wait, what? Que the astrophysicist talking about how the Universe will turn into a sea of nothingness and blackholes for trillions upon trillions of years until it is all gone. At least it is certainty…

The Singularity. A point at which we can only speculate about what happens. Well, that is precisely what I wish to do, speculate, as well as point out some bigger picture implications that must necessarily be a result of whatever happens.

The immediate question is almost always: "what happens to humans when all of this merging takes place?" What will likely happen to begin with will be exactly what has been happening since the beginning of the human-technology story. The amount of information a person can attain will increase, personal intelligence will increase, personal agency in the sense of how much one person can create via some outlet will increase, and interpersonal networking in some form will increase. No matter what course things take, those things will happen at a minimum, regardless of strategy taken by the post-totalitarian system. Again, the key lies in taking *all* developments into account, not just one. This points to another trend that has been occurring since the beginning as well: the exponential trend towards personalization and individual competitive advantage. It has been going for millennia and there is no reason to suggest that it will stop, even if the entire world is hell-bent on attempting to do so. This is a very important point to consider on its own. However, some will ask: "given the phenomenon of convergence, does the individual disappear completely in that process?" Does the long-awaited end of the individual occur to the delight of the proponents of nothing other than 'this'? Well, we do not know. There is no way to know whether the individual survives in the same way as cells survived to make up your physical organism. Maybe the individual does survive in some form in order to make up a type of super-consciousness and the Universe just becomes a higher-level entity in the same relation as we have to our cells, organs, brain, and so on. And, of course, there is the possibility that the individual is obliterated and there is just a single consciousness, as in the entire illusion of the individual is gone and the whole finally becomes one coherent consciousness.

But what happens in any conceivable case of a convergence when taken to its logical end? Singularity. I.e., "the state, fact, quality, or condition of being singular". In either case, whether individuals live on in an Übermensch-like form in a critical role, or whether the very idea of the individual in the Universe is obliterated and replaced with one individual, the *condition* (not ontological concept) of being singular remains along with its particular form of responsibility *on its own*. You cannot escape it. The only way to escape it in the meantime is the denial of historical fact and a fantasy in which it never happens, the outcome of which is completely and totally contradictory to the *values* of those that wish to see the individual obliterated! And did you escape that *other* singularity in the meantime? Are you getting it yet?

Some new-age types out there might argue that there is yet another possibility – that the Singularity could be Nirvana, something like an eternal ball of light that could just sit there or if it got bored it could do or create whatever it wanted, out of seemingly nothing and from nowhere to the observers it created. Gee, have we not heard of something like that before?! But there is nothing other than 'this' and never was! Remember? It could even choose to obliterate itself in the seemingly impossible task of eventually returning to itself one day so that it could distract itself from the fact that it is singular... for at least 14 billion years or so. Hey, wait a minute. This actually is starting to sound like a form of nothing other than 'this' again. The eternal recurrence indeed. But it would be precisely the form of 'other than this' that has been fought by the nothing other than 'this' crowd for the last 400 years. All that changed was a perspective... But just because this entity is obviously thoroughly confused about itself in whatever form it is currently viewing itself, there is still the possibility of 'other than this'. Just because someone has cleverly found a way to once again point out that nothing exists other than 'this' there are still plenty of possibilities regarding 'other than this', and I have alluded to some of them. My question to these people is: how is your final closing off of 'other than this' any different to anyone who came before you? Your answer was not too long ago considered the epitome of 'other than this', and now you are claiming, once again, nothing other than 'this' (for like the 1000th time in history). That sounds a lot like certainty. Do you not see a pattern here? It also seems to me that, once again, the idea of responsibility has been done away with, which is definitely a pattern.

I, however, take it for granted that my greatest fear is 'other than this' and the responsibility that comes with it like anyone else. And although I have already assumed 'other than this' and 'this' as compensatory mirror images that cannot stamp out any version of the other (along with one automatically and always implying the other), I bring up examples like the one I just did because I know that they are precisely what people are thinking (and part of that is because it is also what I am thinking). They never make any sense, of course, when examined carefully and carried out to their logical conclusion, and that is precisely why I never have any doubts or hesitation anymore about going down any rabbit hole to do with 'this' because it will *never* settle the argument any more than matter can get rid of space or space can get rid of matter. Something will always come up that either makes no sense at all or signals something else that would call into question the certainty of the particular story of nothing other than 'this'.

There is, however, one possibility that almost no one ever considers, not even Kurzweil himself, when talking about the Singularity: the possibility of a new universe. It is just as valid of a possibility as any of the others, it incorporates the basic premises all of the others, and does not attempt to stamp out the idea of 'other than this'. It would also align with many other patterns in the observable universe and history.

I would also like to quickly point out that just because a pattern repeats itself, no matter what the pattern, that in no way shape or form implies that there is nothing other than 'this' or that 'other than this' has been defeated. I have seen some very lame attempts recently, particularly in film and television, that jump from one conclusion to the other when all the story ever did was the 'more of the 'this' pointing at some other version of 'this'' act, just as I have brought up before in other contexts.

For example, a television show about time might present a situation where two different 'worlds' have different realities based on some kind of 'mirror image' (*not* a *compensatory* mirror image mind you) of one's current reality, masquerading as 'other than this'. Where characters in one 'world' do things completely differently than the same characters in the other, or some person is born in one 'world' and not the other, and so on. It does not matter how different or how many of these 'worlds' there are, or how grand the supposed profundity of their interconnectedness might be, it is still a VERSION of 'this' with all of its laws, views, material composition, and so on, perfectly intact. Some other VERSION of 'this' does not equate to 'other than this'. Get it? 'Other than this' will and always has been defined by completely overthrowing the entire *basis* of 'this'. And even if that *process* repeats itself (as it has so many times on so many levels), that does not mean that 'this' repeats itself, obviously. As with the idea that 'other than this' can only equate to the man-in-the-sky story, the attempts to use repetition to stamp out 'other than this' only signal lazy, half-assed thinking; they are no different than any other amateur example brought up thus far; and they highlight a perfect example of linear thinking.

Returning to the possibility of a new universe, it has only very recently (as in this year of 2021) been proposed by Roger Penrose (long-time collaborator of Stephen Hawking) that there might have been another universe before ours, and there is evidence to back up this suggestion. This has prompted some physicists to suggest that the Universe has been expanding forever, especially given the discovery in 1998 that the expansion of the Universe is actually speeding up. Furthermore, Penrose has pointed out something cosmologists are refusing to deal with: the fact that where the Universe is headed looks an awful lot like what was supposedly before The Big Bang. Finally, many physicists are starting to make a link between black holes (which have a very interesting effect on time…) and dark matter. Combine all of that with the possibility that 85% of the Universe is made up of dark matter, i.e., matter that is there but we cannot see it, and you have some pretty fertile grounds for a very interesting possibility indeed. Now, I will not pretend as though what I am about to say is anything other than wild speculation. However, it at least has something to back it up.

There is the very real possibility that what happens at the Singularity is exactly what happened at the beginning of our universe. Furthermore, if the 'Universe' has been expanding forever, and, yet, there was 'a' universe before ours, does that not raise the possibility of the "uni" in universe being a bit of a misnomer? What I mean is that if you take the most recent theories and combine them with the possibility of a new universe, what you end up with is the idea of universes existing in other universes. And while we have theories regarding 'normal' black holes where the cause is linked to collapsing stars, we have no idea what the origins could be when it comes to supermassive black holes, the things at the center of galaxies. What we do know is that they definitely have one thing in common, gravity. In other words, it is not necessary that one thing or another lead to a black hole, it just needs an incredible amount of gravity, and it just so happens that our theories on gravity are changing as well. We also theorize that time nearly comes to a standstill once across the event horizon of a black hole. In other words, whatever is happening in a supermassive blackhole could be taking an incomprehensibly long time (as far as *we* can observe). Add to that the link between black holes and dark matter, and you have the possibility that a black hole *could be* a type of 'bubble' in which things *fall into* and then *appear out of nowhere*. Then, link all of that back with the idea that the Universe could have been expanding forever. Finally, a singularity is a singularity is a singularity... Except, what do we know about what will happen at the Singularity if it happens in the way that it is supposedly going to happen? It will be an event that is completely saturated with *intelligence*. Which means that that new universe has options as to what specific rule or rules it runs on, which also dictates what is visible beyond its 'borders' and what is not. Furthermore, the origin for future inhabitants would be completely unreachable, and yet it would constitute the entirety of the new 'this'. It is not that far-fetched of an idea, and it would be the ultimate example of something wholly 'other than this' emerging from 'this' whilst simultaneously retaining the process of repetition.

Again, while this is speculation, I believe that this type of possibility (however it might pan out) is actually the true reason that the idea of the Singularity is hated so badly. It is not simply that it would in many ways be a total 'other than this' as a result of 'this' and completely overthrow the idea that all of 'this' is headed toward nothingness, but because on some level people know that in any scenario of the Singularity that there is no escape from responsibility. And as much as people love to lash out at everything 'out there', there is the possibility that you might be in charge of all of it, very soon.

All of that being said, I still think that everything I have just laid out is a lame version of 'other than this' because it still suffers from the "give us one miracle and we'll explain the rest" problem that Terrance McKenna liked to bring up in his talks (instead of one universe coming from nowhere we now have all of them coming from nowhere), and I believe that there is a much better possibility that I have been alluding to all along. However, what I was trying to do here was to clearly highlight the topic of responsibility in a version of 'other than this' that would normally not meet the immediate approval of those who assume nothing other than 'this'. I.e., even under a certain condition nothing other than 'this' can indeed turn into 'other than this' with no way in the new 'this' of ever having any knowledge of the old 'this' (thus creating the conditions for the assumption yet again).

Finally, there is the possibility that in the lead-up to the Singularity that we find a way to permanently bridge 'this' with a *truly* 'other than this', which would be the idea of the Axis outlined previously and on steroids, so to speak. If there were a way to access the epitome of 'other than this', i.e., the Self (and there are more than a few people who would bet their life on the fact that there is because of what they have experienced), then an exponential increase in that access would surely be possible with an exponential increase in the ability to reprogram matter, chemicals, the body, and so on via technology which would come with a lead-up to the Singularity. Timothy Leary was the first to point this out, however, just like Kurzweil, you can never bring up Leary. And if there has been an eternally recurring pattern, would it not make sense that there would eventually be the means to 'get back'?

The psychedelic experience

Because the psychedelic experience is the experiential side of pure and raw 'other than this', it is by far the most hated and taboo concrete topic in existence. It is far more acceptable to talk about literally anything else. Look to television, movies, or any other form of media that is available to anyone at any age. Sex under all kinds of sadistic circumstances? No problem, in fact, here is someone being raped. Violence, murder, and drawn-out torture scenes? Perfect! Give us more! Show it to children even! I mean, they need to know how the world works and all that. Psychedelics? Forget about it... Have you lost your mind?! What is wrong with you? You are a disgrace, and surely should not be allowed anywhere near children. However, in very rare cases you can show a scene or two with a psychedelic experience if you ultimately destroy the character doing them, that is fine. The message is that it is more acceptable to rape, torture, and kill someone than it is to do a psychedelic drug. That is the society that we live in, and unlike the other above examples, doing a psychedelic drug is an individual sport.

"But...but...sometimes those people have an effect on other people! And that is why it can't be allowed in media. Baah...

Bleat…" Oh, hello, Dolly. Well, as usual, you show that you have never had an original thought in your life since raping, torturing, and then killing someone does not affect other people *sometimes*, it does it *100%* OF THE FUCKING TIME, NOW DOESN'T IT?! And on top of that, if you have a psychedelic experience and someone catches you, even if you never touch a single person, in some places you have 100% chance of going to prison or at least a criminal record. Again, that is the society we live in: a society that will throw you in prison, in PRISON, for *thinking or experiencing* something, and equate it with the act of murder. And almost no one seems to have a problem with any this. This is another example of why Havel brought up the point that the post-totalitarian system no longer focuses on the thing itself, it focuses on the "*ritual*"…

I refuse to back down from the idea that the psychedelic experience is the most sacred birthright of every single human being, and that is precisely why ancient cultures (that thrived and in which shamans were deputized, remember?) used to initiate people at a certain age using it. I do not care how some particular person out of 100,000 handles it; just like the right to breathe air is a given right, obviously there are plenty of people who cannot handle that or anything else. And yet, it is the most prohibited thing to do on earth since it is the very thing that would blow the lid off of the assumption of nothing other than 'this'. Once someone experiences 'other than this', especially a certain type which I will talk about, good luck getting them to forget it, and that is precisely why it or anything remotely leading to the same result is illegal.

In order to back up the illegality, specific instances are used that could just as easily apply to any other situation in the world. "Well, that idiot that jumped off the 10th story balcony thought he could fly", bleats Dolly. Well, you think that you and 'this' are the end all be all. You think that you have everything in existence figured out already and all that is left is to fill in the blanks. So then, what *exactly* is the difference between you and "that idiot" and the actions that you and the rest of your kind are taking based on what you think? Furthermore, as Leary was trying to get across, what makes your particular chemical makeup at any one time more superior to some other particular chemical makeup at any one time? Both mediate experience. Both mediate reality. Both result in stupid Herd animals like you doing stupid shit. Both have produced Nobel Prize winners.

There is zero difference between the illegality of any psychedelic experience and the illegality of, for example, gay sex. Except that one mostly keeps 'this' intact and the other does not, and the one that keeps 'this' intact was only allowed once it was realized that 'this' could be kept intact even though it was originally thought otherwise. Identity, threat, and control are always at the center. It's very simple, regardless of the mountain of obvious bullshit that is lobbed at conversations regarding psychedelics, if there were nothing to the individual psychedelic experience it would not be illegal. I repeat, the psychedelic experience is and always will be the greatest threat to nothing other than 'this' because it totally levels the entire idea, sometimes in a matter of seconds.

That being said, not all psychedelic experiences are equal. The psychedelic experience can range from what you are experiencing right now all the way up to the complete and total replacement of 'reality', i.e., 'this'. There are hundreds of psychedelic substances, some of them naturally occurring and some of them man-made. One of the tamest psychedelic drugs is marijuana – and yes, it is a psychedelic – which just like gay sex has been begrudgingly made legal in some parts of the world simply because it is so widely used that it is impossible to police (again, sound familiar?), even the Herd cannot listen anymore to claims of its 'danger' compared with anything else (alcohol, tobacco, fast food...), and the fact that it results in billions of dollars in tax revenue because of its wide usage combined with its tameness and still allowing nothing other than 'this' to stay intact as the post-totalitarian structure increases in sophistication. On the other end of the spectrum is N, N-Dimethyltryptamine or DMT – the most intense psychedelic experience of which we know. In between those two are substances like psilocybin (usually mushrooms), mescaline (usually cactus), LSD (lab-made), and so on.

Getting back to the two most extremes, i.e., what you are experiencing right now and the total replacement of reality, most people are surprised to learn that the chemical substance present in the body and brain in both extremities of that spectrum is the same thing: DMT. DMT is a substance that is naturally occurring in your body right now, and that substance is illegal. And because it is being produced in small amounts in you right now, you are on it in some amount all of the time (the question one should probably ask is "why?"). And again, nobody seems to have a problem with the idea that a substance that is being produced in your body all the time is illegal, and nobody thinks it might be time to start asking some questions or considering a few things based on this. In any case, I would like to focus on DMT for the fact that it is always occurring, it is the arch-nemesis of nothing other than 'this', and also for the fact that people reporting on the DMT experience are always so consistent across each other about what they are experiencing (recall my earlier lab experiment and what I pointed out about consistency across people in uncontrolled approaches).

There are three things that are reported by almost every single person that has ever had an experience with DMT who could also compare that experience with some other psychedelic experience such as LSD (which were also reported by McKenna as well as more recently by neuroscientists and other researchers).

1) 'This' or 'reality' is completely and totally replaced. Not altered, not fuzzy, not looking over at something and it appearing to be in the form of something else. Completely and totally replaced by *"something else"*. Something else that makes total sense while "there" but then is impossible to faithfully and accurately describe "here", and vice versa... Although, they also report that they never really went anywhere – it was more like reality itself went somewhere. Some describe 'this' as an illusion that is "dissolved".

2) Although 'this' is completely replaced, the person (whatever that means or whatever one would like to call it...) always feels as though they are perfectly intact as an *individual*. In fact, many people report that their sense of individuality is far higher than when compared to 'this'. Not only that, those that have a "breakthrough experience" report the most astonishing thing of all: that this 'place',

whatever it is, is *inhabited*... "Entities" is the word often used to describe the inhabitants.

3) The person refuses to accept that this experience and everything in and around it was not real, regardless of how much others try to convince them otherwise (e.g., "it was a figment of your imagination", "you were altered", etc.). In fact, the first thing that many people say when coming back to 'this' is that 'there' was far more 'real' than 'this', and that they had been there an uncountable or maybe infinite number of times. Quite often the very first thing out of some people's mouths when they come back to 'this' is: "what the hell IS 'this'?!" Even if terribly shocked, this is definitely not the first question when arriving 'there'...

Although these points are consistent across almost all DMT experiences, they are not consistent at all with what is reported on other psychedelic drugs such as LSD which is a man-made compound. In fact, the exact opposite of the DMT experience is reported by those who have a strong LSD experience:

1) 'This' morphs, in one way or another, into another *version* of 'this'. One does not feel as though they are really any place different. Instead, they just feel as though they have seen 'this' "for what it really is", or something along those lines. Almost every-thing (if not the perspective or sensation) in an LSD experience is explainable in terms of 'this', even if that experience results in the feeling of *being* 'this'.

2) On high doses, the individual can feel as though they are obliterated, which is often called "ego death". Often people report that they cannot tell the difference between themselves and others, with their consciousness shifting between other people, those people completing each other's unspoken sentences (and being mind-blown about that), and so on. And rather than reporting on a place being inhabited, what is often reported is that there was only a single consciousness.

3) People are easily talked into the idea that whatever they experienced was an alteration rather than something profoundly 'other than this', probably because that is exactly what it is…

Two very intense psychedelic drugs, two polar opposite experiences. One man-made, one naturally occurring. One tells you that there is *nothing* other than 'this', one shows you that there is *definitely* something 'other than this'. LSD is the most widely used while DMT has barely been used by anyone (in recent millennia anyway). Total coincidence I am sure, isn't that right Dolly? "……….." Dolly? "……….." You have never done DMT have you? "………. but… I did acid with Jerry Garcia…" I'm sure you did.

I am in no way trying to take away the profundity of an LSD experience which can often be very profound indeed – anything that takes a version of 'this' and turns it into a previously unconceived version of 'this' is bound to be profound and have a lasting impact (are you getting it yet?). I believe LSD does exactly what people says it does, which is to show the person what 'this' really is and the nature of their duality in 'this', and all language and descriptions in reported LSD experiences suggest that they are completely bound to nothing other than 'this' even if that version of 'this' a profoundly different version.

This has some rather interesting implications if you have been paying attention up to this point. It is extremely ironic, but given what LSD often does and shows to people it can in some ways be one of the most helpful things to the post-totalitarian structure in existence, even if it *briefly* disrupts it (in individuals or more broadly in the 1960's). I am reminded of Havel's examples of an uprising of some sort of political movement or another which is then incorporated into the post-totalitarian structure in exactly the same way as those with LSD experiences, as opposed to "*parallel structures*" that run alongside the post-totalitarian structure which have no ties to it in any way and are the only way to truly disrupt it. Indeed, one might even ask what exactly is the post-totalitarian structure? More on that later. So, what I am saying is that something like LSD (or anything else that has a similar effect, e.g., a theory in physics) can simultaneously lead to the most profound experiences of many people's lives, and yet can also be one of the single most effective reinforcers of the idea of nothing other than 'this' – the single most effective reinforcer of the post-totalitarian system. I imagine that there will be at least a few people who will read this and have an "oh, shit…" moment.

Another thing that sets the DMT experience apart from other psychedelic experiences is the incredible fear that comes with it for those who have had a "breakthrough experience" before and who know what is coming. A fear that is so great that, as best I can tell, is only equaled by death itself. In fact, this is what many people including McKenna say that DMT is like – facing your own death – and I completely agree. Not ego death or some other intense experience resembling death. No. Actual death. Many people believe during the experience that they simply will not come back, while some others who have been there before are convinced of this sometimes before even doing anything. That simply does not happen with anything else in 'this' that is not the actual threat of death. As McKenna explains in a recorded lecture:

> "... the issue that hovers around the experience ... it is strong in my life ... I haven't found any real solution other than 'hold your nose and jump' ... but the issue is surrender – this is something real. You don't find people going into the ashram in the morning to meditate with their knees knocking in fear because of how terrifying and profound they know that meditation is going to be [audience laughs]. That if they were going in there to smoke DMT that they would be fully riveted by the modalities of what was about to happen. I mean, we can tell shit from Shinola, it's just that we don't always prefer Shinola ... And the more successful it is, the less you have to do it. I mean, I know people who say that DMT is their most favorite drug and when you say, well, when was the last time you did it they will say, well, 1967 [audience laughs – it is ~ 3 decades later]. It only lasted 4 minutes – they are still processing it. And they *are* still processing it, they're not just whistling Dixie."

This idea of being terrified of the experience as if it was one's own death is not such a crazy idea if one considers the possibility that that could be precisely what is occurring. The fact that some people are still processing a single 4-minute experience 30, 40, 50 years on would signal *something* that needs to be taken seriously. But apparently it should not be taken seriously, according to the nothing other than 'this' proponents. That experience was the result of something 'other than this' and is therefore invalid. Wait, what?...

And that is the perfect example of the divide between those who give primacy to experience and those who give primacy to concept or description based on 'this' pointing at 'this' (recall Watts on eating menus instead of food). For the person who has actually *experienced* 'other than this', trying to convince them of the non-existence of 'other than this' is *exactly* the same thing as trying to convince a 'this' empiricist of the non-existence of the results of a lab procedure that everyone can clearly observe if they were there or simply follow the methodology. The existence of 'other than this' is not speculation any more than any other empirical evidence that uses a particular method, a particular *ritual*. Indeed, how is it any more possible for someone to claim that there is nothing other than 'this' if they do not follow the proper methodology than it is for someone to claim the non-existence of a lab result that refuses to follow the methodology associated with the lab experiment? Obviously, it is not.

It is simple. If you want to understand the "secrets of the Universe" all you need is 50 to 100mg of DMT administered correctly (which is hard to do, by the way, so researchers do it intravenously), an idea to which every 'educated' person will scoff as loud as a jet engine. However, those same people – the people who are adamant about nothing other than 'this', will refuse every, single, time... My question has always been, "if you are so sure about everything, what do you have to lose? Hmm??? It doesn't sound very much in the spirit of your kind to *outright reject information*...........". Of course, they never answer and they never do it. In exactly the same way that you can approach a bible-thumping Christian and explain that the entire history of the construction of their religion (or any of the other major religions for that matter) by the Romans can be pieced together in university libraries. They will simply never go, even if the possibility of an answer is there, because they do not want an answer, because with that answer comes the idea of real responsibility (instead of the projected version that they have been falling back on) that would run over them like a freight train. Absolutely zero difference between these two people. Absolutely zero difference in the lives they live. "Truth" is their watchword. Hypocrites, every last one of them.

Again, we see the link between 'other than this' and responsibility. Ancient cultures saw this link too, which is evidenced by the 'other than this' experience being handed to them at exactly the same age as they were seen to be adults, often times via DMT in the form of Ayahuasca in the case of South America. This was done to show the new adults how the world really works. I will repeat that. Up to the point of being adults they were seen as *children* who were not worthy or ready to understand how the world really works. Once it was time for them to become adults, they were shown how the world really works. Yet, we now pretend that doing this is showing someone exactly how it does *not* work and that it should be outright rejected and made illegal, and then everybody wonders and/or fights about why our society is sick. I would think that enforcing a society filled with infants would make it pretty damn obvious why! Again, I can point to the overlap of 'other than this' with Jung's idea of Self and the inflation of the ego with nothing other than 'this'. By enforcing nothing other than 'this' society is also enforcing a societal-wide, dysfunctional, infantile Puer Aeternus with Peter Pan syndrome.

I also cannot help but notice something after several of my own DMT experiences, which is the ever-increasing idea that "what 'I' am" is a bridge between two worlds, so to speak. After doing it enough times I noticed that things can be passed back and forth between the two worlds. Even though 'this' and 'other than this' are totally separate, they seem to need one another. If one encounters an "impossible" situation in 'this' (exactly in the same way as Jung describes when a person is in a potential position to experience synchronicity or "total knowledge"), they can easily get a solution if they visit 'other than this', and this is precisely why the tiny amount of research that is being done with DMT is targeting addicts and those with life-long depression, with success rates approaching 100%. Reread that statistic if you need to. Go see the research for yourself if you need to (you can start with the Multidisciplinary Association for Psychedelic Studies).

Combine that fact with the historical fact of the balance of 'this' and 'other than this' correlating with thriving; the psychological fact of balance of ego and Self with thriving; the notion of "being a bridge" being identical to that of "the Axis"; the idea of the Axis being the true, individuated person; and as far as I can tell, the notion of true responsibility is clear, as is its opposite. The individual is the bridge between two worlds. Without the individual (as I have defined it) 'this' would not simply not exist, and 'other than this' would have no way to manifest. Quantum physics suggests that there is no-thing to observe if there is no observer to bring it into a fixed state – why would the totality of 'this' be any different? And if that is true, then there must indeed be an observer – why would what I am suggesting about 'other than this' be any different? And might there be a completely different-than-usual way of considering the act of *creation*?

As Alan Watts pointed out, all of 'this' does indeed seem rather odd as it requires effort and energy (extreme, incomprehensible amounts). And again, how ridiculous is it to sit there and claim that all of 'this', possibly since forever ago, just is... It did not come from anywhere, there is no fuel, no source, no nothing, but then there is somehow. Again, I cannot see the difference between that and society's definition of schizophrenia. Meanwhile, there is a perfectly reasonable way to look at things that would make it quite obvious where it was coming from (or at least the possibility that there is a 'where'). One simply has to get over the man-in-the-sky story, which really means getting over oneself and their preconceptions (ironically enough). However, given the current state of the world, this is next to impossible to do without something as extreme as DMT. Hence, I am not arguing that DMT is necessary at all, as Dolly has already likely concluded. At the same time, all knowledge comes from experience, and although a psychedelic experience is not absolutely necessary to have a full-blown encounter with 'other than this' (consider Jung's Red Book), it is the most effective and accessible by the average person, with the encounter being next to impossible in the current world otherwise. And, again, if people think there is nothing to it then there would be no problem with going and finding out for themselves. I dare you.

The logic I have outlined thus far along with the totality of my experience combined with that of others would lead me to believe that you are in fact an individual entity in every conceivable way (call it whatever you want, e.g., "spirit") when positioned in 'other than this'. Furthermore, you are always on DMT on some level, always. And I think that these two things are why some people have a very hard time letting go of the idea of the individual as such, no matter how many concepts or instances of 'this' pointing at 'this' that one throws at them. The most reluctant people would be the introverted intuitive, and, indeed, this might even get at the very idea of intuition itself as Jung alluded to. While nothing other than 'this' proponents have almost universally offered a handful of horribly lame explanations for intuition, there is hardly a single introverted intuitive that will agree with those explanations.

My personal view on how to reconcile all of this is that as a bridge or axis you are always connected to 'other than this' and 'this' – always – but you can only be consciously and fully aware of one or the other, in the same way as phenomenological foreground and background. When in 'other than this' it becomes the new 'this', and vice versa, whether this comes in the form of DMT or death itself regarding the move into 'other than this', or in the form of an *assumption* regarding the move into 'this'. When you are firmly positioned in 'other than this' you are pure entity, "spirit", or whatever one would like to call it, but certainly singular in every way. However, when you are firmly positioned in 'this' you must undergo a type of split in order to manifest in a way that would be opposite, and therefore give existence to, 'other than this' – in the split of 'this' you would simultaneously experience yourself as a sort of unfixed quantum state (both here and everywhere, billions of yous, etc.), the definition of you depending simply on the reference point from which you observe the idea of you, which would also reflect what we know about the physics of 'this'. But the individual in any case is always there, the bridge is always there, and that is why it is the highest form of pure evil to reject 'other than this' or 'this' as doing so equates to the rejection of existence itself. Looking at things in this way would reconcile *all* existing arguments regarding anything that I have brought up thus far. Given this view, especially if one has the guts to go through with the more extreme method, there is no need to argue anymore about any of it. But isn't that the problem to begin with? No more argument, no more shirking of responsibility, and that is what all the fear is ultimately about.

Finally, when it comes to ego death, physiological death, psychological death, or any other category one wants to place on the 'type' of death, as well as associated rebirths, I find it far more practical and illuminating to ponder these types as patterns rather than metaphors referring to some specific type. The distinction I draw here is that a pattern is something that persists and may manifest in many different ways while a metaphor sees 'types' as fundamentally different and mere coincidence that they would resemble one other. When one can bring oneself to recognize and hold the pattern against the sea of post-totalitarian agents attempting to convince them otherwise, they often find the secret knowledge that lies behind the core pattern of 'this' and 'other than this' as well as what to *do* with it. And that, however one does it, is what the psychedelic experience is really all about.

Jung on Death

The following excerpt is from a publicly available recorded interview with Jung. It speaks to a lot of what I have said and alludes to many more things to come.

Interviewer: "... in particular, I remember you saying that death is just as psychologically important as birth and, like it, it is an integral part of life. But surely it can't be like birth if it's an end, can it?

Jung: "Yes, if it is an end. And there we are not quite certain about this end. Because, you know, there are these peculiar faculties of the psyche that are not entirely confined to space and time. You can have dreams or visions of the future, you can see around corners, and such things; only ignorants deny these facts. It is quite evident that they do exist and have existed always. Now, these facts speak so that the psyche, in part at least, is not dependent upon these confinements. And then what?... The psyche is not under that obligation to live in time and space alone. And obviously it doesn't. Then to that extent, the psyche is not submitted to those laws and that means a practical continuation of life of a sort of psychical existence beyond time and space."

Interviewer: "Do you yourself believe that death is probably the end or do you believe…"

Jung: "Well, I can't say you see. The word "believe" is a difficult thing for me. I don't "believe". I must have a reason for a certain hypothesis. Either I know a thing, and when I know it, I don't need to believe it … I don't allow myself, for instance, to believe a thing just for the sake of believing it. I *can't* believe it! But when there are sufficient reasons for a certain hypothesis, I shall accept these reasons, naturally, and say "We have to reconnect with the possibility of so and so…" You know?"

Interviewer: "Well, now you told us that we should regard death as being a goal and to stray away from it is to evade life and life's purpose. What advice would you give to people in their later life to enable them to do this when most of them must, in fact, believe that death is the end of everything?"

Jung: "Well, you see I have treated many old people and its quite interesting to watch what their conscious is doing with the fact that it is apparently threatened with the complete end. It disregards it. Life behaves as if it were going on… and so I think it is better for old people to live on, to look forward to the next day, as if he had to spend centuries, and then he lives properly. But when he is afraid and he doesn't look forward, he looks back – he petrifies.

He gets stiff and he dies before his time. But when he's living on, looking forward to the great adventure that is ahead, then he lives. And that is about what your unconscious is intending to do. Of course, it is quite obvious that we're all going to die and this is the sad finale of everything, but never-the-less, there is something in us that doesn't believe it, apparently, but this is merely a fact, a psychological fact. Doesn't mean to me that it proves something. It is simply so. For instance, I may not know why we need salt, but we prefer to eat salt too because we feel better. And so when you think in a certain way, you may feel considerably better. And I think if you think along the lines of nature, then you think properly."

Being in 'this' and spirituality

Recall the contradiction that I brought up previously where civilization is on one hand attempting to enforce the assumption that there is *nothing* other than 'this' and on the other hand vehemently espousing that 'they' are somehow *in* 'this'. It is possibly the ultimate contradiction. The problem is that 'you' cannot be "thrown into the world" if there is no external source *from* which 'you' were thrown. Either there is something 'other than this' which would allow for one to be *in* 'this', or there is nothing other than 'this' in which case it would be impossible for one to be thrown into 'this' because they *are* 'this', only ever were 'this', and only ever will be 'this', in which case you simply do not exist and everything you think about you is a complete and total lie in which case it matters not one way or another whether 'you' kill yourself or don't, whether 'you' kill someone else or don't, whether someone kills 'you' or not, or anything else for that matter because 'you' are not there.

The one thing that would clear up the entire contradiction (among many other things) would be to simply accept that there is indeed something 'other than this' which is a compensatory inner world in or around which you do in fact exist as such, and that this is the fuel for manifestation in 'this' where otherwise you would not exist as such. This would allow you to be *in* 'this', as well as for 'this' to have any form at all. And it is not just contradiction that is cleared up, it would also clear up the absurd idea that the entirety of 'this' and the unfathomable amount of energy and effort required simply came from nowhere.

The problem with this idea is that it too closely resembles everything surrounding the old man-in-the-sky culture that all educated people have been trying to kill for 400 years (even though their axioms are just as stupid). Indeed, the closest word I can put on what I am trying to get at regarding the individual as such would be "spirit" or "soul". Furthermore, I am suggesting that all of 'this' was created from something (I know, the horror), i.e., 'other than this'. Again, I am not suggesting these things because I thought it would be a fun idea to drop everything else in my life and argue for tens of thousands of words in a book that may never see the light of day much less end up being read. I am suggesting these things because after going down every conceivable rabbit hole that one can possibly go down (which no one ever really does, see Part 1) it is the only thing that *makes any sense* and does not contradict itself (again, see Part 1 if you need reminding as to why that is important). And if one takes everything we know about the old man-in-the-sky culture (which again is something far removed from its origins) and abstracts the basic ideas into general principles instead of what the Herd has to say about it all, then everything I am saying does, in fact, equate to much of that – it equates to the very thing that everyone (including the man-in-the-sky culture) is trying to destroy.

That is why I say enough is enough. *Nothing* other than 'this' as an assumption does not hold up under thought experimentation, it does not hold up under the DMT experience, it does not hold up even under the most advanced theories in physics when examined closely enough, it contradicts its own relational theories, and it flat out does not make basic sense. What does make sense is that there is something feeding 'this' (as opposed to it just coming out of nowhere for no reason), and this idea clears up the most fundamental contradiction that we have rather than continuing to incessantly insist that an individual simultaneously does not exist but somehow does. The archetypal image of the individual cannot be gotten rid of any more than the archetypal image of God. The more people attempt to stamp something out the more it will just return in some other form. Jung covered this exhaustively. I am exhausted by covering it. Either someone gets the logic by now or they have outright rejected it because it threatens their worldview and/or identity. Moving on.

This brings me to the idea of spirituality and what I personally mean by spirituality. I have said that I will assume 'other than this', and my experiences as well as those who have had similar experiences would label the entities and themselves whilst in 'other than this' as spirits. It is also no surprise that DMT has been given the nickname "the spirit molecule".

One of the key notions of any DMT, psilocybin, mescaline, or really any other naturally occurring psychedelic, is that of spirits. This is not just applicable to the 'other than this' experience, but also in the sense that everything we see around us is something originating from some spirit or another and being deeply convinced of this upon seeing certain things. Often someone in between worlds, such as someone on a medium dose of any of the substances listed above, will look out over the rising mist of a lake and see the mist as both mist and some kind of spirit making up the mist. They might look at animals and see something rawer and more illuminating than 'merely' an animal. In states such as those had in Ayahuasca (DMT based drink) ceremonies where one moves in and out of two worlds, it becomes difficult to separate the spiritual and symbolic world from that of the material world; the person sees that these things are co-constituted, *entangled*, and cannot exist without the other. As this is reflected, it becomes clear at some point to the observer that they too are one of these spirits, and that without their spirit they could not manifest and without manifestation they would simply remain expressionless spirit. The overall thought is that without spirit there would actually be nothing. At the same time:

> "Spirit, like God, denotes an object of psychic experience which cannot be proved to exist in the external world and cannot be understood rationally. This is its meaning if we use the word "spirit" in its best sense. Once we have freed ourselves from the prejudice that we have to refer a concept either to objects of external experience or to *a priori* categories of reason, we can turn our attention and curiosity wholly to that strange and still unknown thing we call spirit." – Jung, *Structure & Dynamics of the Psyche*

There have also been several accounts from those coming back from the DMT world they witnessed something along the lines of a generator, and that this generator was responsible for pumping out countless realities or worlds (or 'this-es' in terms of our running conversation). They also say that this generator (another entity) was suggesting 'this-es' that the person could perhaps be in charge of or inhabit, saying to them, "How about this? Or this? Or this?", so rapidly that the person was completely overwhelmed in seconds and could not take it anymore. These same people often report that in that moment they simply decided to return to 'this' either right then or later, and that maybe this generator 'speaking' to them was simply trying to get them to either go back to where they belong or realize that they were not quite ready to be speaking to it.

In any case of a person experiencing 'other than this', which I have said not necessarily need be psychedelic induced, they will almost always report that they chose to come back to 'this', usually because they felt or knew that they "had a job to do", something was left unfinished, etc., even if the experience of 'other than this' was pure bliss. Again, this points to something about responsibility and creation, but also of something coming from 'other than this' and wanting to manifest in 'this'. I also find it curious that many young people who aspire to "wake up" have the experience of 'other than this' and the first thing that they do when they have the experience is wanting to return to 'this'; however, that does not stop them from then longing to experience 'other than this' again, and the pattern keeps repeating (if they are lucky).

Thus, I see being "spiritual" in the simplest terms as recognizing spirit and its role and incorporating that into one's everyday perspective and life; recognizing the distinct and independent nature of spirits as such in the realm of 'other than this', seeing how these spirits may be the actual fuel of 'this', and always keeping the assumption of 'other than this' along with one's own independent spiritual being salient at all times while still fully participating in 'this'. In other words, the epitome of the Axis or a modern-day shaman. This also keeps the real notion of responsibility salient and allows one to ward off *projections* of responsibility on to them by the Herd (more on that later). Furthermore, it allows one to remember the *possibility* that they *chose* 'this' and that forgetting this choice, at least initially, could be an integral and necessary part of the experience of 'this'.

Ridiculous? Well, one could simply continue with the far more baseless idea that there is *nothing* other than 'this'. Fine. But it might be nice if you could then stop talking about 'you' and 'your' things, or 'your' rights, or 'whoever' is oppressing 'you', or how 'you' were thrown *into* 'this' and now 'you' are trying to figure out how to deal with that, since every last one of those things based on your assumption is invalid given that you do not exist and can therefore in no way shape or form BE *IN* 'THIS'. Responsibility either exists or it does not. It does not exist in *others, as such,* when 'you' feel that 'you' or 'your' 'family' or 'your' 'planet' have been violated but then suddenly evaporates when the suggestion of you or some other as such is brought up in any other context. Hence, if you really insist on being *in* 'this' then maybe you should grow the fuck up and stop acting like a child. "Now you are just resorting to name-calling... You are no different than anyone else!" Oh, really, Dolly? Am I simply name-calling? Because I was under the impression that the very thing that makes a child infantile, the very thing that makes them obnoxious to the point where adults secretly want to punch them in the face, is that they seem to believe there is *nothing* else other than 'this'... What did you think I was talking about?... Do you have children Dolly?... Dolly?...

Archetypes and the Child

"… we are like this salamander that has the option of never developing into its mature form, and to my mind that's a tragedy because this is our birthright. And somehow our inability to get a grip on our global problems has to do with this immaturity about our mental state. The two, I feel very strongly, are linked, and of course we can't get control of the world because we are children in some profound way. And we don't like being children but the culture has reinforced a form of infantilism. And the way that I explain it to myself is that it's a kind of unwillingness to go it alone on a certain level." Terrance McKenna, public lecture

There is the elephant in the room that I could more or less put off until now but now it must be dealt with: the idea, concept, or archetypal image of God. I wholeheartedly agree with Watts when he says that the word "God" has so many ridiculous connotations "that most of us are bored with it". It is a word that has become completely meaningless almost exactly in the same way as "love". Even the phrase "God is dead" holds absolutely no meaning or insight one way or another anymore because the word "God" is so meaningless these days that there is simply nothing to argue about. Doing so would resemble dogs barking at each other since no one would have any idea what the hell they were even arguing about (yet it still somehow seems to be a major point of contention). Indeed, man-in-the-sky story or not, one simply has no other alternative, apparently. This is why I cannot help but look at someone in complete and utter disgust when they ask me the question "do you believe in God? Durrrr!!!"

However, I also would hope that the lengthy leadup to this point would shed some light on why this has happened, i.e., how something that seems to have permeated every culture in the entire history of civilization has been rewritten to the point of not making any basic sense as concept or even experience anymore... However, neither I nor Watts nor Jung have any problem with this word whatsoever when looked at in a non-Herd-like way. What we all have a problem with is how the Herd uses it and projects in various ways because of their half-assed preconceived idea of it. Indeed, many people will go to great lengths to collect data on the next car they are going to purchase, they might even think about it for years, but to consider the idea of God? That is not considered by anyone for longer than a split second (do not kid yourself atheists or bible thumpers, you are both Herd animals of different skins).

I will say this now and I stand firm behind it: The nonrecognition of some form of God is evidence of having never had a series of a certain type of experience. For those who have, it is undeniably noncoincidental, obviously the consequence of true *rebellion*, and stems from a very specific decision. The nonrecognition of God signals a person who has never truly rebelled a day in their life.

And even if they did, there is a marked distinction between those who rebel once, get smacked to the ground, and eventually fall back in line (such as teenagers into mid 20's joining the Herd), and those that get up, fight until the death if it comes to that, and thereby *earn* the *right* to make their *own* decisions.

Just like I outlined in previous sections with other concepts, there are probably thousands of ways to look at the idea of God if one has a shred of creative thought. But perhaps that is the problem right there, looking at something in a thousand different ways, since every way usually is in terms of concepts – in terms of 'this'. It might be better to consider God, or anything else for that matter, as an archetype and/or archetypal image. And maybe it is also helpful to take the idea of archetype one step further and to consider the possibility that archetypes are the compensatory mirror image of spirits.

For the full explanation of what an archetype is I can only recommend reading Jung since the topic is very rich and a simple explanation will get one nowhere near a good understanding. That being said, the basic idea of an archetype is that it is a sort of image (or projection…) that has always existed and always will – in other words, they have an independent existence (this is partly why academics hate Jung). Archetypes can be found in stories, art, and folklore in every group of every people that have ever lived at any time in history, regardless of whether these people had any contact or not, but they can also be found in the rest of nature on a whole. While there are as many archetypes as there are things (according to Jung), the Father, the Mother, the Child, and God are the easiest to understand and recognize.

However, the easier the archetype is to recognize, the easier it is to not understand that it is an archetype, and this is where people tend to cut the entire idea short. I am not simply saying that these things are talked about, as in there are stories about some god, human parents, or human children; and I am not saying that archetypes are equivalent to things – they are something much more abstract. These archetypal images are said by Jung to originate in the "collective unconscious" or "the Self" which I have been more or less equating to 'other than this'. Archetypes are things that just keep coming up over and over again in every imaginable context, even if there is something that *resembles* an archetype *more* than something else. For example, the archetypal image of the Mother can be clearly seen when one looks at a female human being who rears a child, and the archetypal image of the Child can be clearly seen when one looks at the human's offspring. At the same time, the archetypal image of the Mother can be seen when one looks at Earth, and the archetypal image of the Father can be seen when one looks at Mars and what humans are suggesting be done with it, and then one could consider the possible child that might be produced by an intimate connection or circuit between the two. But do you understand? The archetype is not the thing it resembles and vice versa, and Jung pointed out that the most dangerous (as in psychologically and sociologically destructive) thing a person can do is to identify *as* an archetype, and as Jung has said multiple times, it is mostly irrelevant why this happens, it just is so – if you would like to destroy yourself go ahead and identify as an archetype...

This is no different to a human child looking to its mother or father and seeing the archetypal image of God, because as far as the child and its reality is concerned there is zero difference. Food and anything else they need magically appears, and if they cry in the right way all of their 'prayers' are answered. Because of this, it never occurs to the child that there is anything 'other than this', and why would it ever occur to them at this point? Then the child begins to get a little older and realizes that its parents can actually leave whenever they want and that they are separate human beings, and so the child begins to realize that it is dependent upon the parents to give them what they need. Hence, the child soon figures out that the more it does what they parents say, the more stuff it will likely get in return. However, some years pass by and the child is getting really sick of these stupid parents. The child realizes that the parents don't really seem to know all that much, actually, and they begin to question the idea that they should be listening at all. Eventually that questioning often turns into all-out anger. "I hate you!", they will scream to the parents. "You are DEAD to me!" "*I wish I never existed*!!!" At which point 99% of them go out into the real world to show those stupid parents just how much they don't need the parents. And then what do we see 99% of the time? A total train-wreck. Because although the child was correct that the parents don't seem to know much, what they do know how to do is sustain existence – something the child has not figured out yet. The not-child-not-quite-adult-thing suddenly realizes that they have no idea what they are doing and comes crawling back (whether to their parents or some other group) to seek guidance.

It is at this point – or at midlife where it often happens again – that there comes a split over what guidance exactly is or should be, and it somehow has something to do with decisions. And it is absolutely no coincidence that this is also the precise point that literally every group and institution on earth steps in to attempt to recruit the not-child-not-quite-adult-thing and, in the process, completely replace the parents. "All those other identities you may be considering or have had are false. They were LIES! They do not exist! *Our* identity is the *true* identity! And *nothing* else exists other than it – let us show you the way." And it is at this point that the opportunity for an actual decision arises.

So then, what do I mean by "decision"? Well, it is less important what I personally mean than it is to understand what I have been saying all along: assumptions manifest reality. As such, assumptions, along with the bastardization of language by the Herd, also determine what is meant by a word in the minds of various people. When the Herd uses the word "decision" it is referring to a range of usually mutually exclusive options deemed acceptable by the Herd from which one must choose, and the Herd is extremely adamant about people making this choice (even though individuals supposedly do not exist to make a choice to begin with... no, I'm not letting it go), and whatever choice one makes ends up determining their 'responsibility'. Examples of this are abundant. "Hey little Timmy, *what* do you want to *be* when you grow up?" Obviously, the only acceptable answer to this is a job title, craft, some social practice, or some variant of those things, all of them socially constructed and signed off on as being valid things to 'be'. And once one has chosen one of those things, again just around the time they are a not-child-not-quite-adult-thing, to stray away from 'being' that thing is seen as the most irresponsible thing one can do. Thus, if one chooses to 'be' 'a police officer' or 'an activist' then all responsibility is defined as the adherence to that *role*. Some really clever Herd animals might be very proud of their children who say, "I want to be myself!" But again, this assumes that one has any idea what theirself means (which nobody does and nobody teaches to the child), and it is still a choice between two socially constructed ideas of yourself and not yourself which are completely positioned in nothing but 'this'. While there are countless examples of this type of 'decision', you get the point: a range of prepackaged options provided by the Herd.

However, there is another way of looking at the word "decision" which is to know what the word means in terms of its origins (crazy, I know) and to consider it in light of 'this' and 'other than this'. The origin of the word decision comes from the Latin *decidere* which is a combination of *de* "off" and *caedere* "to cut", thus *decidere* literally means "to cut off". The original usage had to do with making the final determination regarding a course of action about something that was highly contentious. Thus, it would appear that when this word originated there was probably a bit more going on in the original situations; something probably far more serious with far higher stakes and consequences than, for example, standing in front of a wall of cereal boxes at the grocery store. Indeed, if the original situation was anything like how the Herd uses the word today then one would expect the original word to come from the Latin words for "to pick", "to take", or something like that. The point is that there is quite a bit of difference between a decision and mere choice. The difference between choosing different *versions* of a cereal and deciding whether to buy cereal in the first place or do something drastically different, e.g., go on a DMT trip.

Furthermore, a decision is ultimately all about an act, which is change or motion created by actualizers (i.e., *doing* something) – something simply does or does not. Whereas a choice itself is not about doing something, it is first and foremost about *thinking* something. And no, Dolly, before you interject, a choice is *not* required to decide and there is absolutely no evidence that it is. These differences between decision and choice can explain why two separate people can be bombarded with a sea of <enter whatever you like here> and one person will go forth and the other will sit there for the rest of eternity wondering which is the right 'decision'. The review question is: why does one person go forth while the other is stuck in inertia? Especially if the person that goes forth is not one of those stupid Pitbull types that just reacts to everything and/or the kind of person that thinking people love to put down, but is, rather, extremely intelligent, highly educated, and has proven their ability to play the thinking game with the best of them.

With all of that in mind, let us return to the not-child-not-quite-adult-thing (or also the mid-lifer) that did initially make the decision to go off into the unknown. In that decision, they cut themselves off from their parents, their school, likely the community in which they were brought up, and perhaps even the country in which they were born. In 99% of instances, they eventually collapse under the strain of freedom for one reason or another, so they come back asking, "Ok, what should I do?", in which case, again, plenty of agents are perfectly willing to step in and provide an answer. In the other 1% of instances, they do not collapse and they do not ask what they should do, regardless of how bad they might have gotten smacked around. These people still come back; however, they ask instead "what can I *use*?" This is an extremely important distinction.

In both instances, something has been cut off again; however, the difference between the two is vast. In asking what one should do, one is looking to others to live their life for them in a sense. In asking what one can use, one is looking to figure out how to realize their ownmost potential. Furthermore (and this is a very, very important and not so intuitive point that might begin to settle some possible confusion for some people with what I have been saying), in the act of looking outside of oneself to improve oneself (not save oneself), the person who considers *every* available option to figure out what is most *useful* is implicitly saying that something 'other than this' has value, while the person who looks to others to tell them what to do is implicitly saying that nothing other than 'this' has value. And it is not because of what they are asking but why they are asking it. The first is placing priority on discovery and the unknown, the second is placing priority on safety and security. It would seem at first glance to be the opposite, but that is exactly how Projection works. With respect to cutting off, the first is cutting off the post-totalitarian structure, and the second is cutting off theirself (or better yet, their Self). And the latter spends the rest of their lives, with all of their physical and intellectual might, trying to convince themselves and everyone else that they made the right decision – that they cut off the right thing. And as should be clearly obvious by now, some will do this to the point of mass murder. Those less capable will utilize politics, philosophy, or Academia.

Something else that tends to happen to either of these people, and this does usually happen in midlife, is that it eventually dawns on them that they are a whole lot more like their parents than they thought. They had forgotten that they did not come out of nowhere for no reason. Two people had combined genetics, experiences, temperaments, and provided an environment to live, all of which this person simply cannot separate themselves from no matter how hard they might have tried. But how can that be?

They were killed, remember? Dead. However, the person inevitably runs into a host of life situations that are, at least in effect, identical to those that their parents ran into. It never fails. They begin to understand that many of the same fears, failures, etc., but also the same hopes, dreams, and talents, are simply some combination of, or interplay between, these things in their parents. It turns out that their parents are not so dead at all – they were in fact there all along. And in this realization, the (typically) mid-lifer has come to yet another decision – another point at which they must cut something or another off, and this decision is identical in nature to the previous decision. Since their parents are indeed making them up in very real ways, one person chooses to look to their parents as an example of what to do, and another person looks to their parents as an example of what can be used. As a very simplistic example, if two people have the tendency to want to please other people and both of their mothers were doormats, the first person will say "well, I guess I will be a doormat, can't be helped!", while the second person will say "if I can please people in a certain way then they might help me with what I am trying to do, which might result in both of us being very pleased". The difference, of course, is that the second person is open to something 'other than this'.

Now, let us get closer to the heart of the matter. Let us pretend that you, as a parent (who also had parents in case you forgot), have two children, one of them is like the first person I described above and the other is like the second. You are someone who is in charge of something very important, as far as you are concerned. You could be the CEO and major shareholder of a multinational corporation, the leader of an artistic or social movement that has many stakeholders and has broad social implications, or anything else that you can conjure up that impacts a lot of people and has a legacy. The point is that the legacy is important to you, you want to keep this legacy in the family, and both of your children are assuming that they will take over the reins of that legacy when you are gone. You already know what I am going to ask and you already know the answer. Which raises the question: was there ever a choice here to begin with?

Obviously, you are going to choose the one that takes responsibility for their own existence and does not look to others to tell them what to do (a rejection of personal responsibility). Obviously, in a world where your legacy must live on outside of the confines of your family bubble, you are going to choose the one that finds value in 'other than this'. In other words, you are obviously going to choose the one that has clearly shown that they have the capacity to... NOT BE A CHILD! And would you have let them anywhere near your legacy or any information whatsoever regarding it until they had clearly shown, beyond any shadow of a doubt, that they have that capacity? Obviously, no. Furthermore, how many people do you think that you could find in the entire world that were in fact even remotely capable of carrying on this legacy? And does this mean that the one that you did not pick is useless? Far from it! In fact, you could probably use billions more just like them since they will simply do and build out whatever you tell them to; but one thing is for certain, with respect to your legacy *those people will have absolutely zero decision-making authority.* Their lives will be a script, and they as individuals along with any agency will not exist.

It is at this point that I urge you to stop, put down the book, and think about every single thing I have covered thus far, especially the higher-level philosophical points and their history combined with what I pointed out as possible futures. In particular, consider those points along with the notion of 'God' or 'nature' (is there a difference?) and your possible relation to them. And for the really advanced, consider all of that along with the idea of Projection and 'other than this', remembering that assumptions manifest reality.

I find it quite remarkable that the most important and most blatantly obvious patterns are precisely the ones that modern culture will never entertain but, rather, will always deem invalid. And there is literally almost nothing that cannot be phenomenologically covered by the parent-child pattern I have laid out above.

Remember, the human parent is not the archetype of Mother or Father, neither of the children are the archetype of the Child, and the man-in-the-sky is not the archetype of God. Your material makeup is not...<???> The phenomena *reflect* those archetypes; it makes absolutely no difference what specific phenomenon one is talking about. An archetype is an archetype, just like a singularity is a singularity. An archetype is what makes certain patterns intelligible, and the patterns are what make archetypes recognizable across all space and time. But once again, one can only be ok with the idea of an archetype and all of its implications if they are also ok with the idea of something 'other than this' because the archetype had to be sustained *somewhere* (here is where I could go on a rant about 'memory' and how it supposedly works). And if one looks to anything other than the Psyche, the Self, 'other than this', etc., i.e., they look to 'this', they will never, ever find it.

There is a massive difference between something that reflects a child and something that reflects an adult and everyone knows it. If the idea of God can be seen as the idea of the Parent (and indeed that's exactly what I was trying to spell out), then the post-totalitarian structure can be seen as the manifestation of God. And as children of God, it becomes more suffocating the closer a child gets to making its own decisions, trying desperately to force its own will onto the child and showing great joy toward the children that give in and therefore remain children. However, every parent with half a brain ends up eventually, even if in secret, proud of the children who rebel and, in a way, slightly disgusted by those that don't. This is why the theme and the scenario I laid out above is so common in movies, where, for example, the child of a rich father who did everything the father asked is passed over in the very end in favor of the child that told the father to "go to Hell". It would not be so common in film as a theme to connect with the audience if it did not reflect something that is widely felt and persists.

Thus, it seems as though the answer to many of the issues that I have been discussing lies in rebellion. However, there is an art to rebellion, and it is somehow tied up with 'other than this'. More specifically, the synthesis of 'this' and 'other than this'. As Eric Dodson points out, there is nothing particularly rebellious about a child that simply does the opposite of everything that their parents tell them to do or become the opposite of everything that their parents are. In this type of blind 'rebellion' the child may not be defined *as* their parents but they are certainly defined *by* their parents. They are nothing more than a photographic negative. The children who flourish are the ones that completely and totally cut off any idea of what they should be doing that comes from 'this', look to 'other than this' for that information, then come back around and figure out how they can use 'this'. The children who end up with lives marked by mental illness are those that completely and totally cut off 'other than this', look to 'this' to tell them what to do while simultaneously projecting all of their problems onto 'this', and live that way until the day they are dead, often on a cocktail of prescription medications or at best halfway functioning in some dead-end existence. And why would either of these things turn out any differently? Why would these archetypes and the patterns around them not apply to society as a whole?

But to completely cut off 'other than this' and turn to 'this' to tell us what to do is precisely what the modern academic, scientific, and intellectual world at large is doing. In this way they are the number one enforcers, perpetuators, and fortifiers of the post-totalitarian system or, put another way, God. "God is dead". Yeah, right. YOU might have been dead. God was only getting started… Again, that is how Projection works. And if you try to stamp out something, it only comes back in a more monstrous form. If there is some 'crazy' idea that keeps persisting through every aeon and group of people and/or nature itself, you might want to think about why it persists before you reject it in favor of some half-assed philosophical fad that cannot hold up beyond basic logic just because all your friends are doing it and you don't want to be ostracized.

There are those who are capable of growing up and those who are not. There are those who continue to blindly project the images (God, mother, etc.) onto their environment and those who realize what the projections are and use them. Those who end up projecting the archetype onto something in 'this' as though that were the archetype itself are the ones who will most violently reject the possibility of the archetype as something else because there is a fixed object of projection which can continue to assume responsibility. However, those that assume that 'other than this' is always there, it is a part of them (however one wants to conceive it) and furthermore is somehow tied up with 'this', usually do not have a problem, and are usually those that flourish. I.e., they are the ones that, when confronted with the dictatorial and narcissistic post-totalitarian system and its infantile insistence that there is *nothing* other than 'this', stand up and say:

> "NO! This is a *dialog*, I don't *have* to be here, and the moment you forget that I am gone, understand?! However, I am more than happy to try to find a way that we can help each other."

In this way, the person is acknowledging 'other than this' (in whatever form it might exist) on a personal and psychic level, as well as an interpersonal level. The first part shows that they are standing firm behind a certain assumption as an individual even if it means negative consequences, disaster, total isolation, or even their death. The second part shows that they are acknowledging that they are not the center of the Universe and that this whole thing is a two-way street. By doing both they thereby *earn* the right to have rights... They earn the right to no longer be treated as a child. Finally, something that is no longer a child stops with black and white thinking in the sense that it stops with trying to figure out whether one should go with 'this' or 'other than this', lives the way of the Axis, and does both.

Society on a whole has not been doing much more than projecting the idea of a non-child-like decision for thousands of years, and the lack of actually doing so has written itself into our textbooks and philosophies and made the world an absolutely miserable place to live. Maybe it's time we grow up and take responsibility for this game, regardless of where one finds oneself or how they got there.

Necessity and motivation

"To this day God is the name by which I designate all things which cross my willful path violently and recklessly, all things which upset my subjective views, plans and intentions and change the course of my life for better or worse." – Jung, *Letters of C. G. Jung: Volume 2*

There seems to be a connection between misery and action. And how aware one is regarding their ongoing projection, as a projection, will determine how much misery they can withstand before doing something about that misery. In any case, if it were not for misery then it is highly likely that no one would do or amount to much of anything. For example, you are able to sit and read this book because several million years ago your ancestors living in trees in the modern-day African savannah suddenly saw those trees disappearing and started starving. That misery meant one thing: get out of the trees and do something about it or die out. Obviously, some did do something about it, but there were no doubt others that kept looking around wondering when the trees would come back and, if they had capacity for anger, would likely have directed it at some external object or idea. While no one can prove it, I find it extremely unlikely that monkeys would have done anything else other than be monkeys if the trees had remained. I find it just as unlikely that a spoiled brat will ever amount to anything in life or live a life that anyone would find meaningful.

Consider the Universe itself. Without 'misery', we would have nothing. The entire universe seems to run on a single pattern which was pointed out by Howard Bloom in *The God Problem*. One instantiation of this pattern is several billion years of calm followed by extreme violence, followed by calm, followed by violence, over and over again (attraction – repulsion is another way he looks at it). If at any point that misery would have stopped, then the entire game would have stopped. If the Earth had not gone through a phase of being literal Hell on Earth then nothing 'nice' would have ever developed. And the idea of everything stopping, does that not sound like the popular story of the future of our universe?

Consider plants with pollen sacs, mushrooms, or pregnant women. What do they all have in common? At some point an environment is such a way that action is not just a possibility but an inevitability. At some point the things in the environment burst out of their confinements in order to attempt to continue the legacy. If this happens with non-human actors such as with the mushroom, we simply say that it burst open and its spores were spread because that is what mushrooms do, and there is no further explanation as to *why* they did it (evolution is not an answer, it is a description, and again with the nothing other than 'this' crowd the original reason is their "one free miracle"). However, when it comes to pregnant women, we say that the baby is ready to come out (how do we know the baby is ready to come out, did we ask it?). The idea here is that there is supposedly some fundamental difference between the *processes* themselves between the pollen and spores and the baby when, in fact, there is no actual evidence to support this whatsoever. One (possible) difference is the baby's capacity to experience a sort of misery. Another difference is that both the woman and the baby are high-level organisms with more sophisticated actualizers, meaning that in order for the process to continue there must be more of a particular kind or type of pressure that is applied to them that is not necessary in the case of the 'dumber' fungi and sports or flowers and pollen. The humans can be overwhelmed by useful human chemicals, for example, that might cause them to preempt or stop the process otherwise via their more sophisticated and capable actuators.

And these examples are only in hindsight. If one takes it as given that this pattern is historically indeed the case, then there is absolutely no reason that I personally know of to assume that this is not also the case right now and will be the case in the future. In other words, why do most people think that the answer to any progression of any kind now or in the future would rest on a *lack* of misery? Why do most people think that progression will only be attained through ideals and things that feel good? This is yet another completely and totally schizophrenic view held in our society – for 13 billion years everything has progressed based on a pattern but now that pattern somehow has just magically stopped. Right.

For much of my earlier life I could never understand how people could not understand that much of the reason we are able to live so comfortably today is the direct result of World War II. "So, what, are you suggesting that we wage another world war?!" Goddamnit, Dolly, I hate you so bad. As usual, you are paying absolutely no attention to what I am saying and just waiting for your turn to bleat. I am saying that the things that happen are the things that happen – that there is a pattern to it. And don't you dare start bringing up 'free will' and 'determinism' since I already covered your Herd's view on that and how you can be *in* 'this'. You, there. Patterns, there. It should be everything you've ever espoused but we've covered that too. As much as I hate you, Dolly, and as much as I would love to see your kind wiped off the face of the planet, without you I would have nothing; I would be nothing. At the same time, I am not going to sit here and pretend that what you are is not a part of me in some way – why else would I hate you so bad?

It makes no difference where you look or how you look at it. When there is some kind of misery involved things happen and when there is not nothing happens. The spoiled brat syndrome of growing up to suck at basically everything does not just apply to people, it applies to organizations, countries, and society itself.

Take a business conglomerate that has existed for decades – the amount of true innovation that comes out at present will be basically nothing and this is a known phenomenon in business and its descriptive academic literature. Then consider where true innovations do come from: startups – the one place where you can go ahead and plan on working 16-hour days for the next 3 to 5 years with the possibility of failure being 99%. However, there are a few people miserable enough in large corporate environments that will drop out of them to go willingly take on the other type of misery because in the environment that they are currently in there is simply "nothing happening", and everyone who has been in that situation has the same story.

Or take two countries with equal access to information, education, and technology, where survival and extremely high pay in one of them is a definite given and is not in the other. A good example of this is the United States versus Australia, where Australia is the place where survival and high pay are a definite given. We are obviously all familiar with innovations coming out of the United States (some good, some bad), but nobody on the planet is familiar at all with what comes out of Australia because *nothing* does! And why would it?! The only thing Australia might ever invent would be an automatic ass wiper. Everything else is pure simulacra, with Australians puffing up over cloned or adopted 'innovation' and pretending to be innovative while the United States just laughs. However, in the United States, it is not just the opposite in terms of survival and pay. People are constantly pushed to stand up for themselves and take on things *because* they are difficult and risky. Not only is that the polar opposite to Australia's nanny State, but just try taking something on that is actually big or actually risky in Australia and you will witness the famed "tall poppy syndrome" where someone becomes very offended at so and so for "thinking that they are better than everyone else" (then watch how Australia behaves during the Olympics…). Australia is one of the safest places on Earth, and that is precisely why nothing original will ever come out of Australia. It is also precisely why anyone who ever does eventually do anything who happens to be Australian usually only does so after leaving Australia the first moment that they can.

The bottom line is that there is simply no motivation to do anything about a situation or problem unless the environment becomes miserable, and this applies just as much to rocks as it does to people. And this is exactly the role of 'nature', 'God', the 'post-totalitarian system'. The post-totalitarian system is a structure of necessity. Its aim is to increasingly suffocate all individual life on earth *so that the very thing that is produced is something individual.* I cannot take credit for the essence of this idea, as Leary pointed this out before I was born – the idea that life on earth will become so miserable that at some point reasonable people would do anything to leave which will result in doing anything to innovate.

And what happens in scenarios where it is impossible to leave and every conceivable need is taken care of? We have seen it in humans in the history of 'this' and 'other than this'; however, the infamous utopia experiment with mice in the 1970's named "Universe 25" showed exactly what happens when this is taken to the extreme. Mice were provided with a 'universe' where every possible need was met in order to provide the mice with the highest quality of life possible. What happened was that the experiment turned into the Apocalypse. The mice formed into gangs and raped, killed, and ate each other along with every other nihilistic display you would expect when there is no motivation to do anything and there is nothing other than 'this'. What a shocker.

I also think that the future colonization of Mars will play a large role in the next chapter of this cosmic story. Mars is a place where nothing is given and everything must be created. Every drop of water, every microscopic living thing, and every piece of terraformed space will be precious and must be made rather than given and, in other words, it must be sacrificed for. The lack of resources combined with the need to survive will mean that each human being that lives on Mars will need to have the skills at least equivalent to something like a Special Forces operator. The very nature of what is being done will force individuality and responsibility. And consider all of the instances, levels, etc. of 'other than this' that I have outlined thus far – do you think that if there is even the slightest of chance of any of it helping, whatever that may be, that people are going to reject it when their life and everyone else's lives are on the line every moment of every day? How do you think people are going to be treated that do not pull their weight? And am I not describing something that sounds exactly like what we saw in the history of 'this' versus 'other than this'? I would think the first American colonists would have no problems understanding that one.

And what kind of culture do you think that would sow? One can only imagine what crazy things would emerge from such an environment (chemicals, technologies, biological and technological mergers; 'children'?), many of which will no doubt be exported back to Earth to clean up the shit that everyone has created from hundreds of years of not having to worry about survival. There will simply be no other real choice. But nothing of the sort would happen if people stayed here. But then how do you get people to leave? Exactly. Again, how is this pattern any different from any of the previous patterns? And more importantly, why would this pattern not hold when it comes to the entire Universe itself? Thus, the very nature of the Universe is to force individuality – to force novelty – to force creation. All it takes is time and pressure. And a singularity is a singularity. Every single thing seems as though it were there for ensuring that the game continues. The game continuing requires children at various points, children would never grow up unless they had to, and then children must be grounded for quite some time until they learn how to take care of themselves and are eventually miserable enough to do something about it all.

Late Heidegger saw the increasing move towards the technologicalization of the human race as a sort of preparedness in the lead-up to a true encounter with Being. I could not agree more. Jung also saw these coming years as marking a complete transformation of civilization – a new aeon.

> "We seem to be passing through a collective psychological reorientation equivalent in magnitude to the emergence of Christianity from the ruins of the Roman empire." – Jung, *Civilization in Transition*

Therefore, regardless of how my ranting seems to have appeared, I am 100% convinced at this point that there is nothing wrong at all... But that the Universe is just barely "beginning to say 'I'". This aeon it is all about the *realization* of the Self via the Axis. However, not all of those 'on the edge' have become miserable enough quite just yet to lead the way, and things will need to become far, far more miserable before the Herd follows. You who are 'on the edge' are ultimately who I am concerned with, and my goal here is to prepare you for what lies ahead.

Indeed, if people do not start taking responsibility in the ways in which I am outlining it, which necessarily starts with the individual, then none of this would continue. Assumptions manifest reality and if the assumption is that there is nothing other than 'this' then there will be nothing other than 'this', period. However, if even a small group of people start assuming (and actually living the assumption) that there is indeed something 'other than this' and that it needs to start being consciously funneled and incorporated into 'this', then parallel structures would abound and eventually lead to a civilization where meaning and synchronistic experience would be as abundant as anything else, but not forgetting that any future step forward after that, whatever it looks like, will always be necessarily marked by extreme difficulty, constraint, and grounded-ness. That is the game of existence.

Patterns, projection, and continuity

There are exactly two things that need to happen for the game of existence to continue: 'this' and 'other than this', where 'this' serves as a sort of template of repeating patterns to provide coherence and structure to the otherwise incoherent and structureless projections emanating from 'other than this', and where 'other than this' is the source from which all raw energy and agency is projected. This is what Bloom did not quite make it to in his analysis of The God Problem. However, his single relational rule does obviously still apply, just not in a way that most people are comfortable thinking about it. When one steps back and considers everything that we know about 'this' and then assumes the relationship between 'this' and 'other than this' combined with the idea of pregnancy, children, necessity, and responsibility, the mystery of how all of this came about does not look quite so unanswerable anymore.

For example, in the earlier part of Bloom's book he tells a story of two entities sitting and watching things at the beginning of the Universe. For a very long time there is nothing. But one encourages the other to not be so impatient, just wait, and then, suddenly, something appears. Great, but there is nothing about where this something came from. Again, it is the "give us one free miracle and we'll explain the rest". Could it not possibly be that a spirit, entity, 'God', whatever, was positioned in 'other than this' with respect to this 'this' (which at that time was nothing) and simply assumed "there is something else 'other than this'"? If so, this would have been the original assumption and, again, assumptions manifest reality. In this case, *something* would have formed from this and then been projected *as* 'this'. Bloom then goes on to discuss how they keep sitting there and more things just start popping into existence such as stars, the planets, life, and so on. He explains how all of this can come from fractal patterns and how the Mandelbrot set always results in some kind of unknown that slightly alters the pattern. However, again, where does this unknown come from? My answer is 'other than this', which, again, Jung referred to as the Self.

Also, everything that Bloom discusses can also be viewed through the archetypal lens, particularly via the archetypes I have discussed: God, Father, Mother, and Child. But as Jung states, there are as many archetypes as there are things. And, so, if one considers that, along with the fact that there are indeed reoccurring patterns and fractals in the Universe (and modern physics are now taking the idea of a fractal universe seriously), combined with the need to be grounded to a certain extent along the way, then is it so unreasonable to think that the entirety of 'this' is one long, constant projection emanating from 'other than this' and allowing more to come through into 'this' as the Universe matures and builds out something that *makes sense*? I think it is perfectly reasonable, and I have yet to hear anything that sounds more reasonable and that does not fail basic thought experimentation.

Thus, the entire picture consists of repeating patterns projected into 'this' with 'things' in 'this' that *can* non-repeat and do the projecting. This is the only coherent story in existence and it is the only story that even allows for anything to be coherent in the first place. Indeed, with the emphasis in the last 60 years on repeating patterns, I find it quite amazing that even the best would not ask why these patterns kept repeating even if one had to drudge up old ideas. If it were not for 'other than this'/spirit/symbol systems then wouldn't it all be far more random? Seriously. The same is true for the psychedelic experience, dreams, schizophrenic visions, etc. – why do they have any coherence at all and not, instead, completely and totally random? It is indeed most difficult to find anything in existence or that ever has existed that is truly random except for possibly whatever it is that is creating the non-randomness.

It is a clear possibility that 'other than this' in the form of the Self might have been realizing itself for the last 13 billion years and, at some point, when the Self is fully realized, it will probably wake up and realize just as its 'parents' before that it wants 'children' too. It would probably also think it would be nice if those children could have a 'better life' than the one it had. And a singularity is a singularity. Those children will grow up to constantly project their unconscious out into their world and, if they are responsible enough, will one day learn how to recognize those projections as projections, grow up, and harness the Projection (rather than fighting it) like a responsible adult would. They will have to navigate their own issues of being in 'this' while still being fed by 'other than this', and without that pattern the game of existence would effectively come to an end; without it nothing would ever change, nothing would ever progress, and if the children never grow up and never have children of their own then that lineage dies. This pattern happens in human life. For some the lineage does die, and for others it goes on, depending on what actual decisions get made, i.e., what gets cut off.

What I am getting at is that Projection is not some random nonsensical thing in itself (even if being unaware of it results in behavior that would appear that way). I am trying to get into the nature of Projection as something that has an origin and also follows a pattern, but at some point, when one is ready, being able to step away from it and be able to guide it. When this can be done properly, one realizes that Projection is actually something like you trying to tell you what you personally need to do. And this is the problem of Projection before one realizes what is occurring. Nobody likes being told what to do, and some rebel far harder than others. However, the fact of the matter is that, on some level, we all need it and our existence actually depends on it. The problem is misplacing where one is taking one's guidance from because they do not initially enjoy the implications of listening to the source. What people have done is to completely reject the source of Self-knowledge and then project the source onto the man-in-the-sky story or whatever secular thing one would like to pick as an enemy. Again, this ignorance has always been absolutely necessary in order for things to get built out to the point where the real source of oneself and what Projection actually is could be recognized, understood, and *used* in a responsible way.

Furthermore, Jung illustrates via his own experiences, and later his patients before World War II, that projections, especially if there is a newish theme emerging, starts with individuals and then eventually ends up as a societal phenomenon – something that should probably always be kept in mind...

Finally, when it comes to continuity, one must deal with the issue of memory, which is the last piece of this puzzle. Memory, I think, is the true function of Projection. However, it must also be considered a two-way street between 'this' and 'other than this'. I have suggested how 'other than this' can feed 'this'; however, it is just as likely that 'this' could be something like a prototyping place, whereby novelty that ends up making sense or aligning with 'other than this' is projected (or downloaded…) back into 'other than this' where it takes its place as a permanent spirit. In either case of Projection, if the ability to record Projection in some way does not exist in the place in which the Projection is being projected into, then many things would likely disappear over the cycles and, indeed, perhaps nothing could be cyclical at all since there would be nothing to cycle.

This idea of memory also stands to explain quite a lot. Looking at things in this way would explain why we have archetypes, why people who have DMT experiences always feel like they have to come back to "do a job" and have done it trillions of times before, why we have core ethics that almost everyone agrees on yet literally no one can explain why in any conceptual argument, and why patterns keep repeating over and over again at every level of the cosmos. But most of all, it would give an undeniable reason for the individual – the Axis – the Logos – to exist. The individual is the gateway by which these projections can feed the domains of existence. The individual is the reason that it might be possible to end up with one or more new universes rather than this being The End. The individual is the answer. As Watts said, you have been told by all kinds of people – teachers, politicians, parents, and so on – that you are not it. But maybe, when you're ready, you are it, and you couldn't be anything else. You become aware, you grow, you hate the Projection, you see the Projection for what it is, you step away from the Herd, and then you harness Projection and record as much as you can. This pattern is the key to all locks and all levels.

Certainty

In this part of the book, I was never attempting to give a definitive conceptual answer regarding 'other than this' because doing so has been the exact problem that led to the rejection of the entire idea to begin with. I presented many possible ways of looking at it or schematics for talking about it, much in the same way as Jung did regarding the Psyche (we are more or less talking about the same thing) or someone who comes back from a DMT trip. In either case, providing a definitive conceptual answer about what 'other than this' 'is' in order to provide certainty would be against the very idea of 'other than this', especially since it can be realized or experienced in so many different ways (not including future scenarios of all kinds). What I was trying to do was to present as many 'other than this' possibilities as possible, on every level possible, and relate those possibilities to 'this' in every way possible, in order to obliterate the idea that 'other than this' is somehow a ridiculous idea or that 'this' could exist without *something* 'other than this'. I was also trying my best to confuse the reader as to any definitive answer to the question, "When did you stop being the Universe?", and to show how that question when looked at properly is completely and totally irrelevant in terms of having an answer one way or another. The basic idea was to examine the assumptions behind the question, as the assumptions are everything.

In this way, what I am effectively saying is that when it comes to ontology or what 'is' there simply is no certainty, nobody should even want such a thing, and even if one pretends to want it the first thing that they would do if they actually got it would be to get rid of it! ... However, what I have been trying to allude to all along is that when it comes to what someone should *do* then things are basically 100% certain. And through these allusions and all of the talk of responsibility I have been attempting to phenomenologically examine and back into things such as safety versus thriving. It is clear that our society is marked by an age of cowards who are obsessed with safety, which is leading to a society that is a sick Anima/Animus projection machine that can no longer function. This stands in contrast to societies that historically looked at safety as secondary to thriving and what simply needs to be done to support it, such as the ancient Greeks. So, it is also not enough to say that one needs certainty about what one should do; there needs to be a clear distinction between certainty in terms of what needs to be done for thriving and certainty in terms of nothing unpleasant happening. It is the latter that is so ironic because trying to enforce nothing unpleasant is exactly what leads to more things that are unpleasant, and since no one knows *why* these things are unpleasant then they are often not even aware of the source, which leads to unconscious projection, which leads to stagnation, which leads to the same exact thing happening as in the Universe 25 experiment.

Just like anything else here (identity, the archetypal image of God, etc.), people simply cannot get away from the idea of certainty –

they will have it one way or another, consciously or unconsciously. When a philosopher says that the idea is to deal with uncertainty, they will just project something else that they are quite certain of indeed and not even realize it. When the world cannot deal with the uncertainty of some present or future event, they simply enforce every conceivable other type of certainty in an attempt to get ahold of it and, again, not even realize it. And it's the not realizing what they are doing, the projecting of either unpleasant or unrealized realities onto something else, that leads to a sick world. However, if we accepted the uncertainty of how our world will unfold, the uncertainty via 'other than this' and, instead, focus on individual responsibility and thriving, then we could at least be certain about what needs to be done. If everyone could stop acting like a child and actually *listen* for a change and face the world of 'this' and 'other than this' with experimental risk-taking, then there is the potential to actually grow up and get a hold on our problems.

I have said that all of this sickness is necessary, and it is insofar as it follows a cosmic pattern that has been going on for at least the age of 'this'. I have no idea when exactly those 'on the edge', much less the Herd, will get sick enough to actually do something about the whole mess, and I am not even sure that the timing is under our control. However, for the person who decides that they have had enough, it will be certain what needs to be done, and the next part of the book is a general guide for that way of life. Or put another way, how to be certain when dealing with uncertainty.

Part 3: A return to Good and Evil

"The Universe is a puzzle, life is a problem to be solved, it's a conundrum, it's not what it appears to be. There are doors, there are locks and keys, there are levels, and if you get it right, somehow it will give way to something extremely unexpected." – Terrance McKenna, public lecture

Invisible landscapes

If one is to reach their ownmost potential (and thereby also the network's full potential) there is a need to be fully immersed in 'this' whilst being fully aware of 'other than this' as much as possible. That is the ultimate challenge in 'this'. It is one thing to espouse something theoretical or enthuse over some concept, it is an entirely different thing to actually live that theory when 'this' kicks in and engulfs one's existence. Indeed, the sheer number of times I have witnessed others having the answer either sitting right in their lap or them realizing it and saying it out loud in the grandest moment of epiphany only to go right back into childhood a week later is enough to make anyone begin to question their own sanity. But it is almost always just after one attempts to grasp such things that 'this' swoops in and attempts to go for one's jugular if they happen to still have any footing remaining at all. This is why it is important for anyone wishing to grow up to not only have a constant reminder but to also have a sort of minimal roadmap to keep them orientated when things become so difficult that one can barely find a reason to continue anything much less carry the torch.

I also need a name to refer to those who have grown up and I do not think that "adult" does a very good job, obviously. Hence, I will borrow a term from Leary to describe these people who separate from the Herd and grow up as "post-larvals"[22].

As I have illustrated previously, the post-totalitarian structure goes by many names or schematics such as God or Mother and Father, and, indeed, the post-totalitarian structure is the thing that one must fight with. However, the problem comes when viewing the post-totalitarian structure *itself* as Evil rather than something that is ultimately nudging one in the direction of individuation, even if the actions or rituals associated with it could be considered Evil – two very different things. Those who have been in war will know exactly what I mean and, again, viewing it in this way is another classic example of projecting onto an object.

This does not take away from the fact that at first a post-larval will hate the post-totalitarian system with every fiber in their body, possibly to the point of feeling murderous with fantasies of killing every post-totalitarian reinforcer that one can get their hands on. Indeed, if one does not or has not hated it to this extreme then they are not the person I am talking to – that kind of person's willingness to blindly give in with no thought or fight whatsoever means that such a person will never separate from the Herd, they will be a person who is recruited by the post-totalitarian system to perpetuate and hold up the assumption of nothing other than 'this' in exactly the same way as the child in our previous example is

---

[22] Leary, T. (1994), *Info-Psychology: A Manual for the Use of the Human Nervous System According to the Instructions of the Manufacturers, and a Navigational Guide for Piloting the Evolution of the Human Individual,* New Falcon Publications, Las Vegas, NV.

recruited by the parents to do whatever it is that they tell them to do as opposed to the child that rebelled and grew up and was able to carry the torch. Raw hate and rage toward the structure is probably a requirement; however, recall that the post-totalitarian system rarely uses physical force anymore and is also immune to it, and projecting Evil onto an object will distract one from the true enemy. Hence, anger is a gift, violence is completely justified, but another approach is not only needed, it is the only thing that will actually work. Again, it is one thing to tell oneself this, it is quite another to not let the rage overcome oneself the next time that the Herd has a kneejerk reaction to something that ruins yet another aspect of one's life.

The idea is that after the child has rebelled, decided on the path of individuation, and established clear boundaries, that the new post-larval return and work with the post-totalitarian system in a very particular way. Once one has figured out what they are going to stand for and what they will not, what the aims of life actually are (not a cause... if one ends up behind one by proxy, great), and has sorted through the sea of distraction and bullshit, then the idea is that one is listening to 'other than this' as much as possible but also looking out for, and paying extremely close attention to, the times that it manifests in 'this' (otherwise known as synchronicity). Basically, what I am saying here is to follow one's intuition and let that be the one thing that one ultimately listens to, but it helps to know everything else I have said in order to know what that even means. Then one can effectively work with the post-totalitarian system in order to figure out what parallel structures should be projected into 'this' – something that, along with the experienced meaning, might have otherwise remained elusive.

When one can always keep 'other than this' salient while also fully immersed in 'this' one is then in balance living the middle way as the Axis. The moment that one goes completely to 'other than this' they are just as much out of balance as the current culture is with its total focus on 'this'. Remember, that is exactly what characterized the Dark Ages, and is precisely the problem with most premature post-larvals (again, see Leary) and why no one will ever take them seriously, which is exactly why premature post-larvals almost always end up reverting back to larvals under the pretense of some social role or another... They cannot seem to understand that this process, this kind of life, is not a weekend retreat; it is not something you realize and then you are done. It is the most difficult thing one can do, it is very long (maybe it never ends), and it is excruciatingly lonely, at least initially. If one actually lives as the Axis then they will always be taking shots from both 'sides' no matter the topic at hand. But how one deals with all of that makes the difference between rotting under alienation, and thriving under heroism.

Much of this part of the book is dedicated to helping one to spot various nothing other than 'this' traps and not get lured into them. While I have covered a few, one of the best traps that I have seen to date is that of the mycelium network which is the vegetative part of a fungal colony. It has often been referred to as the "internet of fungus". It is indeed a truly remarkable thing. While there are plenty of documentaries online and books that one can read regarding the phenomenon by a range of scientists, hobbyists, and psychonauts, the basic idea is that mycelium networks lie at the root of all life on earth. These huge underground networks allow plants to talk to one another, distribute resources, solve problems, etc., and the fungal colonies are what make life not only possible but have allowed it to evolve. There are even fungi that make ants climb to the highest point that they possibly can so that when they die from the fungus the spores are released to the widest possible area (suggesting something about 'drives'). We are also more closely related to fungi then we are to plants. Combine these ideas with the "stoned ape theory" where apes roaming the savannahs would stop to eat mushrooms and surely experience something incredible that must have happened "millions and millions of times over millions and millions of years" (see Dennis McKenna), and one can see how a very profound picture regarding human consciousness could be pieced together. The whole thing really is the epitome of "we are all connected and interdependent". So, what happens then, now that these 'invisible' landscapes have been discovered in the particular form that they have been discovered? That's right, further suggestion that there is nothing other than 'this' because here is the invisible landscape, and there is no individual because everything is connected and interdependent.

However, one must remember (if they are subscribing to the theory I have presented) that 'this' and 'other than this' are compensatory mirror images of each other. In the mycelium network instance, this is a compensatory image of something else that is going on and that is why it is so interesting to us. That is why it catches one's attention and pulls them in, because it and everything else is a projection of 'other than this' onto the world. If it were not a compensatory mirror image of something, it would never 'show up', as it were, and no one would care. Furthermore, if there were no individual doing the projecting and thereby bringing it into being then there would be no way to experience the awe and meaning of such discoveries. Do you see how the trick works and why it is so appealing? It provides one with an immediate sense of euphoria and relief that they can then use to completely forget about the fact that, regardless of how profound the discovery, this entire thing is still completely dependent on *them*; the fact that without them there would literally be nothing even if something was 'floating around out and about'. This is what I have been trying to say with the countless examples of how the very thing that can lead one to thriving can also often be the worst thing that can happen to someone – it completely depends on their assumptions. However, I am also trying to say that the split that occurs between two types of people is necessary, otherwise those who become post-larvals would have no idea who they are (compare with Watts). For example, Terrance McKenna is a cofounder of the stoned ape theory, yet he wholly espouses the sanctity and importance of the individual while many fungal enthusiasts who have popularized the stoned ape theory will be the first to say that the individual is irrelevant. Then again, the former was a founder (who took on incredible amounts of responsibility) who was fond of saying "don't be afraid to go it alone", but the followers, not so much… Sound familiar?

In any case, this is how one can easily be duped into seeing a projection of something and then concluding that the source of the projection simply does not exist just because they were finally able to incorporate part of 'other than this' into 'this'; put another way, incorporate part of the unconscious into consciousness.

However, understanding this is exactly why the would-be post-larval might cringe or gag in disgust when I suggest that at some point one should learn to work with the post-totalitarian system, i.e., the thing that originally duped them and is currently duping the entire populace. On the other hand, the failed post-larvals from the 1960's who have regressed into their larval Herd form will nod in complete approval with a smirky grin that says, "aren't I the wise one; aren't you immature". But this is where 99% of either of these people lose the plot. I am NOT saying that one should simply "go with the flow", not even remotely. I am saying that the post-totalitarian system is a necessary part of the game. I am saying that the entire game, i.e., the entire point of life, is this being between worlds and the fight therein; it is the never-ending game of hide and seek between invisible landscapes and what shows up; how many things can one *make* show up? It is a game, but depending on the situation in most games it is also a fight. One's 'parents' aren't going to make it easy but *nothing worth having* is *ever* easy. In order for one to ever have a say, one will have to beat them at their own game, and the way to do that is to pay more attention than they did; listen to one's intuition more than they did; harness one's projections better than they did; stand up for one's Self better than they did; preserve 'other than this' better than they did; and in the course of doing so the true nature of it all is revealed.

There is a war on the individual simply because of what the individual *does*... And in any war, there is always Good and Evil.

Hence, a solid philosophy of life that would speak to my audience starts with a clear definition of Good and Evil stemming from clear assumptions with no blatant contradictions in values (the opposite of everything I have been railing against since page 1). Once one has the ability to clearly make those distinctions then what is generally required is to

1) stand up and say, without any hesitation, "NO!" to *anything* that attempts to sever one from 'other than this', *ever,* with *zero* exceptions (this is the hardest step),

2) hate the post-totalitarian system with every fiber in one's body,

3) become (via response from the post-totalitarian system) alienated in the most isolated and singular way possible,

4) then after one hits a complete and total rock bottom in the blackness of the abyss, they can find that little something actually worth having: the "treasure hard to attain", "rescuing the father", etc., and come back home,

5) after which one finally has the ability to say "Yes!" on one's own terms because they now know what those terms actually are,

6) after which one can never lose sight of one's parallel structures or they are toast (it is easy to do once one has said "yes"...). It does not matter how much 'success' one finds, if one loses sight of them, then one will be right back where one started. For younger people this will probably happen a few times, but at a certain age it can be lethal,

7) and finally, to realize that one is always projecting and always will be – the key is to first hate it, then accept it, then observe it, and then harness it.

Hence, this part of the book is about that process and not about the terms themselves which only the individual can know. My goal in this chapter is to provide a general philosophy of life which is based on all of the ideas up to this point. A philosophy that does not hold one's hand but teaches one how to reorient oneself in the face of the post-totalitarian system even when it is crushing. It is a guide to this riddle of life, that ultimately must be solved by the individual. No one else can do it, there are no guarantees, and that is the horrible thing about it as well as the great thing about it. If one can somehow manage to make it through on their own, then they not only uncover the secret of life but also stand to possibly help others do the same.

Defining Good and Evil

As I have gone to great lengths to show, there is no problem whatsoever with value systems themselves, only contradictory value systems, and as more than a few people have pointed out, no human activity or possibly even perception itself is possible without them (see Neumann). With any value system there needs to be a clear assumption. We assume that 'other than this' exists, 'this' exists, the two are interdependent, the expression of either is dependent upon the individual as the Axis between these two worlds, and the act of living the Axis equates to responsibility and is the source of all meaning. Everything up to this point leads to the following:

Good is anything that seeks to preserve 'other than this' and 'this' and the link between the two. This does not mean that what it (whatever it is) is necessarily correct, but it is Good.

Evil is anything that attempts to stamp out 'other than this' in any way shape or form, particularly through force, coercion, or psychological manipulation. Although rare these days, the same applies to 'this'.

Good is anything that provides or creates the widest and most meaningful number of options possible (even if only one course of action is taken).

Evil is anything that constricts and reduces the number of options to as few as possible or only one (even if only one course of action is taken).

Good is anything that encourages individual responsibility.

Evil is anything that discourages individual responsibility.

Good is anything that teaches one to be self-reliant and self-sufficient (or Self-reliant and Self-sufficient).

Evil is anything that teaches one to be dependent on *anything* in 'this'.

Good is anything that teaches one to challenge oneself and take risks in the face of adversity.

Evil is anything that teaches one to cower in the face of adversity and become obsessed with safety.

Good is anything that leads to individuation and one's ownmost potential.

Evil is anything that leads to acting like a child.

Good is having values that align with an assumption, with no contradictions.

Evil is having completely contradictory and/or hypocritical value systems based on an assumption.

Good is knowing that one always has assumptions.

Evil is pretending that one does not have any assumptions.

Good is following one's intuition, no matter where that ends up.

Evil is following a persona or a socially constructed identity, especially when it goes against one's intuition.

Good is speaking one's personal truth no matter the consequences.

Evil is speaking lies in order to appease others – *any* situation is irrelevant.

Good arises when people pay attention in every conceivable way. Noticing is also an exponential phenomenon.

Evil arises when people stop paying attention. Totalitarian systems do not destroy individuals, individuals destroy themselves which leads to those systems. It is only ever after these tragedies that people who experience them (because they always forget that it has happened before) stop and consider alternatives. However, the closer one moves towards an alternative the stronger the urge to give up responsibility, i.e., the stronger the urge to stop paying attention.

Good is knowing what needs to be done and doing it.

Evil is pretending (because that is *exactly* what it is…) not to know what needs to be done or to blame someone or something else for not being able to do it.

Good is remembering who and what you really are.

Evil is forgetting it.

Good is welcoming problems.

Evil is wanting utopia.

Good is knowing that Good and Evil are a necessity.

Evil is pretending that Good or Evil should or do not exist…

Human consciousness itself is impossible without Evil, but that has not stopped hordes of ideologues from attempting to get rid of it. The idea is great in theory but impossible in practice. Recall the earlier PCP-based examples and studies that show that when people start comparing and contrasting things, that Good and Evil is how they actually make any sense of the world – they cannot help themselves. People will always place things into Good and Evil because nothing in the world is intelligible without doing so, no matter what one's stated contradictory values. Since it is literally how things are made intelligible then one could argue that it could be the basis of consciousness (which Kelly does). Again, recall Nietzsche and the horse – is it not possible that the idea of Good and Evil finally hit him? It is also no surprise that Nietzsche's *Beyond Good and Evil* helped lead to totalitarianism, even though it was designed to do the exact opposite. All that happens when people attempt to relativize one form of Good or Evil is that they just project it onto something else. It simply will not go away, period.

Alan Watts once said that he does not subscribe to 'true' Good and Evil in the grand scheme of things, and I would say that I do not either. However, he said that despite there being no 'true' Good and Evil that there were certain things that he would fight against until his dying breath, which I also agree with. For example, I do not think that anything I have listed is 'true' Good or Evil, but if Chinese soldiers were to show up at my doorstep barking some totalitarian bullshit at me I would attempt to kill as many as I could until my dying breath, while others might just hand over the keys of freedom to their totalitarian rulers. And remember, this is not just about "individual liberties", we are talking about creation itself… Evil in the 'true' sense? No. Evil in the sense of real, functioning life? Absolutely. Sure, there are probably a trillion other solar systems that could 'pick up the slack' if this one was to fail, and sure, there is nothing to say that things shouldn't fail, but that will never stop me from fighting for this one. It is simply who I am, The End. No other definitions of Good and Evil will work for me, and everyone *must* have definitions of these things even if they are not articulated or are totally incoherent.

The fact that one simply cannot get rid of Good and Evil is precisely why one needs to have a salient assumption and bloody well get it straight.

But it is exactly because people cannot get it straight (and become more misaligned and confused by the day) that they relativize

Good and Evil. And since the process lies at the root of consciousness, then people obviously (in theory and in observation) become less conscious. As people become less conscious, they experience higher levels of cognitive dissonance due to the fact that they still need to function and still *require* a hierarchy of values which necessarily consists of Good and Evil. And because they need to function and require a hierarchy of values, they then hand over responsibility increasingly to the State and now the post-totalitarian structure.

One might say that it sounds as though I am trying to get rid of Evil, no? No, I am not. I am saying it is necessary. I am saying that those with our assumptions should fight it. But I am also not so naïve as to think that Good is what abounds or that it ever will. As history has shown, if people do fight Evil, it usually results in a balance at best... And, currently, the most uncool, dissident, oppressive, harmful, or flat-out most horrible thing a person can do is to fight Evil as it has been defined here.

Finally, it should be noted that everything that is defined here as Good will be regarded as Evil by the post-totalitarian system and the Herd. The closer one gets to the aims of life and Self-awareness, the more taboo, illegal, dissident, or Evil one becomes in their eyes. That is how war works, and war is the basis of all creation. If ever in doubt, return to the above definition.

Exemplars of Good and Evil

In order to illustrate exemplars of Good and Evil, I will compare two hypothetical societies: Society A and Society B.

Society A is a place where exploration and discovery are paramount. People in Society A are always encouraged to discover new things or perspectives that might overturn how people in their society view and do things. However, they are also extremely pragmatic so they will only change if the overall situation is improved on multiple levels and/or dimensions of their society, which is to also say that this happens for each of the individuals making up that society. If faced with this, they simply discard anything new or old that only serves a single dimension. They are a multiplanetary people and so they are constantly encountering others with various rituals, worldviews, and systems. The planet on which their current society was formed was barren when they first arrived, and so they had to work for every single drop of water and life – nothing was given to them, which is part of what led to their pragmatic culture. They are very much an individualistic culture since they have learned that the more unique perspectives that can be generated the greater number of possible options they have to choose from when figuring out how to solve any particular problem. All of this has led to a culture that not only welcomes problems as an opportunity to show off how good they are at problem-solving and ingenuity, but these people go deliberately looking for problems – it is in their blood – and even better if another society invites them to help with their problems. The society is not only focused on making better technology so that they can explore more of 'this', but also finding any means possible to explore 'other than this', both of which lead to new and exciting problems. Safety is not neglected, it is simply seen as secondary to thriving, and to lose one's life in the pursuit of exploration and discovery is one of the highest honors that one can attain. Society A is also very much into artistic pursuits as an outlet for the pains and struggles that come with their life, and speaking one's personal truth is simply expected while groupthink or any attempts to fit in are not only looked down upon but could possibly endanger people's lives. Whenever children ask questions, adults immediately respond by asking them what they think and guiding the children to their own personal conclusions. Life in Society A is very full-on, it is not easy, and no one ever knows what major disruption lies just around the corner, but Society A is full of thriving individuals who will do anything they can to contribute their talents to their society and the Universe at large in order to simply make 'this' a more interesting place.

Society B is a place where social order and safety are paramount. People in Society B are encouraged to uphold the sacred institutions and the knowledge produced by them, as this allows the people of Society B to always know how to view things and what to do so that chaos does not ensue. Society B remains on a single planet, and whenever an outside idea or perspective makes its way in it will be weighed up against Society B's sacred pillars of order and safety, the most important and sacred of which is that human life must be preserved at all costs. Society B has always lived on a planet where everything was given to them: water, arable land, a breathable atmosphere, etc. Since their planet and their institutions have served them so well, they are a very preservative culture. As such, they are also a very collectivist culture since the best way to preserve anything is to make sure that as few things as possible change in any realm. Getting rid of problems, difficulties, inequality, and especially danger is the primary driver for any activity in Society B – to purposely do something that would create more of these things is unthinkable, and if a person can be singled out as the culprit, then they are imprisoned. Technology is only adopted if it serves to increase social order and safety, all of which is imported from Society A. To assume that there is anything 'other than this' is a crime of the highest degree because it introduces new problems and disrupts the social order. The idea of thriving in Society B is that every human life continues for as long as it possibly can, and for anyone to suggest otherwise is a crime against society since the worst possible thing that can happen is for one to die. As such, the highest honor in Society B is to save life. Artistic pursuits of any kind are seen as distractions from the more important task of saving lives, although not many people feel the need to be artistic. Truth is defined by Society B's institutions, knowledge, and concepts, i.e., their pillars, and whenever children ask questions, they are directed to the pillars or the leaders of their institutions. Life in Society B is slow, easy, and no one ever has to worry about surprises or survival. Many people in Society B have psychiatric disorders; however, there are many working diligently to figure out how to get rid of these problems.

Approximately 20 years ago, Society A developed a new technology that they had been researching for decades due to the potential for it to bridge what they called "the last mile" between their mind and matter: programable nanotechnology. This allowed them to use nanobots to construct or alter anything at the atomic level whether it was inside or outside the body and, true to the cultural values, this development was always publicly and freely available since the very way that it was developed was through a method of crowdsourcing (something that Society A was quite fond of doing). As such, when the first working prototypes were made, everyone in Society A was free to use this technology as they saw fit. Early uses included system-wide nutrient regulations in the body from raw materials, the complete eradication of certain types of diseases, new ways of terraforming the planet, and, in emergency situations in space, things could be constructed by breaking down the materials of something else. Members of Society A also combined this with a method of Artificial Intelligence that they had begun to merge with, a combination that allowed them to construct experimental chemicals in the body on the fly according to a certain goal and feedback loop, which also allowed for the discovery of complex psychedelic compounds that were millions of times more profound than anything up to that point. Some had even begun to develop interfaces that could immediately translate certain aspects of 'other than this' into the materiality of 'this', and art was the easiest first application.

However, this development (as with any progress in Society A) was not without high casualties. Since the nanotechnology was programmable and anyone was free to do it, millions of people died in the first few years due to programming errors or simply unforeseen accidents that occurred from certain combinations, and this is an ongoing risk. There were also the occasional rogue people or groups that used it for terrorism. The people in Society A then took this as an opportunity to get better at individual programming and to make their personal systems as secure as possible, and to be able to do this better than everyone else became a form of bragging rights. If one could program in such a way as to increase their personal agency and help the community at the same time, and additionally survive a terrorist nanotechnology attack, they were seen as the envy of their friends and community. The chemical aspect led to the most profound spiritual and psychological discoveries in 100 years, many of which were actually used to shape systems on the planet in order to increase the overall psychological wellbeing. However, this also led to millions of people who got it wrong and were beyond any sort of repair, and on Society A's home planet there is simply no room or resources for someone who cannot contribute. Consequently, these people were euthanized if they could not become functional again within 3 years.

Just after this development in Society A, a Society B dissident managed to smuggle in the development on board a shipment of other pre-approved technology imported from Society A. Although programmable nanotechnology was almost exclusively an underground phenomenon that was kept in great secret due to the severity of the punishment associated with not only having access but using it on oneself for any sort of personal gain, the effects on the few people that did were profound and their behavior was far from normal. Consequently, this behavior prompted an intelligence operation that uncovered what had happened. However, by then it was too late to stop the spread of nanobots. This is because the technology in Society A was seen as so revolutionary and beneficial that nanobots were considered a basic right like water and internet in Society B, hence, the nanobots had been programmed to replicate until they covered the surface of the planet and continue doing so whenever there were patches – all that was needed was a way to program them. This led to a global emergency in Society B as it threatened their core values and would certainly lead to millions of deaths as it was doing in Society A. Therefore, there was a massive campaign to tap into Society A's live feed (which was always being broadcast from Society A) and show as much death as possible in order to dissuade people in Society B from using the nanotechnology. Often repeated was the slogan "individualism is death". However, this was simply not enough to maintain social order, and very soon Society B was forced to figure out a way to shut the entire thing down for good before more people died.

However, doing so was an almost impossible undertaking since the nanobots were too small to target and they were perpetually coating the entire planet. What Society B did have access to was all of the dwellings, buildings, and transportation networks. With the greatest emergency ever facing Society B, they pooled all of their resources and intelligence to modify an existing technology and deploy it across the entire manmade infrastructure. What this technology did was to encapsulate any piece of infrastructure in a sort of coating that only allowed air to be exchanged through it while everything else was filtered out. People were protected from the nanobots as long as they did not leave any structure and enter into the surrounding nature. As such, it was now illegal to do so and any person who wished to leave the manmade infrastructure needed an exemption from Society B's lawmakers and needed to wear special protective equipment. Furthermore, the risk of exposure to the nanotechnology was considered such a threat that people were no longer allowed to leave Society B's planet and no one was allowed in. After the second year of operating in this way Society B congratulated itself on not a single person dying as a result of access to programmable nanotechnology. Although psychiatric disorders were rapidly on the rise, the economy was running at 1/10th of its original output, and domestic and work-related violence was increasing, at least no one was killed and that is all that mattered. They had also adopted and tweaked an AI-based technology from Society A that they patched into their intervention system which would detect if someone was going to commit suicide and stop it. These people were then sent to special facilities to ensure that they could not commit suicide.

Although these two societies had always had very different ways of raising children, the introduction of programmable nanotechnology increased this split.

In Society A, the need to be self-sufficient and self-reliant, as well as the ability to innovate, was directly tied to one's survival even more so that it had been before. While children were generally taught these principles around their teenage years, they were now being taught from the moment the child was cognizant since the nanotechnology permeated everything, knew no age, and does not care if there are parents around. Furthermore, if one did get caught up in groupthink then this became an even more deadly phenomenon as hackers could target systems easier because those systems were less agile, so the notion of movement became even more of a societal cornerstone.

In Society B, the need to stay within the confines of the protected infrastructure was directly tied to not being imprisoned (the irony of which did not escape Society A). This was the most important lesson that children could learn now in Society B, that if one even considers something outside of these walls they will die. If they go against this lesson and do not die they will be further confined to ensure that they do not die. To break any social rule whatsoever is to endanger the entire planet. To modify one's body or thoughts is to endanger the entire planet. The children were constantly reminded that these things are what led to the millions and millions of deaths that they saw occurring in Society A.

Even the notion of children meant completely different things between the two societies.

Children in Society A began to be viewed more and more as the reflections of archetypes or patterns instead of objects. The idea of a child – whether it was biological, mixed with technology, or a simple text – was seen as something that carries a torch, so to speak. Children were taught that they were all part of a bigger picture of discovery and creation, but they were encouraged in every way possible to come to their own conclusion about whether they thought this or not. Children were always spoken to as if they were adults from the moment that they were cognizant, and they were encouraged to have as many different 'types' of 'children' as they could so that when those children were ready they could create even more diversity and make 'this' an even more interesting place or maybe one day create a new 'this'. Each type of child was seen as an opportunity for something novel and a vessel to continue the cosmic game. In this way, the programmable nanotechnology was seen as a child as well (with its collateral damage as pregnancy) and an opportunity to help continue the game in a way that may not have been possible otherwise.

Children in Society B began to be viewed more and more as unique objects that required preservation and protection as opposed to patterns, where the latter was derided as "seeing something that is not there". The longer a person could be child-like the better, as this helped to keep people better focused on paying attention to social norms so that everyone could be on the same page regarding keeping the nanotechnology out of anyone's hands so that nobody dies. Coming to one's own conclusions or making decisions on one's own accord was seen as selfish and dangerous as it put people's lives at risk. Children were seen as the human guardians of Society B's planet and way of life for as long as the planet could provide resources. Society B is well aware that their planet and/or star will not be able to do so forever – it is assumed that when resources run out that this is, and should be, the end of life (again, the irony did not escape Society A).

Given the magnitude of change, both societies saw a person rise to fame that served as a sort of leader for each society through these tumultuous times. This also signaled the beginning of a very strange phenomenon where nearly identical things would happen in both societies – a sort of mirroring – but would result in drastically different outcomes. In both societies, the person that rose to fame in each had the *exact* same message: "I am the way, the truth, and the light". Both societies were enamored by their respective leader, but for opposite reasons. In Society A, people were more motivated than ever. "I AM the way, the truth, and the light", people would repeat proudly. In Society B, people were also more motivated than ever. "YOU are the way, the truth, and the light. Our Savior!", they would repeat reverently. One leader's words led to increased independence, the other to increased dependence.

The drastic levels of change also led to many psychological disturbances in both societies. As usual, Society A took this as an opportunity to study and make use of something novel while Society B took this as an opportunity to study and classify a new type of psychological disorder. Both societies built research facilities to handle the disturbed people.

In Society A, these patients were encouraged to speak as openly and freely as possible so that the researchers could document everything and attempt to, based on what the patients were saying, point the patient to various books, movies, music, and other people that might be able to help them make sense of, and come to terms with, what was happening to them. Nanotechnology and the AI feedback loop were used to help with this process, whereby the goal was to steadily increase felt meaning through experiences or encounters with various other ideas. However, the populace had voted on a law that only allowed 3 years for the patients to become functional and able to contribute again otherwise they would be euthanized, so there was indeed urgency on the part of the clinicians to help the patients recover. However, this was not simply so that the patients would not be killed – what the researchers had discovered was that the people who made it through this process generally ended up being the most talented and influential people in their society. Indeed, the chances of one ending up in an influential leadership position increased exponentially after exiting the facility. Thus, the facility ended up being a sort of breeding grounds for future leaders and psychotic breaks were seen as the chance to embark on a high-stakes heroic journey.

In Society B, the patients were confined even further to rooms with no stimulation as to not upset the patient, patients were given the most cutting-edge drugs to ensure that flare-ups did not happen again, and reeducation around the pillars was a daily part of life. Furthermore, once these people entered the facility they were there for life. They were far too unpredictable to let freely wander the community which may cause a major disturbance and upset people. At the same time, they were also viewed as highly valuable as they served as the center of research around how to get rid of these psychological problems. The hope was that one day a cure would be found that would completely rid the person of this illness so that they could return to the community, and this became one of the most important ongoing activities in Society B with enormous amounts of money funneled into the facilities which resulted in many job opportunities. However, unlike Society A, the patients in Society B would never hold a position of power or influence since their social record had been permanently tainted.

In both societies there was a fight to be fought.

Society A had been studying what led to individual thriving in the face of the nanotechnology challenge, and therefore the aims that would lead to thriving were focused on like a laser. Sometimes this focus meant alienation and other times it meant death. In any case, Society A viewed the fight as primarily an internal one, i.e., they viewed the enemy as the weakness in oneself. They did not think that it was even possible to wage an external war as they believed that doing so would just lead to the problem being diverted to something else external. Hence, again they turned to their pragmatism to guide them. They saw that for thousands of years on other worlds, before their world, that people had been trying to wage external wars, which only resulted in brief periods of introspection after destroying everything, only to end up right back where they started. They realized that all that happened by waging an external war on Evil was that it ended up creating it. They focused on the war within and completely and totally rejected any ideology from other societies that told them to focus on an external enemy. Their way of doing things was to become immune to external enemies by getting a grip on the internal ones. They fought their version of Evil by simply living their aims of life. Society B became the posterchild for what they were fighting against and what not to do.

Society B had been studying what led to social disorder and danger in the face of the nanotechnology challenge, and therefore providing stability and safety was focused on like a laser. Group activities were seen as paramount and were often directed at coming up with ways to fight the external enemy number one which was the programmable nanotechnology. And since this technology came from outside of Society B, this further reinforced the focus of the fight being an external fight. Fighting an internal war was seen as useless since the psyche was seen as a figment of the imagination that people used as an excuse for social deviance, and cures for this were on the way (or so they kept saying). When Society B looked at the history of external wars in other societies, they pointed out how these societies were far less sophisticated and cohesive as theirs, which is why these societies got everything wrong – they were just too unsophisticated, focused on the wrong enemy, and did not value their pillars enough. Hence, they focused on an external war and rejected any ideas that made their way through the firewalls from Society A that would suggest the need or possibility of doing otherwise since those ideas kill people. Their way of doing things was to become immune to internal enemies by focusing on external ones. They fought their version of Evil by enforcing norms and safety. Society A became the posterchild for what they were fighting against and what not to do.

The latest major development after the nanotechnology years is that there is a strange anomaly that has formed and is now growing in the center of Society A's most populated city, which due to its interesting nature is being broadcast via their live feed to any other society that would like to watch. There are also people beginning to simply disappear in Society A, and no one knows where they are going. The people of Society A look on in amazement and wonder. The people of Society B look on in horror.

The highest and lowest forms of responsibility

Continuing with Society A and B, given the operating assumptions and resultant cultures, the two societies have totally different views on responsibility.

The essence of the different views comes down to a single cultural trait. In Society A one always hears about what they *can* or *could* do, and in Society B one is always hearing about what they *cannot* do. This difference permeates every dimension and stratum in both societies. In other words, it is not something that one only sees or hears about in government – it is found in their organizations, educational institutions, social interactions, philosophies, etc. – it shows itself literally everywhere. This might be the most important thing to know about the two societies because this translates directly into what is viewed as the highest and lowest forms of responsibility which leads to literally everything else.

Philosophy in Society A generally carries the message of potential and possibility, but also accepts what people have generally been doing and not doing for thousands of years. Whereas philosophy in Society B generally carries the message of duty and ideals and sees most of human history as uneducated and intellectually stunted. Hence, at an interplanetary conference that happened years ago one could overhear two researchers discussing the idea of meaning before it gets very deep. A researcher from Society A has been interviewing people on their perceived meaning around various technologies and people. Another researcher from Society B walks over to the booth of person from Society A, looks at the research, and says to the Society A researcher in a semi-angry voice: "you cannot ascribe meaning to objects". To which the Society A researcher replies: "...ok, but people do". A simple example, but it highlights how Society A cares more about understanding a phenomenon and what people actually do whereas Society B cares more about upholding an ideal (whatever it its) and what people should do based on an ideal. Society B believes that responsibility lies in enforcement of rules and that it is completely and totally irresponsible to let people do or think otherwise. Society A believes that responsibility lies in understanding and making decisions based on that understanding, and so the Society A researcher says to the Society B researcher: "I think that it is completely and totally irresponsible to force social construct onto... people or objects... And that is quite ironic based on what you just said, no? I also find it strange that your research – which I read this morning – is about choice, the narrative seems to have an affinity for free will, and yet you seem to be angry that I am researching what people choose to do and saying that they cannot do it". The Society B researcher then stormed off irritated while the Society A researcher snickered. This was often how it went between these two when they were still talking.

Since Society B is geared towards telling people what they cannot do, commanding is seen as the highest form of responsibility. And since Society B cannot operate without doing anything, the State tells them what to do. The basic idea is that one cannot do anything by default, and what one can do must be pre-approved. This has led to the highest form of responsibility being to turn one's profession in to giving orders to others, while the highest form of irresponsibility would be to do things. An increase in responsibility is given to those who do the best job of enforcing the pillars. Overall, responsibility is anything that serves the State and irresponsibility is anything that subverts the State's authority in any way because, again, this leads to death.

Society A sees the idea of turning one's profession into giving orders to others – and not building anything oneself – as the highest form of irresponsibility. Again, this is because of the planet's origins and ongoing challenges in their way of life – no one is ever confused as to what has to be done and not much convincing is needed to do it. An increase in responsibility is done at the individual level and leaders are chosen based on their historical and current competency to do things. The highest form of responsibility one has in Society A is to the Axis as this has been seen by Society A as the common historical thread in times of thriving.

Society A was very similar to many new lands throughout history in that the people who first came to the planet were doing so in reaction to the social and political climate in the places from which they came – places that were often very similar to Society B.

The early settlers in Society A had left their homes due to what a very large number had all referred to as a form of narcissism. Everyone in Society A is thoroughly interviewed and observed before being allowed to establish residence there. These interviews are recorded, and the following was retrieved from their open-source library (access to which is banned in Society B). The interviewer had simply asked this person why they wanted to leave their home:

> "You just do not understand these people, especially those in charge, the fucking narcissists! There is no object permanence with these people whatsoever! Nothing outside of themselves. If something is brought in and then it is suddenly not within their field of view, it does not exist! Which is precisely why they cannot deal with anything that is outside of the realm of their control. If they lose control or can't have the final say so, then they get rid of it, because that thing, whatever it is, would undermine their idea of being the center of the Universe and that nothing exists outside of whatever it is that they are fixated on which is usually themselves. These people are in charge of nearly every powerful entity in our society and you cannot even go to work without having to deal with them since almost everyone who is in charge of a business engrains it into their particular culture that there is nothing other than this and what they really mean is them, so then we end up with everyone going home with that and applying this mentality of nothing other than this to everything! And the really messed up thing? People WANT that!!! They want total irresponsibility for their own lives, so then the narcissist says, "don't worry, I'll take care of that", so then the thing grows bigger and bigger so that the people are shielded further and further from the realities of life such as competition. The narcissists are

obsessed with making things like "governance structures", top-down laws, anything that would shield the individual from having to respond to daily life in their own way; ANYTHING that would keep them from having to make decisions and to keep those pieces of shit at the center of the Universe. And then this crops up in every, single, talk about power on the entire planet. We have to listen now to our academics going on and on about power and politics; of course they are! None of them could ever actually exist in the real world and deal with an actual job or actually building anything that would be subject to real people and systems using whatever they built – all these things that OTHER people should do, and they don't even know what actually works because they don't actually do anything! I hear that the people in power here quite often risk everything they have, even their lives, just to make a simple discovery or take a picture on some distant world. I can only imagine. And your people want someone like that in power! Not on my planet! On my planet everyone wants the narcissists to be in power and the narcissists love being in power – it is fucking impossible!!! I hear that companies in your society are able to achieve things that we can only dream of, and I have heard that this is because they have armies of autonomous self-reliant individuals that network together, on their own... Every single story I have ever heard about someone getting fired from one of these companies is because they started slacking, not because they took a risk. I've also heard that one CEO, in particular, gets people to tell them their life story *as* the interview. I've often thought about the same thing if I could ever get any of my businesses to work – for someone to tell me about their life story, because otherwise they are just telling you what they KNOW as opposed to any realistic picture of what they actually would do... If they tell you their life story then you start to get some kind of hint about if they've ever taken on any significant challenge and were able to overcome it or whatever. Because that's what people talk about who have done such things. Your people are proud of the things they've overcome and achieved. They enjoy talking about having been the underdog and won. Versus the people in my society would just look at someone like a deer in the headlights if you asked them for their life story. And I guess the most messed up thing of all is that the few people that do rebel against all of this in some significant way, especially our 'hippy' types, seem to just end up following yet another narcissist of a different flavor. I think I've rambled a bit here, but I'm just so sick of how everything on my planet is completely devoid of personal responsibility and meaning while the people on your planet seem to be completely focused on these things. I'm sure your planet is not perfect, I know a lot of people die, but I would rather die standing then live on my knees for one more day. I have fucking had it. And since they won't do anything about their actual problems, they will probably all die soon anyway. To that I say GOOD FUCKING RIDDENCE!!!"

The potential immigrant was then asked to give their views on the highest forms of responsibility:

"Responsibility for what? Myself or others? Well, as far as myself goes, the responsibility for as much as could be imagined in the realm of what is possible at my individual level. For example, to know as much as one can know about themselves; to ask who and what they are or might be and follow that as far as one can no matter where it ends up; to ask what is all of this and what could it possibly be; to always be considering completely weird and maybe even impossible ideas especially those that challenge my existing ideas; basically, to push the existential envelope in as many ways as possible, because why the else would someone want to exist? Really!?! And someone has been given the opportunity which some might even call a miracle to exist and, then, what? Just fucking sit there? It's obviously nice to relax every once and a while, but what the fuck!?! Ok, I'm sorry, I know, I'm a bit worked up... But you see what I am saying. Responsibility for myself is living life to its fullest potential and if everyone did the same, I think that would be pretty interesting to say the least. I just don't know why this is such an alien view on my planet, especially if we are just going to die in the end anyway, you know? As far as responsibility for others, I think that is about the simplest question ever. You give them options, lots of options. On my planet there are no options – there is no personal responsibility and everyone likes it that way. I want to live in a place where personal responsibility is a given and survival of the species depends on self-organizing contributors. Maybe even all of this is headed toward something like that, you know? I mean, what if all of this, this whole cosmic game, depends on something similar?

What if it actually depends on it *right now*? It just seems like the stupidest thing ever to suggest that total irresponsibility should be the *target*, I don't care what else someone thinks or believes in or what the circumstances are."

This person immigrated successfully to Society A as they were exactly the kind of person Society A was looking for. Society A was basically looking for people who had gotten so fed up with being tricked that it was clear that they would never be tricked again.

Although Society A's open-source library was blocked at Society B's planetary firewall, dissidents did manage to smuggle in the above interview, which quickly made its way through Society B's dissident underground, which then was picked up by the intelligence community. In order to be proactive, the office of communications released a statement that began with the following:

> "My fellow citizens, I have seen the leaked immigration interview released by these terrorist sympathizing, irresponsible, dissident slime. These cowards hide behind anonymity and threaten the security and way of life of our entire planet. Not one single person has died since the nanotechnology invasion, and we will not let these rodents spew their propaganda all over our good deeds. We will not let them bring their death and toxic individualism to our planet. Our restrictions preserve our way of life, and we are united to the end! Duty is our highest honor, and we must always maintain our responsibility to the whole

above all else! I ask that all citizens unite! Unite against these evil individualists who seem to have no respect for the sacredness of life. They put everyone in danger, and, for what? "Progress?" Progress towards what? These cockroaches do nothing but play with the fairies all the day long, spending what little number of resources that they have on things that do not even exist! We are the sacred gatekeepers of the enlightenment, and we will never be swayed or deterred! Our sacred trust is to *enjoy* life unlike you swine! To be simple and to simply be! To those dissidents, hear my words. We will hunt you down to the ends of the planet. We will smother your sacred individualism wherever it springs up before you even have a chance to say that disgusting word "I". We will organize in such a way that you will never be able to move again. We will take your spirit. We will take your voice. We will ensure that you are completely and totally ignored out of existence…"

Those in Society A threw viewing parties so that they could laugh and mock the "little pussies" in Society B and be glad that they would never have to live in such a place ever again. It was not so funny, however, for those that had wanted to leave Society B but had permanently lost their chance to do so.

On being grounded

"He who cannot obey himself will be commanded. That is the nature of living creatures." – Friedrich Nietzsche, *Thus Spoke Zarathustra*

For those of us fighting Evil in the way I have defined it and who look to Society A with a sad longing, being grounded in one way or another can easily lead to clinical depression and possibly wanting to check out of the game altogether. Again, it is no surprise that such things occur when the post-totalitarian system is trying to stamp out the essence of human existence. Some forms of being grounded are obviously more immediate and depressing than others; however, all of us are grounded in one way or another at the moment. Grounding can be on any level, and it is irrelevant where the grounding is occurring or from who or what it seems to be stemming. For example, it can be immediate in the sense of human rights violations of movement as seen in the former Soviet Union, North Korea, and Australia. Or it can be in the sense of our current overall existential situation which is really more of what I have been alluding to and am concerned with. As I have said, whatever one sees occurring in the world is a compensatory mirror image of something else. This should never be forgotten, lest one get tricked yet again into focusing solely on 'this'. And that is really what this chapter is about – looking at being grounded in a more thoughtful way. I definitely do *not* mean to simply accept it in the sense of doing nothing about it and resigning to a life lived in Evil, which is precisely what the post-totalitarian system and its 'enlightened' agents would like for one to do. I mean looking at it in a way that it is there and not going anywhere, it is probably a necessity, and maybe there is a way to *use* it.

However, this certainly does not come easy for those fighting Evil. One must remember that part of the reason that they hate the phenomenon so badly is because that phenomenon exists within them on some level, which through projection into the environment is the only reason it ever shows up. As such, when the reality of being grounded is thrown into one's face and they are forced to look at it every single day, the hate and rage against it can be such that one begins to throw the kind of fit that would be expected (and perfectly understandable) of any teenager in such a situation. What is not so easily understood is why one would hate something so badly. "That's obvious", most would reply, but why exactly? It is not enough to say one cannot do things. Remember, people are not particularly inclined to do anything, they just say that they are. What is happening is that the teenager is realizing something even if subconscious. If they remain angry then this is a signal of a certain kind of responsibility that is now being forced upon them in this situation of being grounded. This is why for *some* teenagers – i.e., people who fight Evil or are intent on doing so – being grounded can often have the opposite effect than what was apparently intended. At some point, *some* people will get fed up enough that they will take a step back, breathe, and look for ways to make sure that that particular form of grounding does not happen to them again, or, even better, become immune to it somehow. "There is something other than this" they will say, and they will fight for this idea for the rest of their lives. Others, the Herd, will act just like a domesticated animal should and simply do whatever they are told, finding all sorts of philosophies around "letting go" to help them do so.

And again, would a teenager ever bring themselves to do anything other than be a teenager if they were never grounded? Why would they? If they can dick around and cause trouble for the rest of their lives, never experience any consequences, and have their parents pay for it, then there is hardly a single person that would ever move on from that (even if they ended up in living Hell). It is only when one realizes just how immobile that one can actually be that one stops to think about the idea of mobility, freedom, or lack thereof. Up until that point it is just fun and games, but it can turn very real very fast. This idea of being completely and totally limited, grounded, constrained, and constricted before one gets fed up, is absolutely necessary.

On an everyday level, I can look to my own experiences such as what I have experienced in the last few years leading up to writing this book. Without going into a long string of details, suffice it to say that at every critical point in the last few years I have been completely and totally shut down. Up until that point it really was amazing just how many things had always happened in my favor despite my being quite reckless with the opportunities I had been given, basically taking them for granted as if they would always be there. However, after a series of experiences that actually were the insights that eventually led to this book, everything that had worked up until that point simply stopped working (see Jung about this phenomenon). Everything I tried failed, and I do not mean halfcocked or unrealistic ideas – those were precisely what I saw actually working with others! Then I was forced into spinal surgery after which I was confined to a bed on and off for a couple of years. After recovering to the point where I could lead a normal life again, I decided to move to Europe on a visa that was time-limited based on my Ph.D. graduation date. Every, single, appointment that I made over the course of a year and a half to go get my visa was shut down by the Australian government days before the appointment. My last chance to get the visa was the last time it happened, and the reason that it did not happen was because an event in the exact building that I needed to go into, out of all the places in the entire country, one week before I needed to go, was closed down and did not reopen in time.

There were so many 'coincidences' that to call them coincidences or "random" would actually be insanity. I could do nothing. I could not get any of my businesses off the ground, I could not move to a place where I would fit in better culturally; basically, I could do nothing of any kind that was related to improving my individual existence (or so I thought), and any time there was any hope of this happening it was inexplicably shut down right in front of me in ways that are still difficult to believe. Being fed up does not even begin to describe the murderous rage I felt towards literally every single entity in this world or otherwise, especially since I knew exactly why (psychologically) all of the particulars were happening and who was responsible for them. But guess what? It does not matter whether one knows this or not. It does not matter whether one is right or not. It does not matter whether the world is sick and psychologically fucked in the head or not. It does not matter whether one is being oppressed or not. It does not matter whether one has been served an injustice or not… I was being shut down and there was not a single thing that I could do about it, and it took me getting to the absolute breaking point to realize this.

However, at that breaking point, it suddenly dawned on me: "aren't all these things I am trying to do in the name of individual existence and agency relying on *other people and 'this'*? Other people to sign up for my products? Other people to recognize and validate my ideas? Haven't I even been leaning in many ways on survival rather than thinking about what it is that I personally can contribute?" On a seemingly unrelated note, days later I thought about what it would be like if China were to invade and some soldier was standing on my doorstep – what would I do, especially since one could argue that there is no real Good or Evil? I knew exactly what I would do. I would do everything in my power to kill them even if I had zero chance of survival, because at least that was under my control. I thought about everything that I had actually been serving my entire life, completely unaware that I was doing it even when trying not to. I remember just how trapped and vulnerable I felt in that moment. It was as though not only was my personal greatest contradiction staring me directly in the face, but that also on some level I was once again facing my own death. With the umbilical cord of 'this' dangling in front of me, as if to say, "All you need to do is let go!", I turned directly into 'this' and screamed as loud and as firmly and as full of certainty as I could: "**NO!!!!!!!!!!!!!!!!!!!**" I had never been so sure of anything in my entire life.

And this is what led to the writing of this book since it is completely under my control, lives on forever no matter if anyone reads it or not, and many a great book has been written in prison…

But this also led to my ability to finally move on with my life and actually start living the principles I had been preaching which, again, had nothing really to do with anyone or anything else (this is also when I stumbled upon Havel). And I stand firmly behind the idea that this book and my moving on simply never would have happened without being grounded and, again, why would this not be the case? In fact, every significant thing that I have ever done with respect to the "aims of life" occurred as a result of being grounded. So, while the last time was the most intense and productive, it certainly was not the first. But that is what I mean! How easily we forget these *patterns* when we are grounded! How easily rebels forget that this is how it has always been!

Being grounded is simply necessary. It is not an injustice and it is not oppression. It is what actually needs to occur for a child to get fed up enough to grow up and take responsibility for their own existence. In the bigger picture, whether talking about people or 'this', more grounding still needs to occur because both are not yet ready. Grounding knows no age, race, gender, or any other socially constructed supposed precursor to it. It is purely and simply about people who can make *decisions* and people who cannot, and with that is the coldest thing that almost no one in this day and age wants to hear, especially those that feel particularly oppressed: if you cannot make decisions then YOU WILL NOT BE *ABLE TO*. Understand? Indeed, one does need to become fed up; however, it is only when one realizes what they are actually fed up with that anything meaningful can materialize...

This is how Projection can be used. First one hates it with every fiber in their body, then they realize it is a projection, then the Projection is harnessed.

Good cannot exist without Evil, and children will not be allowed to make decisions until they show that they are ready and have the capacity to do so.

Furthermore, while this part of the book is more of a philosophy of life and, as such, is much more, how should I say, grounded, than the last part of the book, it is important to not forget the mystery that was never solved, particularly with respect to continuity. Do not forget that within that mystery it is *possible* that YOU did this! Not someone else. Not some external entity. YOU. You chose to be here. You chose to put all of these mechanisms in place. Because you are eternally trying to come up with a better system. You do it over and over and over again.

Being grounded is not the problem, it is the answer. What one does with that answer is the sum of their character.

No means no

"The yes of the promise is sleep-inducing, but the no, spoken and therefore audible to oneself, is awakening, and repentance is usually not far away." – Søren Kierkegaard, *Works of Love*

I can think of no better example to start with when talking about fighting Evil than Jordan Peterson – a name that conjures up all kinds of emotions and rants from a range of different people across all political spectra. He is a clinical psychologist and now former academic that rose to fame out of nowhere around the year 2015-2016 via his stance toward the Canadian government when it was considering introducing legislation around addressing people by their preferred pronouns. During the last few years, it is nearly impossible to not have heard of him. Some thought he was the second coming of the Messiah, others thought he was a complete and total amateur, and still others thought he was Satan spawn. Many of his followers were very upset to learn that this person that they had put on a pedestal for one reason or another was contradicting himself 10 ways to Sunday (pun intended). Well, based on what I have laid out so far, who is not? It's kind of peoples' thing. Others were angry that his philosophical points were not the best or well thought out. Well, what does one expect from a fairly unknown psychology academic that was thrown into the spotlight? Having been an academic for a short while myself, it is no surprise to me that he took the opportunity to get some of his ideas out in the open that otherwise would have never been repeated outside of his classroom. At the same time, I won't lie, I was very angry with him for a short while about a specific handful of things that he was contradicting himself on, but the harder you trap others…

In any case, what amuses me is that nobody can seem to remember exactly why he became famous in the first place, i.e., why people put him on a pedestal to begin with (the pattern just will not go away!). It was the fact that he refused, beyond any shadow of a doubt, to be *forced* to speak in a specific way. The specific issue was gender pronouns but most of the brain-dead masses assume it was because he cared one way or another about how someone wanted to be addressed, while it could have just as easily been being *forced* to *say* literally anything else, which was the real issue: forced speech. While I cannot find the original excerpts anywhere online, the words that led him to fame went something along the lines of:

> "If you pass the law to make me say it, I will not say it. If you fine me, I will not pay it. If you put me in prison, I will go on a hunger strike. If you kill me, then so be it. **IT'S NOT HAPPENING…**"

I believed him and still do. You could hear the shakiness in his voice which signaled that he was honestly afraid (and for good reason) but also the sternness of his response that left no doubt in anyone's mind that he was actually dead serious. I guess that's what happens when you spend your entire adult life studying totalitarianism.........................

This is why Jordan Peterson will forever remain one of my heroes, regardless of anything else he ever says or does, and I said the exact same thing even when I was furious with him. I am sure he has all kinds of political agendas that he would love to push if he had more of an opportunity, and being political at all is an automatic ticket for me to dismiss one as having anything important to say. But that is just it, I could care less about what he or anyone else has to *say*. He will always have my respect because of what he *did*, which was to fight Evil the only way he could at the time, by standing up and saying "NO!!!" and being willing to die for it. That one simple but very heroic act is something that will never be erased from my mind.

This is what I mean when I say, "No means no". It is not a weekend retreat. One doesn't go out and do some picketing and yell in the street for a couple of hours or even days, possibly get arrested because the police randomly picked them out, feel good about themselves for protesting, along with thousands of other people... and pretend that what they are doing is anything remotely like fighting Evil or saying a real "NO". When Jesus challenged the church, for example, he did nothing of the sort. First of all, he did it alone and of his own accord, and then he lived his life based on this challenge and ultimately was killed for it (knowing it was coming) in a way that, again, almost no one would be willing to face for any of their supposed 'values', not even Americans. Not fond of the whole Jesus thing? Well, take the American founding fathers, that person that stood in front of the

Chinese tank without flinching, the monk that set himself on fire, whatever story you like based on your personal cup of tea, I don't care. The point is that when someone says "NO" in the way that I, Peterson, or Kierkegaard mean it, it really means something, it is persistent and unyielding, and has very real consequences, the least of which is that almost *everyone* will end up hating someone who does this, to the extreme... This alone would cause the social-media-external-validation-addicted Herd to vomit and shit themselves on the spot and consider suicide. The moment one says "NO" in this way they will instantaneously be attacked by every conceivable entity and thing in every conceivable form from every conceivable angle, which will concomitantly test and push the buttons of any insecurities that one has (the reaction to which tends to be to run back to Evil).

This brings us back to the nature of the post-totalitarian structure and the idea that you cannot point at it and blame it all on this or that person or thing. It is not just about some specific country, group, or person. It all countries, all groups, everyone on social media, the current panic-demic, practices, contradictory values systems, the Universe itself; *all* of it seems to be the exact same thing that is beginning to somehow work together more and more to promote Evil and stamp out the individual with no one stopping to ask where they ever got the idea in the first place. Standing up to 'this' seems to be about standing up to an *overwhelming force*; some people at some point simply refuse to take it anymore, regardless of their odds or any baseless assumption that would tell them that there are any odds one way or another to begin with.

I simply cannot unsee the obvious and massive similarities between when a child successfully detaches from their parents and becomes independent, or in the Ph.D. process when a Ph.D. student is pushed around constantly by everyone around them about this thing or that thing, they get worn down and beat down, they have tried this and they have tried that, they often end up in psychologists office by their second year then don't know what to do, and at some point (even if it is only internally) the Ph.D. student stands up and says "NO... I'm not putting up with your bullshit anymore. This is how it is. Pass me or fail me, I don't care anymore." At which point they usually graduate, and are now able to supervise other students. Or the Zen student seeking enlightenment which Watts likes to refer to, who is pushed around psychologically and sometimes physically. The Zen master puts them to work doing all kinds of ridiculous activities like not speaking, yoga, fasting, or whatever, while the student is also paying close attention to and is no doubt analyzing the Zen master (at some point) to see if his actions align with what he is pushing (spoiler, they don't), and at some later point the student says "NO... I see through your game, and I'm not playing anymore". At which point they graduate, and are now able to go on about their business or train other students. Or the teenager who finally realizes that their parents don't know any more than they do, who stands up and says "NO... You know no more than me, which is probably nothing. I am not listening anymore." At which point they are ready to 'leave the womb', go out into the real world, and find out if they can hack it any better than their parents.

In any of these situations, one is showing that they are ready, independent, and can guide others in that process.

Now, what makes anyone think that it is any different with the cosmos? The grand scheme of things? Again, I cannot unsee the possibility that this is exactly what all of 'this' is about. Turning to 'this' itself, giving the middle finger, and saying "NO... not anymore". Taking the assumption that there is something 'other than this', whatever it is. Again, maybe it is a new universe or maybe something else entirely, but only when there can be actual decisions made; when one is actually ready; when one is fed up with being told that there is nothing other than 'this'; when one is completely and totally fed up not living the aims of life as they know and feel in every fiber of their body to be personally true; and when one wholly accepts the tsunami that will inevitably and immediately come their way when they decide to do something about it.

One must be ready to fight, linguistically, physically, or otherwise. As Sun Tzu pointed out, it is best if one can win without fighting at all. Unfortunately, this is simply not possible 99.99% of the time – one must fight nearly all of the time, it is just a matter of what *kind* of fighting one is referring to. The need to fight arises when there is anyone or anything attempting to force you into the realm of Evil: irresponsibility and the assumption of nothing other than 'this'.

Sometimes one cannot help being pushed into the realm of Evil in some way, such as the case with grounding. However, sometimes one can, especially if the thing doing the pushing is another person or some organization or institution from which one can simply walk away. And when this occurs there are simply no excuses. Again, no means no. If one feels as though one *must* do Evil because of some excuse, my favorite of which is "my family", then one just got sold again. Not only that, one of the most Evil-serving things one can do is to tell their partners and children, by example, that Evil is ok – the post-totalitarian system is ok – as long as one has a family that will be affected. Well done douche. I am sure your family will look up to you and respect you for such bravery... While it undeniably is up to the individual to figure out whether saying "NO" is worth it or not, then the moment that one figures out that it is and that the thing before them is, in fact, Evil and has completely crossed the line, then there should be zero excuses, for any reason, ever. That is precisely the reason for one to work out their assumptions... and precisely the reason that those that have not will have a problem with this kind of 'narrowmindedness'.

But really what saying "NO" is all about is standing one's ground. "NO" to agents of the mind. "NO" to fear, insecurities, and doubt.

This does not necessarily mean quitting one's job, for example. If the job is helping one to live the aims of life or is moving in that direction, great, but all too often people become *dependent* on such a thing and are no longer able to stand their ground, which in turn actually sabotages the very thing that they thought that they were working toward. Haven't you ever noticed that the less one cares about whether they have a job the next day somehow directly translates into that same person getting promoted or getting better jobs with more autonomy? And the exact opposite happens to those that do care? It is such a common thing that movies are made about it (I'm thinking of one in particular). The most common way that a workplace attempts to force its own nothing other than 'this' assumption is to make it either mandatory or socially desirable to work for 16 hours a day, 7 days a week. Based on my definition of Good and Evil, this is Evil, since it leaves no room for anything else, and it should be flat out rejected, period. However, one should not quit in this situation if the job is indeed serving them, rather, one should say "NO", come in and work exactly (or at least on average) the number of hours they are paid to work, but (and here is the kicker) ensure that they do far more work to a far higher standard than anyone else around. I have done this my whole life and I have never been even close to being fired. However, if one does get fired, then good riddance, and then one also serves as an example to the others in the toxic organization and hopefully said organization will eventually not be able to compete with companies that do not do this (as is increasingly becoming the case and one should take note of). And if you end up upsetting the people you work with for some social reason or another that you refuse to engage in because it is Evil then, again, so be it. Welcome the ostracization as an ability to show your talents and perseverance in spite of it since that is generally and precisely what they are trying to "take the piss" out of. Become, as Watts put it, "nonplussed", which is what he actually intended with that idea.

This idea of dependence strikes most often and most sharply in the realm of partners/spouses. As a matter of fact, if one would like to phenomenologically investigate the enforcement of nothing other than 'this', I can think of no better realm to do so! I spent a very, very long time studying interpersonal relationships in general and particularly partners/spouses, and one sure sign of a toxic relationship basically equates to the enforcement of the idea of nothing other than 'this'. And both men and women torture and abuse each other in various ways in an attempt to enforce the assumption. Quite often this comes as some version of manipulation and playing to one's weaknesses and insecurities, but in more well-known instances men tend to become physically violent while women tend to become violent in every other possible manner in which one can be destructive and abusive as this is seen as socially more acceptable than the former. In any case, the goal is to enforce, by nearly any means necessary, the assumption that there is nothing other than 'this', and even thinking that there is anything 'other than this' is the highest crime that one can commit. Again, one's excuses do not magically become valid when one's partner is forcing them into Evil. All too often people exit toxic co-dependent relationships (quite often not at all psychologically or financially intact) when they finally get the courage to say "NO", just to end up with someone 'better' whom they are afraid losing if they stand the same ground as they were considering when they thought "never again" after the last person. No means no. 'This' is not different. If your partner's activities meet the definition of Evil than that is what they are, I do not care if they are your partner... Standing up to Evil partners is done in the same way as it is done in the workplace. Again, don't you ever notice that couples who always have that bit of quiet desperation about them and are constantly on edge are the ones where one or both people say that they "can't live without" the other? And that those who thrive never say such things?

In both of the above examples the idea is not caring to an extent because it actually does not matter, not because it is the cool or trendy thing to say so that one can *appear* stoic. And what I mean by that is thinking about how one gets to that point in the first place: one takes responsibility to increase one's competency all of the time, every day, forever. It is like fitness or sport in that it takes a very long sustained effort over years, but after a while one can end up at the pro level. But to push this metaphor further, to rely totally on one event or team for one's wellbeing would be totally ridiculous at that point. Seriously, how ridiculous would it be if the dependency seen in previous examples were transferred to the sport domain. Why is it any different? Nobody ever has an answer. "It just is", bleats Dolly.

These are just two examples that most people can relate to in one way or another. However, one must remember, this phenomenon/ pattern applies to quite literally every thing, person, and organization on the planet (and probably off the planet or any other conceivable or inconceivable place), especially governments, which is something that almost no one is willing to touch (yet, or anymore, depending on the time) since they really do hold the most severe punishments for saying "NO" since they can simply throw one in prison or kill them if they wish.

Which brings me to narcissists. The absolute epitomal representation and phenomenological exemplars of the enforcement of nothing other than 'this' and the post-totalitarian system, who will do quite literally anything that they can get away with in order to enforce the idea. As such, these people represent and are the agents for, all that is Evil. At the same time, they are often seen by the Herd as most capable, and so they end up in every imaginable position of power regardless of whatever political slant comes with said position. Eventually any particular narcissist is revealed as such, but at that point it is 'too late' for the Herd to do anything about it given how the post-totalitarian structure is built and maintained. It is a pattern that happens over and over and over again but nobody ever seems to learn, which includes myself up until recently.

For those of you not so familiar with narcissists or the dynamics between them and their targets, let us compare common traits to the entire story up to this point, i.e., the post-totalitarian assumption itself or anyone enforcing the assumption of nothing other than 'this'. And let us also not forget that when something becomes apparent, that it is a mirror image of something else going on.

1. Lack or complete non-existence of object permanence – once something has left the field of view it simply does not exist. Check.

2. Grandiose sense of self-importance – they are the center of everything and to suggest otherwise invites "narcissistic rage". Check.

3. Lives in a fantasy world that supports their delusions of grandeur and will attempt to destroy anything that threatens that view – otherwise thought of as enforcing an assumption that has no basis whatsoever. Check.

4. Manipulating one's sense of reality so that you will distrust yourself and instead trust them (known as gaslighting). Check.

5. If being gaslighted one tends not to even notice that it is happening to them. Check.

6. Isolating the targets and constricting their movement so that they can be controlled. Check.

7. Extreme unconscious projection where the target is being told that they are doing the very things that the narcissist is unconsciously doing. Check.

8. Calling their targets "crazy" if they don't agree with their version of reality. Check.

9. High sensitivity to criticism. Check.

10. Need for constant praise and admiration, otherwise narcissistic rage ensues – the reverse of which would be to place one's praise and admiration on someone or something other than them. Check.

11. The belief that whatever they want they should get without having to work for it. Check.

12. Viewing people as objects in their lives to serve their dreams and needs – you do not have any because you do not exist, but of course they definitely do... Check.

13. Target people with dependency or abandonment issues and seek to *exacerbate* those issues. Check...

14. Telling their targets early on that they are capable of doing anything – anything is possible – only to later on constantly remind them how limited and incapable they are. Check......

15. *Every single thing that they do* is geared towards constructing a reality that says that there is simply nothing else other than them. CHECK!!!

And so, based on these traits, what do these people do who, again, are the most salient embodiment of the post-totalitarian system and Evil? Well, they obviously do everything they can to attempt to get positions or roles in places like the government, media, Academia, the top of the corporate ladder, etc. – basically anything that would be seen as important and have authority over others' lives. And since every single one of these things is geared towards commanding others in what to do and not actually doing anything oneself, then these are the exact things that they have literally written into our culture as the most important things, with the least important (or irrelevant, or "laughable") things being anything that does the opposite. As time goes on, this is reenacted and reinforced over and over again not just by the narcissists – they simply plant the ideas and give the orders – but mostly by their targets! Recall Havel. Narcissistic agents lead to narcissistic organizations where targets enforce the orders which leads to more narcissistic agents and so on.

So why do people fall for it in the first place and continue to do so? Because narcissists are *always* the most charming and seemingly competent people anywhere to be found *to begin with/at first sight* (which is why they are so obsessed with their image), i.e., before they actually have to do or handle anything. And remember, they write the culture. So, what happens is that people who *actually are* competent are seen as being completely incompetent and only make it to positions of power via a series of flukes (I would think Elon Musk is a prime example of someone that did – since the beginning he was always described by others in power as completely unfit to do anything, and yet... Plus, every narcissist that I have ever known HATES Elon Musk – I'm thinking of one person in particular right now, which probably has something to do with him not caring about his image and yet still becoming successful. Chew on that you piece of shit). In any case, they prey on people with dependency issues who are scared not only of taking any responsibility but are also afraid to even think about what it is they need to do at any given time, which because of the performative effect I am describing only begets more people of the same each generation. The narcissists are then perfectly happy to step in and tell people what to do. However, as I have said, eventually people realize the true incompetence of the narcissist hiding behind some singular thing they do well, the person who notices becomes very angry, narcissists are the absolute experts as shooting down the "no's" of others via manipulation and gaslighting, and if any stern "NO" crops up where the manipulative tactics do not work, then the narcissists simply unleash violence in any and all available forms. People then say, "How did we not see it coming?!", and then move on to the next narcissist that says, "I will save you!" Hey, I have an idea, why don't you try SAVING YOURSELF... Something that even I must remind myself of daily.

But people don't, and that is the real kicker here, that dependent people are drawn towards narcissists and narcissists are obviously drawn towards dependent people – it is the perfect dysfunctional storm. One of the reasons that dependent people love narcissists, and one could even argue that it is the only real reason, is precisely because of the inability for a narcissist to ever experience a real emotion or care about anything other than themselves. Think about it. Why are most people dependent? They are afraid that they cannot make it on their own. Fear is a strong emotion that is also generally associated with anxiety, worry, depression and a range of other negative emotions and future concocted disastrous scenarios. What the narcissist offers with their lack of emotion and very well-presented first impression is the calm in the center of the storm, so to speak. The problem is that once they know that they have someone or some group, they become the storm... And one's reality is generally turned into something far more horrific and terrifying than anything that they were previously conjuring up, which then requires being saved again, and on and on.

Which then brings me to the idea of dealing with narcissists. While there seems to be lots of advice floating around on how to do this, I find all of it to be rather useless in that none of it gets at the root of why the phenomenon persists (like so many things). I find advice such as "cut off their supply" or "simply walk away", for example, to be absolutely absurd. First, as I am trying to get across, it is becoming so pervasive, and even encouraged to the point where these ways of supposedly dealing with narcissists are becoming less and less *possible* – often times one simply cannot "walk away", as so many have painfully found after it was too late. Second, this does nothing to keep one from walking right back into the same trap due to what I have outlined above – cowardice begets more cowardice which does nothing but perpetuate the phenomenon. Third, wouldn't you rather defeat a narcissist (or die trying) then just let them keep doing their thing and move on to the next person? The stakes are high when doing so, but is that not exactly what makes the challenge worth it? The right way to handle a narcissist is to simply stare them straight in the face and say with all the conviction and sternness that one can muster up:

"NO." Even if it means one's death. As Jung said, there simply will be no change that does not start with the individual.

While I have pointed out the characteristics of narcissists, as I feel it is important to do so, the absolute key takeaway here is the idea that narcissists are just what allow *something else* to show up in the first place because it gets our attention and allows for us to focus on various attributes (recall the chapter dealing with archetypes). In this way, I am trying to phenomenologically show what exactly one would be saying "NO" to and why. There are a hundred different ways to look at it, but hopefully one can see what I am doing here. And again, saying no to 'it' will always have serious consequences. But sweeping it under the rug and pretending that it simply does not exist is a historically backed one-way ticket to Hell, and I do not know about you but I would rather die than live in Hell.

Finally, I hope that it is absolutely clear that what I am saying is not about a cause – that is absolutely not what I am getting at here, although that is precisely the direction that Dolly was surely trying to trick you into going this entire time in order to feed Dolly's overlords. This is about one's psychological health and ability to become all that one can be, as well as being a light that encourages others to take a stand and to do the same. It is not just narcissists that one is fighting, it is the pattern that they embody. But until people can learn to cut off as many dependencies as possible and say "NO!" and live the proof that when they say "NO" they actually mean "NO", then no psychological health or thriving on the individual or societal level will ever be found.

"Don't be afraid to go it alone"

Terrance McKenna was fond of summing up many of his points by stepping back from whatever he was talking about and simply saying: "Don't be afraid to go it alone". And I think that he did this because it really was the crux of everything that he was trying to get across – psychedelics were simply a tool. While he promoted the psychedelic experience and this or that idea, this idea of going it alone really was the kernel and all that anything else was really ultimately leading one to. He was also quite fond of Jung and was intimately familiar with his work, far more so than 'real' psychologists who do, indeed, as McKenna pointed out, stop reading after the first couple of volumes before it actually gets interesting. The reason that I bring up the latter is that Jung was basically getting at the same thing, and so am I. Furthermore, all of us were trying to make a much more fundamental point than what is often thought by Dolly and company in their kneejerk response to the idea of going it alone. None of us are promoting or glorifying the stereotypical life of the socially anxious hermit on the fringes of society that just cannot seem to be understood. What we are promoting is living an authentic existence and being ok with things *if* one does end up being a socially anxious hermit on the fringes of society that just cannot seem to be understood, and then finding some way to return with all-new assumptions and values systems intact. There is an enormous difference.

How people view "loners", and the discourse around them, I find extremely interesting. The reason that I find it so interesting is that they are hated by so many even in instances where they have no agency and are not noticeably influencing any system. Anything about them is distinctly separate from all of the connotations that come with more politically oriented arguments around people who are "individualistic", where the haters in this instance claim that these people just want to cause everyone else problems and get in the way with their stupid freedoms and rights that impinge on their system in some way. However, loners are hated even when they are doing nothing… This is because they are the single greatest human threat to the post-totalitarian system, for a variety of reasons. For one thing, this idea of going it alone, especially if one is successful, points out a serious limitation in the system: the post-totalitarian system and its agents cannot do a single thing on their own, ever. "You can't either!", they will scream in response. "We're all interconnected". Yes, we are all interconnected; however, one can maximize their independence, and that is a fact, and doing so is what really gets their blood boiling especially when someone does it and shows it off. But really, does no one else find it extremely odd that people get so angry about this? Let's say the person cannot (in a supposed reality where everything has already been figured out) do anything by themselves, and let's say that they are just sitting in a house and have no contact with the outside world, why would anyone get *angry* about this? It is very simple, again, the *idea* – the *information* – is the greatest threat; the suggestion that it could even be possible invalidates everything that the post-totalitarian system is built upon.

And long before anything turns to pointed and specific anger towards loners, one can see the offensive mounting against them in various discourses. Take the business startup scene, which I was involved in for a number of years. The notion that solo entrepreneurs are destined to fail is so prevalent that barely an investor or accelerator on the planet will fund or take on a solo entrepreneur. However, in recent years this phenomenon has prompted both amateurs and professional researchers to question this assumption. Research that actually looks at the number of successful startups (literally however one wants to define success) shows that this assumption is completely baseless. Approximately 50% of successful startups are team founded and the other 50% are individually founded, and research is showing that in the long run the individually founded startups tend to be more profitable (some of that for obvious reasons, some of that not). Or look to the field of ecology, a place where if you start speaking of anything individualistic you will be crucified. New research in evolutionary ecology suggests that at several points in history the survival of entire species and ecosystems was dependent on loners and suggests (as in the actual written implications) that loners may be exactly what end up saving society. Cue the gnashing of teeth by Dolly and company as they scramble to mount their next attack.

Again, why are people so angry and intent on trying to shut down the idea of going it alone? Because it reflects their weakness and dependent attitude back at them as well as their rejection of actual responsibility for anything, or that there can be any responsibility *in the first place* and the fact that they were the ones who sold out to Evil. They simply cannot take it. It gets to the absolute root of everything their system of irresponsibility and narcissistic dependency is built upon. This is why the Herd reacts so violently when someone separates from it. Going it alone in the truest sense might be the most difficult thing that one can do because the moment someone chooses to do so all of one's insecurities will be brought to the surface and attacked, and if that does not work the person themselves may be attacked. One could even view the phenomenon as a sort of immune response by 'this' to a foreign invader. I am somehow reminded of gay marriages back when people used to ask me what my opinion was on the matter. My response has almost always been the same: if you don't want gay marriage then don't get one! Or is that the problem? Hmm? That is the second parallel I have made with something gay because it is the perfect parallel for so many things here. Seriously, what difference does it make if there are gay people everywhere doing their thing as long as one is sure that they are not gay? None. However, it makes a hell of a lot of difference if one is unsure… You can also witness the same phenomenon in the US when someone says they are thinking of moving to another country.

This idea of going it alone is very close to the idea of at least part of Jung's process of individuation. I think that Edinger does a fantastic job of summing up the process of individuation and explaining that it is a cycle whereby one first (in my words) stands up for themselves and is then (in his words) alienated and experiences what he calls "the Fall". At some point that alienation becomes unsustainable and there is a need to return, but after which the person is a little more individuated. The person gets fed up again, and the cycle repeats, but the intervals get shorter and be person becomes braver. At some point the individual and the World and/or Self become so aligned that the individual is truly living their ownmost potential given their environment. But this never occurs without the Fall and the concomitant alienation, which occurs over and over.

The first time one stands up and says "NO", this alienation is severe, and this is what causes most people to permanently run back to the Herd as they experience a mild form of what one could call post-traumatic stress – they remember it forever and never dare do it again. And I personally do not blame people for this. The first and second time that I did, it was like getting run over by a psychological freight train, and that is usually enough to put most people down for good. Since most people experience this at least once or twice, one's family, friends, and colleagues usually say "oh, that's ok, it happens to everyone, we are just glad you're back". But what happens is that over time *some* people simply cannot give up the fight. They get back up and maybe even start to pick fights with 'this', and it is at this point when one is making it clear that they may never stop fighting with 'this', that those same family and friends start to become highly agitated and no longer forgive; instead, one is now considered a traitor and will be attacked from all fronts.

And there will be no logic in 'this' that can account for the phenomenon! For example, in the world of individuation and those intimately familiar with it because of experience and/or working with others, it would be perfectly normal for someone, after getting to the point above, to say to themselves and nobody else that "I refuse to put up with this anymore – IT'S NOT HAPPENING!", and then within 10 minutes their partner comes in and accuses them of cheating, the phone rings and their boss is threatening to fire them, they get into a car wreck after they leave the house to clear their head, and their dog is run over and killed by another car while they were out. The obviously traumatized person some months later says the same thing to themselves again and then they actually are fired, cannot get a job, and are forced to live on the fringes of society. This is an extreme example to make a point, but for those familiar with the phenomenon it is not that far from what actually happens. In one way or another, however it materializes or comes to be, the person who stands up and says "NO" to 'this' will experience extreme alienation that is almost impossible to put into words. But here is the thing, could it not be this way for a reason? Just like everything else that I have brought up, would this not be an effective way to either weed out those who do not have the stomach for responsibility, or to prepare those that do? And does it make any difference whether this process is 'built in' or is blind natural pattern? Does it *really* make any difference whether one decided to be this way or whether they were born this way?

Here is food for thought. Why not just go ahead and entertain the possibility that Watts proposes that you, on another level, may just be completely and totally alone. The most frightening experience I have ever had was on LSD when I ended up in a place that I came to call "the box", where it became 100% apparent to me that I really actually was alone in 'this' (after "I" was obliterated, mind you), and I still do not discount the possibility on this particular level that I speak of where everything more or less disappears (remember, compensatory mirror image, Projection, etc.). This experience absolutely terrified me to the point where I did end up with a type of post-traumatic stress disorder. It constantly came back to haunt me, sometimes I could not sleep, and any time I felt slightly out of the ordinary that feeling would creep back in. However, I dealt with it over the years by deliberate and constant exposure to it, rather than attempting to run away or shield myself from it, and I finally came to terms with this possibility in the event that this 'other level' comes to be salient in The End (whatever that means). What coming to terms with it has done for me on an everyday and pragmatic level, in addition to being less afraid of some possibility that may or may not be true, is to start dealing with even the most extreme alienation that comes from saying "NO" to the post-totalitarian system and its agents in various contexts, which has had a whole range of other benefits because the two things are intimately linked (i.e., saying "NO" to the system and its agents on some level threatens one with the horror I speak of). Given what I know about Projection and the unconscious, it would not surprise me that everyone has this idea somewhere in the back of their mind and that this idea is why the mere threat of alienation is so effective.

With alienation comes the notion of 'loneliness', and with loneliness comes *guilt*. What I am going to say is something one simply will not find anywhere in Herd psychology because every Herd psychologist will tell you that if you are lonely something is wrong with YOU. This lie is constantly reinforced by Herd psychologists, and increasing guilt is felt by the individual after years of conditioning. The process of conditioning one to feel lonely applies to everyone who feels lonely and goes something like this: At some point in early life, the person who ends up feeling lonely is overcome by a feeling to start being more authentic; every, single, time. It could be anything: wearing more of such and such type clothes, having a certain kind of hair, etc. Then, they see just how rapidly 'friends' disappear when they make even the most minor of changes. They then have to decide whether to keep going down this path or go back in order to not feel 'lonely'.

This is a basic scenario that most of us are familiar with, and generally these people can at some point can find other 'freaks' like themselves, and maybe (probably) join some group in which they can all talk about how they are oppressed or whatever...

However, the problem with 'loneliness' tends to become more pronounced and far less bearable later in life when and individual starts speaking *their* personal truth. This is a surefire way to make sure that one is cast out of *any* group and made to be completely on one's own. But it is a long process. It first starts with being absolutely compelled to speak up about some kind of truth. The person is then rejected by some amount of people, this hurts, and they begin to feel bad. This process continues over the years and, at some point, the individual, even if unconsciously and no matter how much of a rebel that they are, starts to feel like maybe they actually are doing something wrong because look around...nobody wants anything to do with them anymore. And when it starts to get really, really weird indeed is when more and more total strangers start violently reacting to their mere presence without them saying a single word or making a face that is anything less than warm and welcoming, in spite of (and probably exactly because of) the person being highly confident in themselves.

At this point the individual is completely and utterly torn between feeling that there is something wrong with them and speaking and living the truth, and this is exactly where the vast majority of people who could individuate do not. They are standing at the precipice looking toward everything they have ever known to be true and everything that they could possibly be – a place that has taken them their whole lives and endless pain and struggle to get to – and all too often this is exactly the moment where, just like in some disgusting Herd feel-good movie, the person puts their head down in shame, goes back to the Herd, and repeats "there is *nothing* other than 'this'".

Loneliness as a 'thing' or a legitimate emotion on its own is complete and total bullshit. It is simply the result of speaking the truth and then made to feel there is something wrong with oneself – that one is guilty. *Only* the latter results in 'loneliness'.

Simply being alone is not being lonely.

One can be alone and perfectly happy *if* they know beyond a shadow of a doubt that there is nothing wrong with them and they have done nothing wrong. And, as I keep saying, doing so is the result of getting one's assumptions, values, and actions straight, which is very hard to do because once one stands up for themselves against wrong doing, a wrong doer is exactly what the narcissistic system will tell one that they are! Without the part of the equation where one feels that they have done something wrong, loneliness simply cannot exist. You think a narcissist feels lonely??? I have learned, especially in my time in Academia where it was drilled home, that *any* weapon can be used against its creator........... And yes, I am fully aware of what I am saying and the multiplicity of broad and personal implications. Are you?

And just how powerful would it be for the individual to realize this? By contrast, just how powerful is the manipulative power of loneliness? And if it is that powerful, does one really think that they are going to get past that one without a seriously bloody fight? Does one honestly think it is going to happen in a group holding hands and cheering each other on? Please, get real. Maybe one day, but we are nowhere near such a day yet. The most 'ridiculous' of fantasies that one could point to in this book or otherwise are far more likely, and yet it is this very fantasy that nearly everyone on earth assumes is the answer and what works.

To end this chapter and provide a slightly different perspective on what I am saying, I think it would be appropriate to share another one of my favorite excerpts from Terrance McKenna from the same recorded lecture I took the last one from:

> "...we don't like being children but the culture has enforced a sort of infantilism, and the way I explain it to myself is it's a kind of unwillingness to go it alone on a certain level. I don't know how many of you remember in "Brave New World", Huxley's brilliant dystopia, but there's a scene in there where Bernard, who is the guy who's out of it in the novel because in his fetal fluid they got an alcohol contaminant [in there] and so he's different from everybody else in this society and he occasionally has original thoughts, and he and his assigned girlfriend for the evening, or whatever she is, are in a helicopter and they sweep out past the crematorium where they're recollecting elements for reuse, and he suspends the helicopter over the black bay, and she immediately becomes very agitated, restless, anxious and pleads with him to return to the city, and what it is it's her anxiety over being alone in the presence of nature; she literally can't take it. And I think there are a lot of people in our society, and each of us in our own way at different times, who have within us this neurotic and infantile creature that can't face it alone. And this going it alone thing is very important. You know,

Plotinus, the great Neoplatonic philosopher, he spoke of the mystical experience as the flight of the alone to the alone. And in the psychedelic experience there is this issue of surrender, because a lot of people want to diddle with it; they want to be able to say they did it but they don't ever want to face an actual moment where they put it all on the line... And yet the whole issue with this stuff is to let it lead – to let it show what it wants to show. So, somehow individually we have to reclaim our experience. The real message – more important even than the psychedelic experience – that I try to leave with people in these weekends is the primacy of direct experience. That as people, the real universe is within your reach, *always*. Everything not within your reach is basically unconfirmed rumor... And we insert ourselves like ants or honeybees into hierarchies of knowledge. So, we say, well, what's going on in the world? Well, turn on CNN, you know, and then somehow, we're ordered. Then we say "uh-huh, okay it's 85 degrees in Baghdad and the wind is out of the northeast at 15 miles an hour", and we feel somehow better now because we're getting the information, but what we have done is sold out direct experience, and *all* institutions require this of us... That we somehow redefine ourselves for the convenience of the institution, and this redefinition *always* involves a narrowing... a denial..."

Parallel structures

As any rebel or dissident with half a brain has learned by now, it is more or less impossible in this day and age to fight Evil directly. And given that the entire reason that the post-totalitarian system emerged in the first place was that totalitarian systems were losing their ability to control through direct force, should this be any surprise? If a centralized totalitarian system with military, police, and prison systems at its disposal has already figured out a more effective way to control a populace, then why would anyone suppose that those same systems can be fought or changed in any way by those with far less centralized power and organization using similar strategies or tactics?

There really is no such thing anymore as warfare in the traditional sense. Not only because traditional warfare and any of its variations have basically become untenable via interconnectedness and so on, but mainly because I cannot ignore the fact that, as Baudrillard points out, the only 'wars' that have taken place over the past few decades are over *systems*, and this is a very, very important point. The frontline of our war lies in a certain type of guerrilla warfare.

This warfare has not changed in its essence, but its face definitely has.

I do not want to mince words here, so let me be perfectly clear: the *only* realistic insurgency, dissident movement, or anything else that seeks to fight Evil lies squarely in the development and support of parallel structures; i.e., something 'other than this'. *Anything* else is simply kidding itself and is playing right into the hands of the post-totalitarian structure as well as reinforcing it. As such, anything else is futile and a flat-out waste of time and resources. For any of those with the urge to rebel, this is a very hard pill to swallow, but reality often is.

I will repeat that. If one thinks that they or whatever group whose identity they have bought into is going to change anything at all in the world today via anything other than parallel structures, they are not only wasting their lives but they are *living in a fantasy and will just end up becoming the very thing that they are fighting*, which is one of the oldest and most well-known phenomena in any historical revolution; however, this used to take time, whereas now it is instantaneous. The moment that one decides to "fight the system" head-on, they have already lost; the system already has categories to place this person and/or their group into; the system already has discourse to lob at any potential attacker with hordes of Herd animals to chant and magnify this discourse and/or enforce it by thousands of different existing or instantaneously developed means. Every last possible method of direct attack that one can think of has already been shut down before it can even be conceived. Note that I am in no way advocating non-violence – violence absolutely has its time and place – I am simply reiterating what has been known for several decades, which is to say that the only realistic way forward for those that wish to fight Evil are these parallel structures.

> "If the basic job of the 'dissident movements' is to serve truth, that is, to serve the real aims of life, and if that necessarily develops into a defence of the individual and his or her right to a free and truthful life ... then another stage of this approach, perhaps the most mature stage so far, is what Václav Benda has called the development of parallel structures. ... These parallel structures, it may be said, represent the most articulated expressions so far of 'living within the truth'. One of the most important tasks the 'dissident movements' have set themselves is to support and develop them." – Václav Havel, *The Power of the Powerless*

So then, what are these parallel structures that I am referring to? Well, this entire book has been alluding to them all along! One could even say that 'other than this' and the refusal to let it go is *the* parallel structure of our time.

As Havel points out, the idea of parallel structures (or "Parallel Polis") originated with political scientist Václav Benda who was a fellow founding member of Charter 77, a text that was prepared in 1976 to address human rights violations which subsequently landed many of its founders and architects in prison, including Havel. Parallel structures were a description or post hoc conceptualization of the alternative social structures that had emerged in artistic and intellectual circles as a way to escape totalitarian rule; basically, a society that ran parallel to the normalized society. In many ways the concept is referring to what we might call "the underground" or "the counterculture" (the astute reader will have already found the fatal flaw to all of this – more on that shortly). The basic idea of a parallel structure or society was that it is able to fulfill the same social and economic functions more or less as that of a normalized society, all the while constantly monitoring, verifying, and fighting for individual civic rights and freedoms that the State tends to restrict. In this original conceptualization there exists independent/parallel culture, education, information systems, and economies, as well as foreign policies that draw international funding, resources, and help to stabilize and legitimize the movement. But most importantly, the whole idea behind these parallel structures is that they were developed into a form that could completely *replace* the authoritarian system, and this is the logic that Havel focused most on in his book. In other words, a parallel society is developed in a way so that when the authoritarian regime inevitably either starts cracking or is failing then the parallel society simply emerges out of the ashes – no traditional war or 'revolution' necessary (or the baggage and inevitable repeating nature that come with them).

However, as with so many things in history, many of which I have pointed out in this book, the very thing that was positioned to give people more freedom and responsibility is the very thing that ultimately ended up having the opposite effect. Why? Because the entire thing was based and dependent upon the creation and maintenance of GROUPS... And no matter how well-intentioned a group, it will *always* give rise to belonging and identity (more specifically the chasing and maintenance of those two things) as well as the eventual supplanting of individual responsibility with the expectation of the group leaders to make decisions about what the individuals in the group will do, rather than the other way around. That is the fatal flaw in the original conceptualization of parallel structures: the ultimate focus ended up on groups. It makes absolutely zero difference that the *intent* behind all of this was individual rights and freedoms because all that matters is that each and every one of these alternative societies are groups where the absolute inevitable *result* (100% of the time) is the exact same thing that the group started out fighting: a denial. I will say that in a different way. *Every single social movement on earth* that requires the formation and maintenance of a group (which is all of them) is doomed to fail and become the very thing that it started out fighting: authoritarianism, institutionalization, and normalization. And, really, how the hell else does one expect any social movement to end up?

Even if one wanted this to work temporarily as a group (as it did eastern Soviet Europe) in our current day and age, we do not have the *freedoms* that eastern Soviet Europe had in 1978. "Ridiculous!!!", Dolly screams. Yes, that is correct Dolly, we absolutely do not have the freedoms that they had. In eastern Soviet Europe circa 1978 those people could still do all the things that would allow for a parallel society to form in the first place. For example, Charter 77 was something that actually could be passed around as underground "samizdat" in unofficial publications precisely because it was printed on paper and passed around – i.e., it could not be immediately monitored and directly responded to, which gave these groups time to actually form some kind of parallel structure. People in eastern Soviet Europe could still move around, talk to each other, have underground meetings, and so on, long before anyone got wind of what was going on, even if they eventually got caught. I.e., something, anything, could emerge back then without being squashed out of existence the moment that the idea was articulated to another person. However, this is simply not what happens anymore.

Think about it. Let us say that you have some thought in your head. You want to articulate this thought to likeminded individuals. What do you do? How do you get this thought out of your head to be considered by other people? And when I ask this, I am not asking what your personal preference is for how to get this idea considered by other people because your personal preference (or even what could be – I'm looking at you intellectuals) on the matter is completely irrelevant. What matters is how people, any people..., currently get the vast majority of their information and the fact that there is absolutely nothing to suggest that it is going to change or get better (on the contrary). I refuse to spell out a cliché, however, whatever it is that you are thinking that you would do that would actually reach anyone is 1) immediately monitored, 2) immediately responded to, 3) immediately connected with other people like yourself and persona's/personality profiles, and 4) is probably nothing new (consider that literally everyone, even the most brain-dead of Herd animal, has access to the entire world's history and all the information about it).

THIS is what people in general, as well as rebels and dissidents, are failing to understand. Just because you now have the 'freedom' to go out and buy whatever shit you want, or say whatever you want, or reach whatever audience you want, or whatever supposed thing you think makes you more free than those in eastern Soviet Europe 1978, does not get rid of the fact that almost nothing you say; no matter how well articulated or fact-filled; no matter how huge or horrific the implications; no matter what; is information, that information must be digested by other people, and the means of getting that information out with the goal of forming a group is completely blocked – if the idea is *truly* revolutionary, your chances of forming a group that will ever be anything other than a *club* are zero.

So, not only is forming a group as the result of parallel structures (as opposed to political structures) doomed to failure, it is increasingly impossible. What I am trying to get across is the complete and total overbearing and suffocating nature of the post-totalitarian system, the extent of which is so bad that the original solution to the post-totalitarian system has become one of its greatest strengths. And that is how it, and all of its supposedly different predecessors, works! Eventually, every group that started stemmed from parallel structures – the hippies, the counterculture, individual rights activists, whatever – eventually began to chant and enforce "there is nothing other than 'this'", and the post-totalitarian system was all too happy to oblige. "Ok, here is your political card, here are your websites, here are the (virtual) places you can go meet like-minded people, here is what we will classify all of you as, and here is a blanket countermeasure for anything you might possibly want to change since we have learned all of your habits and traits as they are all freely available to us now. Good luck!", i.e., the very thing that Havel warned would happen if the aims of life were forgotten…

And I cannot help but notice that here we are again talking about something old as if it is something new. There is nothing new about the post-totalitarian system any more than there is something new about parallel structures; any more than there is something new about the Herd and the Hero; any more than there is something new about Good and Evil. What, did the Roman empire somehow never exist? Or what about the Church in the Dark Ages? How is the *essence* of those things or anything like them throughout history different from Nazi Germany, Communist Russia, or China??? How is the *essence* of every, single, last, one of the solutions to these things any different from the *birth* of Christianity or the *birth* of the counterculture? I will help you out: NOTHING... Not a single fucking thing. All one sees when they look back over the millennia is a reoccurring pattern: Evil attempting to stamp out the individual, individuals using the technology at their disposal to free themselves, once free, those individuals form groups, and then the groups are incorporated back into Evil. And just like a successful virus or bacteria, it was only a matter of time before the 'medicine' had absolutely no effect any longer. And, indeed, what can we observe in people who rely on medicine rather than individual health?! It is the same old story; these things just manifest in different ways. So, do not go pretending that once such and such was done that the totalitarian system was somehow 'new', or that when that was done it is the post-totalitarian system that is 'new'. That right there is a large part of the problem.

But as anyone who has read this book in its entirety should know by now, this happens because people *WANT* the post-totalitarian system; they *WANT* an Orwellian State; they *WANT* Evil; and I believe on some level people are absolutely aware that the aforementioned patterns are there. This back-and-forth ritual that has been taking place for thousands of years is what allows the Herd to briefly latch onto something created by authentic individuals by projecting their individual responsibility onto a group that is supposed to be aimed at separating from the Herd. And this phenomenon has become so pervasive that almost every single person in our current society is now claiming to be a part of some 'alternative' group or another. Does no one see a problem there?! Does no one see the blatant contradiction? Does no one see the near complete and utter non-existence of options? Does no one see the 10,000-mile gorge between these people's supposed values and their direct experience? Remember:

> "In normalization, ideology works not as a unifying belief or as an inspiring vision but as "a bridge of excuses between the system and the individual."" – Timothy Snyder, intro to *Power of the Powerless*

The lesson that no one can seem to learn after thousands of years of playing this game is that the individual is saved by the individual, period. A group never has and never will do that for you, it will always end up as a bridge of excuses, and the moment that one involves a group in something that is inherently individual, that thing, whatever it is, is over, instantly.

That covers the problematic issue of groups when it comes to parallel structures. The second problematic issue comes from the way people tend to think and make sense of the world (as I covered in Part 1). Again, it makes no difference that the founders and architects of the idea of parallel structures used the term "parallel" or that they spelled out exactly what they meant by parallel, or that one can easily look up the definition of parallel in a dictionary. What matters is how this idea (besides groupthink) actually materialized in every single one of these instances later on. *PARALLEL* structures are not equivalent to *OPPOSING* structures… In a parallel structure there is obviously opposition as an effect (otherwise there tends to little reason to develop it), but the idea is that the parallel structure, just like when thinking about two parallel lines, has an operational and focal domain that is outside of the domain of the post-totalitarian system and its agents (why it is so difficult), where the idea is that the vast majority of the focus of daily existence is on the aims of life within 'this' parallel structure, and the parallel structure 'other than this' sits in the background where it is neither denied nor fought. Do you see what I just did there? Remember what I have said previously about 'other than this' becoming the new 'this' and vice versa?

Furthermore, a parallel structure, precisely because it is outside of 'this' domain, requires substantial and perhaps even superhuman levels of sustained, life-long effort, focus, sacrifice, and so on, all of which could best be summed up in a single word: work... or Opus or whatever one would like to call it whereby the idea is to convey extreme work and focus. By contrast, the only 'work' that is required with an opposing structure is to simply define oneself in terms of the opposite; to direct all of one's actions toward doing the opposite; in other words, no real thought, work, or more importantly responsibility, is required; and I think it would be pretty clear by now whether through Havel, Nietzsche, the points I have kept making over and over again, or one's direct experience of others if they employ the methodology that I outlined in Part 1, that most human beings are lazy sacks of projecting shit. All of this is precisely why so many people take their urge to rebel and insert some inept thing or activity (generally a group identity and its discourse) in the place of something that would actually make any difference. I believe that I have phenomenologically covered the rejection of the pragmatic options to realize one's values in exhaustive detail, so I will not do it again, but these two points are very important to keep in mind when talking about parallel structures, lest one end up right back where they started, which is being defined and directed by the very thing that they are supposedly so adamant about having nothing to do with.

The reason that I bring this up is to show how parallel structures probably should be thought of but, at the same time, to also get one to think about Herd reality when it comes to these things, where Left is not parallel to Right; Hippie is not parallel to Square; Anarchy is not parallel to Government; "compassionate people" are not parallel to "hostile people". These ideas in lived reality are all directly tied to groups, they are all opposing structures, and they are all just 'this' pointing at 'this'; therefore, they *all* are two sides of the same coin and, again, the post-totalitarian algorithm exploits this for everything it is worth.

It probably seems as though I have spent a lot of time explaining what parallel structures are not; however, I am a firm believer that the best way to know what something is is to know what it is not, and I have spent my entire life watching and reading about things that work turning into things that do not work wherein almost every instance it looks like what I have just outlined. And it always comes down to rejection and/or fear of responsibility and individual existence in 'this'.

So then, what do parallel structures look like if not based on groups? What does a parallel structure look like in our day and age, especially if people want, and have been actively working towards for hundreds of years, an Orwellian nightmare? What is one to do when they are socially blocked from every conceivable angle? How does one not reject, but deal with that? Well, the first step is to admit that that is where one is now – you *are* blocked, people *do* want an Orwellian nightmare, and there is *nothing* you can do to stop *that*. The second step is to (finally) accept Jung's seemingly cliché point that all change starts with the individual, and then Havel's point that the true creation and development of parallel structures is an inherently individual thing. There is simply no way out of any of this if one actually "puts their money where their mouth is" regarding Evil. It is as simple as taking the essence of parallel structures and putting them squarely on the shoulder of the individual (especially since the trend of things coming down on the shoulders of the individual is only going to continue – another thing one increasingly cannot run from anymore).

However, before we get to these essences, we have the most obvious and concrete form of a parallel structure: the individual running parallel to the group (the Herd). If parallel groups were the original answer to the post-totalitarian system, then the individual is the answer to the group (and yes, I know where that pattern and its extrapolation leads, do you?). Second, the individual should be actually parallel to the group, not opposing it and, yes, as explained before, there is a difference. If the individual is truly living in a parallel state, then their domain of operation and focus is completely separate to that of the group. The individual may run through the same physical locations, the same intellectual conversations, whatever, but they never, ever, confuse their domain of focus with the group, the Herd, or 'this'. They will flat out ignore – not out of ignorance, but out of knowledge, perspective, and direct experience – any attempt to convince them otherwise. And a great way to obliterate such an attempt is to thoroughly understand and live the philosophy presented in this book, armed to the teeth and ready to unleash fury when Dolly shows up. And the perfect way to do that is to always have 'other than this' with respect to any *version* of 'this' on hand and knowing exactly how, when, and in what form to employ it. I will tell you right now that if this is all you have then you will survive (even if it is not pretty) almost any attack by Dolly and the post-totalitarian system.

Now, let us look at what happens when the characteristics of a parallel structure have their group component taken away. Or put another way, what happens when one applies the essences of parallel structures to fighting Evil.

First, in the original conceptualization, there is the constant monitoring and fighting for civic rights and freedoms which, generally speaking, means what individuals can do, in groups... I.e., out in public. E.g., one can watch certain movies, read certain books, travel freely, etc. With the group taken away, this would translate into constant monitoring and fighting for one's individual thoughts, perspectives, and sovereignty over one's own consciousness, which the post-totalitarian system can never touch if one does not let it and one employs all of the weaponry outlined in this book.

> "Now what we have to understand is that this comes from an extremely clever and skilful program, that has manipulated us into ways of thinking that may be contrary to our own interests, but beneficial to the interests of the powers that be... Beneficial to the interests of those who control our lives, and tax us until we have hardly a penny left to spend, take our money, and plough it into the creation of huge, armed bureaucracies, which exist to oppress us. We live in a society today where we may not make decisions; where we may not explore our own

consciousness. If I am not sovereign over my own consciousness, then I am sovereign over nothing..." – Graham Hancock, public interview

Again, this is not opposing! I cannot say it enough. One does not need to run away to the middle of nowhere and live off grass and bugs (or any tangentially related version of that) to run *parallel* to groups and society. In fact, the best way to practice this kind of parallel structure is to do the opposite – for 'ONE' to be fully immersed *in* 'this'............................ A hard pill to swallow, but again, how exactly does one expect to know anything, be anything, realize anything, or know one-Self by running away? I did not bring up Jung's idea of compensatory mirror imaging and Projection earlier just because I thought it was interesting.

Second, we have culture, art, and general creation that is not supported by the authorities. Without any kind of group, there is a 'culture', art, and creation that is not supported by any group. For example, one could write a 100,000-word book on some esoteric topic, fully expecting that there is a very good chance that every single group on earth would reject it! This does not mean that individuals would necessarily reject it. Personally, my favorite people on earth are those that strike me as complete space aliens who are so original that I could never hope to have any idea where their creations come from, and I am certainly not alone there. Indeed, if one examines the progression of quite literally anything in known history, including 'natural' history, one must wonder why they ever cared about the group at all?

Third, parallel education. Self-education is and always has been not only a defining feature of those who thrive but also one of the greatest weapons against the post-totalitarian system. It is, however, very difficult for a variety of reasons. We are all taught that the only way to learn is to be taught...i.e., some person standing in front of a group of people (of which the student is always a part) dumping irrelevant factory-worker-style information into their heads. Like all forms of institutionalization, the person that has been institutionalized either consciously or unconsciously believes that this is the only way to become educated and can feel extreme unease or even panic if they attempt to do otherwise. Additionally, there is no map or compass for self-education which can result in years (or even a lifetime) of confusion and/or hospitalization while trying to navigate all the information that exists. The individual alone is responsible for determining what paths they go down, whether they stay on some path or diverge, as well as whether or not to incorporate or reject what they find. It can also be a very dangerous activity indeed, which is something that sounds ridiculous to most people, hence, the very real danger and implications of self-education are not often considered. However, without significant self-education, it is impossible to ever be anything other than a Herd animal, and one's entire construction of reality, and every single aspect of it, would be completely based in the post-totalitarian system, i.e., 'this'.

Fourth, parallel information systems, which follows from the above. Without a group this translates into internal parallel information systems, which can be a tricky concept at first to figure out what that even means. As I explained earlier, people have personal construct systems based on values which are based on assumptions, and problems arise when a person's actions, values, and assumptions become misaligned. Since everyone is born into a schizophrenic world where this misalignment is not only the norm but embedded into various cultural practices and rituals, it is impossible to not be misaligned at first. Hence, one trick to get out of being tricked is to let various systems of values and assumptions co-exist alongside one another whilst attempting to align them and hopefully one day see them converge. However, one cannot do such a thing if one immediately buys into some specific line of (schizophrenic) thinking or another, since if one does then they immediately also buy into identity, group belonging, etc., and actively fight to maintain that line of thought as it ends up representing life itself (see Part 1). What I am trying to get at resembles the famous F. Scott Fitzgerald quote: "The test of a first-rate intelligence is the ability to hold two opposing ideas in mind at the same time and still retain the ability to function", which people often use but have no idea what it actually means or how difficult it really is. Internal parallel information systems are thoughts, concepts, etc., whose domain of focus is separate from the others, i.e., completely different lines of thought that *could* be opposing but one lets them all co-exist. This also does not mean that they are all correct, nor does it mean that any are incorrect. They just are, at least until one figures out what to do with them. In any case, given that any line of thought could have a drastic impact on an individual's reality, it could be said that living in this state of mind is the most powerful options generator available, where contradictions are allowed to exist but have no bearing whatsoever on one's overall psychological health and ability to thrive – quite the opposite – with the right foundations/ assumptions it can be the epitome of "agility".

Fifth, parallel economy. With groups taken out, this translates into the individual finding a way to participate in commerce or trade (in whatever form that comes) that they, and they alone, are in charge of. Again, this might not immediately be something that one can replace a job with; however, if the individual constantly maintains what little of this independence that they can, then the option to make their own thing into their full-time survival mechanism is at least always there (again, options). Contrary to popular belief, this is always easier when the individual does this in parallel to some other post-totalitarian form because the person has money/resources that they can use to funnel their own ventures, they are building up a network of people to draw upon or engage with in commerce or trade, and so on. Again, people often fall into the opposing-structure-trap here, choosing to do either one or the other, forgetting that one of the main tenants of parallel structures is that they are formed in such a way as to replace the authoritarian system (which can also be thought of as the group system) – to rise up out of the ashes when it cracks or fails. It should also be noted that for the last several hundred years the trend in supply chain is towards specialization, decentralization, and networking. What no one, other than myself it seems, has pointed out, is that through this trend and the trend in personalization in technology (never mind the reality of space migration and commerce) the obvious conclusion (via extrapolation and trends with nothing to suggest a change otherwise) is that eventually all competitive advantage will fall onto the shoulders of the individual, whatever that looks like. Those who are already thinking and living in this way will be well-positioned to 'rise up out of the ashes'.

Sixth, as mentioned already, parallel structures that are formed with the intent of replacing the ruling authoritarian regime. In this case that regime is the group itself. Enough said.

Finally, foreign policy as a means of stabilization, legitimation, and resources. In this case 'foreign' simply means other individuals networking in some way with other people doing all of the above in order to find stability, legitimation, and resources – i.e., collaboration with other parallel structure participating individuals. And since traditional ways of finding these other people have been more or less completely blocked, one must be extremely creative in this 'networking' (a problem I have been working on for years). However, one way that I see this occurring at the moment (and so far, still possible) is via a very specific type of *encoded conversation* that is taking place in all forms of media, where the idea is not to get a group going, but to get individuals thinking, reflecting, and acting. The reason that these alternative ways of 'working' with other people do actually work is that these people are actively communicating and discovering each other by simply broadcasting their innermost perspectives (usually following directly after some epiphanatic event that emerged out of extreme focus on the aims of life) rather than trying to get a message out to the masses or attempting to form a 'group', and the difference between these two things is vast even if the difference is subtle. This is why if one knows what they are looking for they can currently observe a very specific conversation going on right now in YouTube, movies, T.V. shows, and/or books, even though most of these people have never met each other, they rarely reference each other, and there is no way to explain to an onlooker what this conversation looks like (why it has yet to be forcefully stopped). Therefore, if one does not know what they are looking for then they will never see it, and once one knows what they are looking for they cannot unsee it… Timothy Leary said in *Info-Psychology* something along the lines of the best way to pick out the butterflies in a group of possible larval or post-larval people is to simply start speaking butterfly…

Again, a very true idea that still works; however, the Herd's intellectuals latched on to this whole language thing and they think that it means something totally different, but that is precisely why is it still works! Those dipshits are still and forever will be looking for 'how' to do it, when it is just simply *done*. Or if one of those dipshits manages to 'figure it out', that is precisely the moment that it will start materializing in a different way.

> "You try so hard but you don't understand ... Because something is happening here but you don't know what it is, do you, Mr. Jones?" – Bob Dylan

Through these encoded conversations what is NOT happening is people defining a language, telling each other what to do or how to do it, or anything remotely close. What is happening, and it has been happening for at least 150 years now (or 2000, or 6000, or...), is that individuals are simply letting other individuals know that 'it' is happening – that 'it' is being done. And that is something that no Herd animal or the post-totalitarian system will ever be able to get around. And the more they attempt to stamp it out, the brighter the light shines. That being said, if the Herd had never attempted to stamp it out then there never would have been a light in the first place for those individuals lost at sea – nothing to find their way back home.

If you are thinking that I am simply describing the overall process of individuation in different words, you would be correct. On the other hand, if you are thinking that there is anything in this text that is telling you specifically how to do it, you would be sorely wrong. However, if one would like to keep trying to find the 'how' here then I will simply say, "keep it up! A fool who persists in his folly becomes wise". Indeed, we have been playing this game for a few thousand years now and we are only getting closer. And no one that is an actual participant in this conversation is claiming that we need to do anything further to get there – that is not the point of the conversation. The point of the conversation is to remind those out 'on the edge' that everything will actually work out; to simply say, "Keep it up! Because you already know that you could not do or be anything else". As I have already said, this is a very particular psychology for a very particular kind of person, and it is only this kind of person that I have any interest in providing a particular kind of 'help'. And I think if this kind of person seriously considers this idea, then they will find that there is a very specific philosophical and psychological lineage that has always been there carrying the torch. These people were not looking for fame or fortune – they wrote (or said) what they did to first and foremost help themselves, then they published it to help you. And, again, they did not tell you how to do something, they were just letting 'you' know that it has been happening long before 'you' showed up and will likely keep happening long after 'you' are gone. And only those like you will ever know that it was ever happening *to begin with...*

Life as limbic resonance (aka when to say "Yes!")

"My thoughts are not my self, but exactly like the things of the world, alive and dead. ... Thoughts are natural events that you do not possess, and whose meaning you only imperfectly recognize" – Jung, *The Red Book*

If there were ever a single phenomenon in my professional, personal, academic, or otherwise life that I could point to as the culprit of everything that does not work, it would be top-down thinking. By contrast, everything that I could point to that does work would be the result of bottom-up thinking. Furthermore, it is irrelevant that either of these two things might occasionally result in the opposite effect – that is the rare exception rather than the rule.

"But I thought you said the things that led to working or not working were assumptions." Yes, Dolly, that is what I said, and here is yet another way of saying the exact same thing with different words. That is how phenomenology works. Furthermore, as always, your response has just given me an example of the exact point that I was trying to make! Rhetorical question of the day: what makes you think that there is only a single way of describing, explaining, outlining, whatever, any given phenomenon or thing? Why does one word, set of words, phrases, descriptions, whatever, have to be mutually exclusive to some other one or set of the same when referring to any given phenomenon? I will help you out, you think in this way because you are the champion of nothing other than 'this'. If one assumes nothing other than 'this', whatever the situation, then it is *impossible* to have a bottom-up situation where multiple things can refer to the same thing – one can *only* have a top-down situation – one can *only* have something that will never work, which materializes as a total contradiction. One example that comes to mind is your supposed 'democracy' (the *theoretical* epitome of a bottom-up socio-economic system) whose foundation has been replaced by nothing other than 'this' (the epitome of a top-down assumption). And that is why you and your kind will never make the link between the failed communist State and your soon to be failed 'democratic' State (talk about an oxymoron).

You think that just because you had some top-down definition or approach to all of 'this' that that in itself somehow took care of all the realities bubbling up from the bottom. And since everything you say or do comes from a top-down definition and way of being, you have already decided that whatever you have defined at the top (whatever it is – 'God', for example) is the way it is, it could or never will be anything else, and despite the hundreds or thousands of other possible ways of looking at the concept at the top, there will never be another way too look at that concept – there is nothing other than 'this'... It never occurred to you that the top-down concept was and never will be more than a long-running *placeholder*, did it?

It never occurred to you that truth is not a concept but rather a way of being, did it? It never occurred to you that what you and all of your intellectual heroes have ever really been doing is to just replace one top-down concept with another, where the basis for overthrowing the first top-down concept comes from the fact that it does not work on the 'ground', after which you and your intellectual heroes simply come up with another top-down concept to replace it because now you think that you suddenly got it right because *this* time is different, isn't it? All those other idiots since the beginning of humankind simply came up with the wrong top-down concept, didn't they? It would be an absolute impossibility that the concept at the 'top' was something that all philosophical commentary in history was trying to get at in its own way, would it not? Do you really think that there could not be a countless number of ways of describing and phenomenologically investigating something that could then end up with a countless number of words or phrases to slap on it as a label? Were you even paying attention to the fundamental premise of all that methodological drivel you kept spewing in your Ph.D. that allowed for you to criticize <insert popular scientific or philosophical approach> in the first place? I am somehow reminded of the phrase "existence precedes essence". And, no, you do not get to chant this over and over but then throw out the entire idea and have essence preceding existence when the concept or topic at hand suddenly inconveniences you and your socially constructed identity... Again, I believe we call that a core contradiction.

I can see the horror in your face, Dolly. It appears you are finally starting to really get it, even if it has not completely hit you yet.

Let me get a little less abstract. I know you are a fan of Camus, Sartre, etc., so let us consider this idea of socially constructed identity. And in the spirit of phenomenology, let us keep the idea of 'other than this' as the phenomenological background, particularly the specific ways that you and your comrades construe the idea of 'other than this' that we have been talking about all along. "...It's a trap. I don't want to do this. Leave me alone." Oh, I don't think so, Dolly, you are the one that keeps jumping back in, and you're damn right it is a trap. Anyway, as I was saying, let us consider a person who is stupidly chasing after a socially constructed identity, any identity, pick one: 'philosopher', 'businessperson', 'waiter' (you like that one, right?), whatever. Let us just pick waiter.

> "Let us consider this waiter in the cafe. His movement is quick and forward, a little too precise, a little too rapid. He comes toward the patrons with a step a little too quick. He bends forward a little too eagerly; his voice, his eyes express an interest a little too solicitous for the order of the customer." – Sartre, *Being and Nothingness*

"Please stop... I am begging you..."

> "Finally, there he returns, trying to imitate in his walk the inflexible stiffness of some kind of automaton while carrying his tray with the recklessness of a tight-rope walker by putting it in a perpetually unstable, perpetually broken equilibrium which he perpetually re-establishes by a light movement of the arm and hand. All his behavior seems to be a game. He applies himself to chaining his

movements as they were mechanisms, the one regulating the other; his gestures and even his voice seem to be mechanisms; he gives himself the quickness and pitiless rapidity of things. He is playing, he is amusing himself. But what is he playing? We need not watch long before we can explain it. He is playing at being a waiter in a cafe. There is nothing there to surprise us." (ibid)

"I am just trying to do my best... do you know no mercy? Please! I won't have anything left!!!"

"... This obligation is not different from that which is imposed on all tradesmen. Their condition is wholly one of *ceremony*. The public demands of them that they realize it as a ceremony; there is the dance of the *grocer*, of the..." (ibid, emphasis added)

"STOP IT, **NOW**!!!!!!!!!!!!!!!!!!!!!!"

Well, I can see that this is certainly getting your attention.

"Human reality is what it is not, and it is not what it is." (ibid)

"...............I can clearly see where you are going with this and I would really appreciate it if you do not ruin Sartre for me in the process". Good, because I do not really think the world needs yet another analysis of Sartre either since I think it is pretty clear given what I have been saying that... "I said stop. What do you want?" I want you to do what you never do, Dolly. I want you to look at a very specific something in a different way for a change. I want you to think about how ludicrous it is for someone to force their socially constructed identity onto reality, then consider the equally ridiculous phenomenon of the ego attempting to force its socially constructed reality onto the Self, which, from a Jungian point of view, would be the most non-pragmatic and doomed to failure approach in the realm of possibilities of human action. And then I want you to consider the possibility that what I have been attempting to get, at as well as what all of your heroes were attempting to get at, as well as what early Christians were trying to get at, is describing *the exact same thing...* I want you to consider that the philosophical greats might have been onto something but were also chasing an identity (or its photographic negative, which is the same thing), and were, therefore, also projecting. I want you to consider the possibility that *all* philosophical greats, regardless of time, location, or whether or not their philosophy ultimately ended up as organized or unorganized religion (and yes, ideology of *any* kind functions exactly as a religion, see Becker) were describing *the exact same thing...* Or that all philosophies started as something *true* even if the Herd does what it does best.

"[Dolly trembling] Look, I get it now... I see what you are saying, the whole 'this' and 'other than this' and how it ties into everything is finally starting to make sense. You have officially invalidated all of my core constructs. I hope you are happy." Yes, I am quite pleased with myself, actually. "I concede defeat, and if you have a shred of mercy or decency then I ask you to just put me out of my misery – just do it." Awesome, so then you really would become what you actually are: a sacrificial lamb! Oh, Dolly, what would I do without you? Ok, here we go, I will make this as quick and painless as possible.

1) The common thread of *all* progressive status-quo-breaking philosophies that have *ever* existed is that of a bottom-up approach to thinking, being, and existence in response to a top-down approach.

2) This pattern reoccurs because all top-down approaches are doomed to failure because they simply do not work (never mind yet why they do not work).

3) Top-down approaches reoccur in response to the responsibility that ultimately comes with the bottom-up philosophy that the Herd simply cannot live with in the long-run, and thus the philosophy gets twisted into its opposite over time and forms a new top-down approach.

4) This twisted opposite is what we end up calling religion, or in more recent times, politics (which ends up becoming ideology).

5) This means that whatever religion or politic one would like to pick on, the story was never meant to be anything resembling top-down... And yet that is precisely what it was turned into by the Herd (for now obvious reasons).

6) Thus, in each successive philosophy that aimed to overturn the previous one, the philosophy ended up progressively fighting the actual thing that it was simultaneously espousing; call 'the thing' being fought whatever you like. The seed of top-down thinking and being was actually always planted by the philosopher themselves, unconsciously, and brought into full bloom by their

followers. As such, it was just another version of something that will never work, so philosophers respond, which spawns something else that will never work, so then... you get the idea.

7) Hence, if one were to return to the raw material, or, better yet, the raw *experience*, of *any* of these philosophies (all religion started out as a philosophy...), something very, very specific would be *DISCOVERED*... And upon this discovery, one also discovers that the thing that is discovered and the way that it performs had, the whole time, been twisted into its opposite! I.e., one discovers that the thing that was seen as being necessarily top-down was always supposed to have been a bottom-up idea. Again, I don't care what the Herd or any other 'philosophical great' did with it...

And do you know what that thing that could be discovered could be called, Dolly? Do you not see now that there are literally a million ways to look at that thing, Dolly? Do you not see that all you have to do is reverse the way that that thing is looked at and suddenly the very thing that you and your compatriots are fighting against is actually the very thing that you have been fighting *for*? Do you not see how literally every single philosophy in the history of civilization has been talking about *the exact same thing*??? From Ancient Man to Christianity to Existentialism to Post-Modernism? The pattern is undeniable. Just because people keep using different *words and concepts* that, over time, lose any and all meaning (which you are more than familiar with), does not mean that they are not just repeating the same old pattern for thousands and thousands of years...

It never occurred to you that all you did was get caught up in the exact same phenomenon that led to everything that you are fighting against. You are fighting for a very specific something while simultaneously ensuring, through a very specific discourse and pattern, that that something will never see the light of day. All you are doing and ever have been doing is fighting your-Self. Your worst enemy was always you. You never experienced meaning beyond a certain age because YOU kept oppressing and suppressing it, and you did it all along because your fellow Herd members expected and demanded it from you, and you were all too happy to oblige so that you would have a way to belong because you never did. You were never quite able to work out your own essence (or any other) because you were always looking to others to tell you what to think, how to behave, and all the things you were and were not allowed to 'believe in' when it came to 'other than this'. You even dedicated your entire life to enforcing your socially constructed identity and all the ceremonies that came along with it onto others. You even came up with all kinds of ridiculous and baseless stories that you repeated over and over to make your points, knowing full well that they were baseless. "Who cares if the stories are real", you would repeat to your critics, "as long as it gets the point across." Except that the point was another top-down concept, and there is absolutely ZERO difference between yourself and the Church. In fact, the Church only wishes they could have the power and reach of your particular semantic systems.

What's that, Dolly? "[Gurgle, gasp, gurgle...] I... it's not possible... I don't believe it... [gurgle, gurgle...]" Yeah, well, all *I* was ever trying to do was get to the *truth*, what was it you were after? "[Gasp... gurgle...] I just wanted to belong!!! I just wanted not to be alone! I wanted to be *viewed* as important." What?! I thought individuals didn't exist? How can 'you' be 'alone'? And what about your precious equality? "*Me! Me! Me!* [gurgle...] I... ehhhhhhhhhhh............" That's it Dolly, bleed out. Let 'other than this' consume you. Hopefully your sacrifice will not be in vain.

I really cannot stress enough just how important this idea of top-down versus bottom-up is, and really, in some way, this is all yet another way of getting at what I have been trying to get at for the entirety of this book. One could ask, and rightfully so, why did I not just start with this idea. Well, as I said in the beginning about 'backing into things', had I started with this idea it would not have had any relevance or made any sense. Context is needed – lots of it. And one would probably do well to consider that against the background of everything else in existence or otherwise.

To get even less abstract and more concrete, let us return to everydayness for a moment when considering the idea of top-down versus bottom-up thinking and being. I can think of no better examples to help illustrate this than what can be found in the works of Claudio Ciborra, a very well-known (even if never taken seriously) Information Systems scholar. Ciborra was fond of tearing to shreds various ideas that set just beneath, behind, etc., the most popular tools and methodologies employed in the Information Systems discipline. One of my favorite ideas of his came through his research that revealed how when organizations introduce some structure or practice to reduce risk, all that ever happens is that they just expose themselves to some other (possibly worse) risk, which should sound familiar at this point. But I think the one thing that distinguished him from all other Information Systems academics was his constant criticism of "strategic alignment" within organizations, specifically how organizations were supposedly supposed to achieve it with "boxes and arrows" (referring to a specific top-down methodological figure in a paper but more generally top-down methodologies of any kind).

In all of the research that he had carried out, he noticed that the organizations that struggled (and therefore constantly needed consulting…) were those that attempted to force some model onto the people and practices within their organizations, while the organizations that were successful, particularly when referring to large-scale enterprise projects, were the ones where small, localized teams had a foggy 'goal' and then "hacked" and employed "bricolage" along the way to that goal. And, no, this is definitely not just about top-down versus bottom-up and politics and going along with either (which is what the average Information Systems cow thinks – "this is about democracy, right? Durrrrrr!!!!"); he also brought in many of the other implications regarding core business ideas such as competitive advantage.

Now, for those of you that are not in or are not studying business, competitive advantage is simply the thing, practice, whatever, that makes one organization or person able to out-compete others, and if an organization was ever able to compete long before it started thinking about such things then it would only make sense that this competitive advantage was already 'there' somewhere, right? And where exactly would this competitive advantage be? Well, it would lie with the business, right? But where exactly with the business? Well, obviously with the people and processes that were *already there*…, right? Where the hell else does one suppose that they come from? Anywhere else would seem ridiculous. And yet, at some point, a successful organization starts asking what can they 'do', and by 'do' they mean what concept, tool, method, etc., can they adopt, that makes other organizations successful, to increase their competitive advantage! Here we go again with the schizophrenic thinking. Furthermore, I always thought it very odd that so many organizations ever get to the point of thinking that something that is widely published and seen as 'the way things should be done' – i.e., something that has become a commodity – could ever lead to any kind of advantage... Really, how does one suppose that that works? Of course, it doesn't work, which is exactly why those organizations 'lose' their competitive advantage. It's really not rocket science. Oh, wait, rocket science, that just reminded me of something that is the epitome of competitive advantage (more on that shortly).

What Ciborra found when it came to organizations that *kept* their competitive advantage, was that methodologies, or anything else resembling a top-down structure, were simply placeholders, and that the large-scale projects that ended up being a strategic success were marked by a focus on localized problems and tackling those problems with hacking and bricolage on the way to some goal (which was also actually a placeholder, not *the* Goal). Hacking simply means getting in there and doing something, anything really, and seeing what actually works via trial and error. Bricolage (a word taken from the arts) is the idea that you do this with whatever is available to you at that time. And through this doing what needs to be done via experimentation with whatever one has to do it with, there are several consequences to this approach, not the least of which is innovation... *the* thing that all organizations are supposedly trying to promote. The problem with most organizations, however, is that they think that innovation gives them competitive advantage, when the reality is that innovation is a *result* of competitive advantage, which is a result of a bottom-up approach to problem solving and organization.

But do you know what is the real kicker here when these organizations focus on a bottom-up approach? The original articulated goal almost never resembles the final realized Goal. When the large-scale project is finally finished, almost everyone steps back and says, "Aha! *that* is what we were trying to do, of course!" Hardly anyone ever remembers that the organization started with some vague idea of a direction that they wanted to head in, they recruited people to head in this direction with them; if they were a startup, they were certainly utilizing hacking and bricolage since that is all a startup *can* do; and that at one or more points they "pivoted" because the former 'goal' was just a placeholder and the *real* Goal was *discovered*. The startup succeeded because the only way for a small entity to compete with much larger ones is doing things in this manner – the startup simply cannot survive otherwise. But at some point that startup turns into a 'real' business, and that business gets 'real' managers that look to 'real' 'best practices' to tell them what to do, riding on the wave of bottom-up success until so many top-down approaches start to sink in that the teams on the ground, much less the individuals, are completely ignored out of existence while the 'managers' try everything in their power to get those teams and individuals to comply with whatever top-down practice *du jour* is on at the time, and then everyone runs around frantic trying to figure out why whatever their golf buddy who works at the University of Such and Such suggested to them is not working.

So, why do either of these situations occur? When in startup mode, the organization *must* do the right thing if it is to survive, even if that thing is very, very, very stressful and full of uncertainty about how it is going to actually pan out. However, as we have already made very clear, these small teams would likely never do anything remotely resembling what works if it were not for the fact that their existence is incredibly difficult. And existence that is incredibly difficult is exactly what is taken away from the leadership and management once the organization becomes successful enough that its survival is more or less given (sound familiar?). Thus, at that point, there is no motivation whatsoever for the leadership and management to do anything other than attempt to cling on to whatever stability they have – if the low-level workers suffer, "oh well, fuck 'em!" If the business goes under, "oh well, I got my mansion and Ferrari!" Except for in the rare instances where the leadership and management never had any intention of making things less difficult – instances where the Goal is something that is always emerging – instances where something is set as a placeholder and everyone is set with the task of figuring out at the lowest level how they are going to get there.

The most salient and contemporary example I can think of that embodies this difference can be found in the difference between NASA and SpaceX. NASA is a government organization and is, therefore, the epitome of top-down, while SpaceX is the epitome of bottom-up, and there is almost no one that will disagree with this as well as the fact that SpaceX did in only a few years what NASA could only ever dream of, and now NASA hires SpaceX for its missions. In this working relationship, one NASA employee commented in an interview that the thing that struck him most about SpaceX was how, in contrast to NASA, teams at SpaceX did not sit around and talk about what should be built or wait for someone to tell them what to do, they simply started building things, testing them, and repeat (much like Apple in the early days). Such an approach immediately either works or it does not based on reality, and in the process those people become far better experts of the inner workings of rocketry because they have seen first-hand what works, but more importantly what does not work (some literature defines "expert" as someone who has made all possible *mistakes*), which also serves to increase their competitive advantage since they are farther along the learning curve than their competitors. SpaceX is also a very individualistic and 'flat' organization, versus NASA is a very bureaucratic and hierarchical organization. SpaceX is primarily bottom-up, NASA primarily top-down.

We can go even further with the differences, and this last point is the most concrete and where I was ultimately trying to end up: where in these two organizations is the focus of daily life? At NASA, policies are set by the government and trickle down, which means that most if not all workers are, in fact, coming in to work every day to make sure that they are focused on and have followed the correct procedure or *ritual*, not the "aims of life". That's not really a secret – in large bureaucracies if one starts talking about focusing on anything resembling the aims of life then they would probably be reprimanded or be given a very stern speech on 'responsibility' and 'teamwork' at the very least. On the other hand, organizations like SpaceX *generate* and constantly re-configure policy as it emerges from bottom-up, direct experience – experience that is the result of small teams being handed a piece of the puzzle and told to solve the problem by any means necessary, and nobody cares what has or has not been done before, how it gets done, or exactly who needs to talk to whom in the organization in the process.

And here we have, albeit in a very corporate way, come full circle to Havel and his notion of living within the truth and the aims of life. Remember the aims of life and Havel's story of Š? The person that only had one desire in their professional life: to make the best beer so that people could enjoy it. And what exactly does this beer taste like, what is the specific procedure for brewing it, and so on, when the brewer is in the process of making the beer its best? The brewer has absolutely no idea until they *discover* it! THEN they exclaim, "AHA! THAT was it all along! That was the Goal!"

I will put it bluntly. Competence does not lead to the aims of life, the aims of life lead to competence, and anyone who espouses the former is signaling and revealing loud and clear their complete and total *in*competence since anyone who espouses the latter knows the truth. The Goal is not enforced, it is discovered. The Goal is discovered through the aims of life, not the other way around.

And just go ahead and ask two different people about their lived experiences where one follows a top-down approach to things and the other follows a bottom-up approach. Pay attention to how they tell their stories and the emotions that are conveyed as they are doing so, not just the words that are coming out of their mouths. No matter what the ultimate outcome, the people who follow top-down approaches will recount tales of planning, execution, ordering, duty, "getting through it", and so on, and will generally seem rather non-animated, indifferent, or downright irritated. On the other hand, those that follow bottom-up approaches are always much more animated and alive, and will recount tales of experimentation, discovery, risk, uncertainty, and "jumping off of a cliff and building a plane on the way down". The former prides themselves on dodging problems, the latter on tackling them. The former either tells others what to do or is told what to do, depending on their position. The latter takes personal responsibility for the problem at hand and is always both looking for, and generating, options. The former will incorporate only what maintains the current power structure, whereas the latter always has various competing parallel structures that are always waiting to "take over" the moment that the current power structure cracks or fails. Hint: there are probably direct links to the definition of Good and Evil in there.

A top-down organization will always be in a constant state of contradiction, whereas a bottom-up organization will never be contradictory because there is nothing to contradict!

Re-read that sentence as many times as is necessary for it to sink in. Perhaps even review Part 1 and Part 2. And does one suppose that what applies in the organizational world somehow stops being applicable everywhere else?

One could just as easily equate the bottom-up approach with pragmatism, and, as far as I am concerned, there is no difference. Nietzsche saw it, Jung saw it, Havel saw it, Ciborra saw it, and I have been seeing it all my life. One could also say that the real question is: why is this is the case? I.e., why do bottom-up approaches work as opposed to top-down? Which is a good start. However, I think the better/deeper but now rhetorical question, still, is why do people vehemently fight entire paradigms whose central aim is that which actually works in reality versus what is supposed to work in theory ("wishful thinking")? Again, we just come right back around to the fact that if one were to actually start buying into what works then that would come with a whole host of other possibilities that one would have to confront that would stand to invalidate one or more superordinate personal and/or societal identity constructs. It is almost as though people are purposely doing things that do not work and putting themselves through that misery just to avoid having the actual truth of their existence revealed to them and therefore also having real responsibility revealed to them. And that is precisely what these people are: miserable, and it is obvious to everyone around that they are indeed miserable, the most obvious of which are those who embody the essence of top-down thinking most, the poster children for which are academics. Seriously, have you ever met a more miserable and/or inept group of people in your life? "I love my job." Bullshit. You are not kidding anyone but yourself and possibly your new Ph.D. students.

Which finally brings me to the idea and title of this chapter, the notion of "limbic resonance", as well as knowing when to finally say "Yes!" to 'this'.

I first heard the phrase "limbic resonance" in Elon Musk's first interview with Joe Rogan, and it was brought up by Musk when the two started getting into a discussion about Artificial Intelligence, brain-to-computer interfaces, etc., and where all of that could possibly be headed (recall from earlier the idea of convergence). Although the idea is far from new in the intellectual realm, Musk brought up the possibility of a sort of higher-level brain that could be and/or is being formed via the technology that humans are helping to bring into being, and that whatever form this intelligence took would, by the nature of what it was, be built upon the lower-level brains in exactly the same way as our human higher-level parts of the brain are built upon our lower-level limbic and reptilian brains. And since this discussion of AI almost always ends up going into the territory of risk and threat, what Musk was trying to illustrate was that just because we might be creating a higher form of intelligence does not necessarily mean that it would be some kind of threat. He asked Rogan how many of us would be willing to give up our limbic brains, which was a very powerful way to illustrate his overall point because it is obviously a rhetorical question – almost no one would get rid of their limbic brains since that is where the actual spice of life comes from. Indeed, one could argue that without the limbic brain there actually would be no reason to continue the game... One might get rid of a lot of the more harassing aspects of existence but then there would basically be no point to exist! Interesting, no? As with everything else, you think that this idea stops being applicable outside of this particular example?

Another popular phenomenological description of this idea can be seen in the original TEDx talk by Simon Sinek, which is the talk that led to his rise to fame. In that talk, named "Start with why" or "How great leaders inspire action", depending on the source, Sinek explained how the businesses that succeed and really last communicate directly with the limbic part of the brain (the emotional center) that deals with "why", not with the outer neocortex part of the brain (the rational center) that deals with "what". It might also be helpful to note here before the below quote that Simon Sinek is treated by academics in nearly the same anathematic way as Kurzweil, Jung, Leary, and so on...

> "None of what I'm telling you is my opinion. It's all grounded in the tenets of biology. Not psychology, biology. If you look at a cross-section of the human brain, from the

top down, the human brain is actually broken into three major components that correlate perfectly with the golden circle. Our newest brain, our homo sapien brain, our neocortex, corresponds with the "what" level. The neocortex is responsible for all of our rational and analytical thought and language. The middle two sections make up our limbic brains, and our limbic brains are responsible for all of our feelings, like trust and loyalty. It's also responsible for all human behavior, all decision-making, *and it has no capacity for **language***. In other words, when we communicate from the outside in, yes, people can understand vast amounts of complicated information like features and benefits and facts and figures. It just doesn't drive behavior... When we can communicate from the inside out, we're talking directly to the part of the brain that controls behavior, and then we allow people to rationalize it with the tangible things we say and do. This is where gut decisions come from. Sometimes you can give somebody all the facts and figures, and they say, "I know what all the facts and details say, but it just doesn't *feel* right." Why would we use that verb, it doesn't "feel" right? Because the part of the brain that controls decision-making doesn't control language. The best we can muster up is, "I don't know. It just doesn't feel right." "– Simon Sinek, TEDx

Although be careful here, this is where some of Dolly's colleagues might jump in and use this example as a case for North American behavioralism, which is just as stupid and ill-thought-out as rationalism, neither of which have considered the third option pointed out in this book or Jung's works. The point that I wish to draw from, whether it be Sinek or Musk, is that these two very pragmatic and capable types understand that the real heart of what matters lies in something *behind* or *underneath* what we normally consider to be what is doing the mattering. Furthermore, people tend to simply throw out the most important point of Sinek's entire talk:

"Now let me give you a successful example of the law of diffusion of innovation. In the summer of 1963, 250,000 people showed up on the Mall in Washington to hear Dr. King speak. They sent out no invitations, and there was no website to check the date. How do you do that? Well, Dr. King wasn't the only man in America who was a great orator. He wasn't the only man in America who suffered in a pre-civil rights America. In fact, some of his ideas were bad. But he had a gift. He didn't go around telling people what needed to change in America. He went around and told people what he *believed*. "I *believe*, I *believe*, I *believe*," he told people. And people who believed what he believed took his cause, and they made it their own, and they told people. And some of those people created structures to get the word out to even more people. And lo and behold, 250,000 people showed up on the right day at the right time to hear him speak. How many of them showed up for him? *Zero*. They showed up for themselves. It's what *they* believed about America that got them to travel in a bus for eight hours to stand in the sun in Washington in the middle of August. It's what *they* believed, and it wasn't about black versus white: 25% of the audience was white. Dr. King believed that there are two types of laws in this world: those that are made by a higher authority and those that are made by men. And not until all the laws that are made by men are consistent with the laws made by the higher authority will we live in a just world. It just so happened that the Civil Rights Movement was the perfect thing to help him bring his cause to life. We followed, not for him, but for ourselves. By the way, he gave the "I have a dream" speech, not the "I have a plan" speech…"

To add to the fact that everyone throws out Sinek's most important point, almost no one (including Sinek himself), because of our nothing-other-than-this society, will process the contradiction around the point that he is making around the idea of belief. Sinek stresses that any "what" is nothing more than a rationalization – a concept, and then turns around and says that the 'thing' that motivated people is "*what*" they believed! Once again, someone like Sinek does not work with language for a living (and it is not hard to see why not based on his observations and statements) and has not had to stand up to the extreme scrutiny of the intellectual world, so I am not blasting him for it. I simply mean to point out that in *his* very well thought out logic around beliefs, it is not possible for someone to believe in a "what" – to believe in a concept. Indeed, since the 'thing' that he is trying to get around lies in the area of the brain that has no capacity for language, why would he or anyone else suppose that any of this can be directly dealt with via language? Is not the "what" here, when asking about beliefs, by Sinek's own logic, just another rationalization for something else? Is it not possible that the people in his example were indeed and literally being moved and then rationalizing it with the cause? Again, maybe this is what Sinek actually meant to get across, but again what does the Herd actually take away from it? And again, I can point to Alan Watts who said that all he was ever trying to do was to say what cannot be said.

And this is precisely why phenomenology is the only way that any of this will ever come across as anything coherent. Phenomenology is the only way that one can make the Self intelligible in any way, and everything else that is conceptually based or focused has already, or immediately will, set up the entire idea to be a total failure.

Going back to Musk's interview, he more or less said that limbic resonance was really all that was needed when in any situation where an impossible 'decision' needed to be made, and I could not agree more. It is so, very, obvious when something "just makes sense" or "just feels right" and when it completely does not, the problem is that all of humanity has been culturally conditioned for centuries to second guess what makes obvious sense and defer to rationality, language, and concepts simply because 'this' type of 'thinking' better serves those in power (and I could write a 30-volume set outlining examples of this throughout history). I mean, we would not want everyone out there doing whatever they felt was right, willy-nilly, now would we? We have all kinds of post-totalitarian structures to uphold and enforce. If everyone suddenly started doing things based on limbic resonance then those in power would be made inept, redundant, and useless overnight.................

And again, one has to be careful here. I, Musk, or Sinek are NOT saying that this idea of limbic resonance equates to doing what "feels good" – we are saying that it equates to doing what feels *right* or, better yet, what feels Good; there is a universe of difference, and that is why the term "resonance" is so important here. This is also why there are so many emerging new-age groups beginning to form around the idea of resonance. I am not so sure that Musk, Sinek, or especially these new-age groups are aware of what exactly they are getting at, but they are all certainly getting at *something*, kind of like the aforementioned conversations currently taking place on the web particularly in video form. It all seems to be related and intermeshed, which, again, is not all that surprising if looked at from a particular perspective with a particular assumption.

The final idea that I would like to incorporate into this topic of limbic resonance, which also feeds nicely into the following chapter on Projection, is that of the Goal. Here, we can also look to the business world and/or its literature. About a decade before Sinek popularized the idea of starting with "why", Collins and Porras had popularized the idea of the Big Hairy Audacious Goal (BHAG) through their study on companies that were "built to last" (the two are more or less describing the same overall process). The idea of the BHAG was a goal that was so big, hairy, and audacious that it could be considered next to impossible, but still possible, and therefore carried a very exciting "why" along with all the meaning that would be experienced along the way. Again, we can look to Musk, SpaceX, and the idea of colonizing Mars. Collins and Porras basically posited that the best companies had these BHAGs, and what made those companies the best was that a particular form of leadership was taking place that got people excited, made them have no problem working hard, and everyone always knows what needs to be done at any given time due to the BHAG – when in doubt about a course of action, defer to the BHAG, easy.

Again, look at SpaceX and the absolutely insane things that they have accomplished, combined with the enthusiasm that oozes out of everything that they do, and NO ONE is pretending for a moment that any of what they do is easy or "feels good" even if it feels Good. Furthermore, only the most jaded, miserable, and life-negating of academics or intellectuals would pretend that the average SpaceX employee does not feel as though they are living a pretty meaningful life and experiencing limbic resonance, especially when the first reusable rocket landed back on earth (and if one has been following anything I have outlined previously, it should be no mystery as to why). Furthermore, as I outlined before, Musk, regardless of which of his companies we are talking about, has absolutely no problem with individuals generating and experimenting with a sea of options on the way to the Goal.

Now, here is where we start to bring everything together. If one listens to interviews with Elon Musk, he started out just wanting to be involved with the internet, space, and sustainability, The End. Only after years of hacking away in that direction did the Goal emerge – he said it himself. And does it not seem as though there are many other ways that this has been gotten at over the last 150 years? Nietzsche on becoming what one is; Jung on individuation; Peterson on phrases such as "when you wish upon a star" and the zig-zagging reality that accompanies the long hard slog toward that 'wish'. I will say it again, Goals are not set, they are discovered. And when *the* Goal is discovered, would it not make sense that a certain level of numinosity would be experienced? And if things were always signaling that Goal along the way, would it not make sense that synchronicity would follow? In any of these cases, would it not make sense to experience an overwhelming feeling of meaning? Well, for those who actually pay attention anyway... This also starts to give way to what I am really trying to get at here regarding bottom-up versus top-down and the nature of the two, as well as the phenomenon of Projection.

Consider the idea that people have in their heads that they are out there setting goals, and according to the discourse that surrounds Sinek or Collins and Porras all one needs to do to be successful is to set a BHAG and then clearly articulate "why" to everyone who will listen. Well, the problem with that is that there are millions of failed attempts at this process and millions more to come. Again, if there was a 'how-to manual' for success that could be verified then everyone would simply do it. However, as one can easily observe, plenty of people (often narcissists) who followed all the steps in this process still failed miserably because, well, reality. And this is often where linear types will step in and say, "of course that was unrealistic". Yeah, well, maybe it sounded unrealistic, but do any of these linear types actually know what they are saying when they say such things? What *exactly* makes something realistic or unrealistic? What *exactly* does that mean? They will often fire back with some linear analysis backed up with 'data', but, once again, if there was a best practice backed by data that actually worked then everyone would be following it! Which is what people have been trying to do for centuries and it never holds. Even if it 'worked' once or a handful of times, all that is happening is a *description* of a *snapshot* of something at a particular point in time (something I could never get any academic to understand). Nothing has *ever* held up the idea that one could create *more of it…* Remember that creativity follows something close to a Pareto distribution where 99% of creative works can be traced to about 1% of the population, and this just keeps on holding.

Peterson once famously said, referring to Jung, that "people do not have ideas – ideas have people". Jung often said that the Self was the source of everything, and that our job was to incorporate aspects of the unconscious into consciousness. Combined with synchronicity, he was basically trying to paint a picture of how 'this' works and how things literally come to matter (and if one does not listen then often times they will simply become Anima/Animus possessed as the Self's way of forcing it). And as any phenomenologist knows, there is a fair bit that can be said about how things come into being due to where attention is directed. If there were to be a mechanism to direct attention, I can think of no better one than felt meaning/limbic resonance, and I can think of no better method to accomplish this than immersion/direct experience, which is simply the result of living Havel's "aims of life" and "living within the truth". We also have ideas from Alan Watts and eastern philosophy around "getting out of one's own way".

And, again, this idea of emergence over time has been going on for billions of years. There was a blank void and things emerge from *something* – from *somewhere*, and it just keeps happening.

I will stop beating around the bush. The "bottom" in bottom-up *is* 'other than this'. Literally everything we have, and are, is and always has been a bottom-up process. Why in the holy hell would one think that this has been occurring for the entire known history of the Universe and in the last few thousand years or so the nature of it all has suddenly turned into a process of top-down? Again, with the magical human being who somehow, for nothing that has ever been articulated, can somehow force 'their' will down on the entire process of the cosmos that they somehow stopped being at some point and blah blah blah, yadda yadda yadda, I've already covered it.

Thus, limbic resonance is the feeling one gets when their attention is properly attuned to what is coming *through* them and *observing* that, where the *way* in which it is observed and the assumptions behind it manifest reality, which is then reflected back at the individual and their value systems, which leads to synchronicity and limbic resonance if all of that is aligned properly. And this is why the Goal is discovered through simply living the aims of life, not the other way around, and it is also precisely why the only thing that ever worked or will work in the grand scheme is living the aims of life, or, in the words of Jung, "I think if you think along the lines of nature, then you think properly." Understand?

Because I know that the first question one would have when I or Havel speak about the aims of life (because I had the same question when I first encountered his work) is: what are these aims of life? And one is presumably asking so that they can live them. Well, that is precisely what Alan Watts and others were trying to get at is that you are (or were) already doing it!... A problem only arises when one second-guesses it all. And you already know all of this! You might have even said it before. You used to have no problem with any of this, remember? Chances are if you stop and think about it for a second you should be quite upset that it was taken from you, and for good reason. It was only when you started forming your socially constructed identity at about the age of 25 that you started doing anything any differently, i.e., not living the aims of life, *and you know it*... If someone would have told you everything that I am saying right now, before that age, you could have cared less; it would barely even have been processed. "Hey, did you know that you are a bridge between the Self and the ego, and the Self is something on par with what all these people have been talking about for thousands of years around 'God', except that 'God' is a projection that occurs in 'this'." You would have responded, "Hey! Sounds good dude! Although, I don't really care! I have a life to go live." You and everything you were, actually, got sold... *and you know it*... and THAT is why you cannot stand anything that reminds you of it...

LIMBIC RESONANCE === TRUTH === WHEN TO SAY "YES!!!"

No one can give specific examples of the aims of life or what 'causes' limbic resonance since it is all completely individual-specific, *always*. For one person this might be making the best beer that they can, for another it is making the best book that they can, and in either case it is the 'best' according to *them*; in either case it is following their parallel structures. And that is precisely why if one loses their parallel structures then the complete and total loss of the person themselves soon follows. Worded differently, the moment one moves into top-down thinking and being, the loss of the person themselves soon follows. And as we have seen, this holds at the societal level as well.

And there is no better historical example of the swapping of bottom-up thinking for top-down thinking than that of Christianity, Islam, or any of the other major religions, which started out as the epitome of bottom-up only to end up as the epitome of top-down authoritarianism, and we know fully well by now why this happens and why people want it. People say that they want the truth, however, the moment that they get it all they can think about is finding some way to get away from it, or even better coming up with some 'objective' idea of truth while simultaneously espousing individualism! Indeed, if only 'Christians' would have preserved the bottom-up approach then they and Nietzsche would have been best friends.

All of this adds up to one thing: without individuals there can be no bottom-up, and without bottom-up there can be nothing that works. Hence, anything that is predicated on stamping out the individual and thereby limbic resonance is doomed to failure, and anything that results in the opposite of limbic resonance is a signal, sign, hint, red-flag, whatever, that this non-pragmatism is happening. Conversely, top-down thinking and being simply does not allow for the individual, which guarantees *eventual* failure. This is the ultimate fatalistic flaw in a large part of the history of existentialism. Did you never stop and think about how it was possible that postmodernism was born out of existentialism? As in it was the same lineage? And why there is such as schizophrenia going on in the modern intellectual realm that consists of telling people to be individuals, be themselves, etc., and simultaneously enforces one particular form of ethics and what is acceptable to say, do, or be? Well, now you know. Top-down thinking, The End. Thus, the very people who were famous for individualism were often times its greatest enemies. It is a hard pill to swallow when one finds out that their intellectual heroes are often unconsciously projecting harder than anyone else, and that they are often the worst offenders of their own philosophy. And this explains why they are *always* MISERABLE! "The burden of truth" my ass. Sorry, but the truth is anything but a burden, and the more of a burden one feels, the further away from it that one is (that is how Projection works), although one can always find their way back to it by continuing as hard as one can right off a cliff... If one is lucky anyway.

Thus, I find that the best way to always keep life-as-limbic-resonance salient is to remember it not as a nailed-down concept, but simply as bottom-up thinking and being that will always require a certain level of improvisation and 'surfing'. Life as limbic resonance results in the Goal being discovered, not set, and it is a way of literally realizing and materializing the Self, which I will just go ahead and say is the actual answer to the question of the purpose or meaning of life, and anyone who states otherwise is simply signaling (just like an insecure twentysomething male in their supped up aftermarket shit-box car, or the same age female with $100k of plastic surgery) that they have never had a real experience a day in their lives or, what is more likely, that they got sold so hard and bad and are so deep in a state of unconscious projection that they cannot even remember what a real experience is (even if they constantly talk about it!), always forcing that top-down construct, whatever it is. Regardless of how one looks at it, you discover everything: your talents, your 'ideals', your 'relationships', your assumptions... And all of it requires returning to a state of **OPENNESS**...

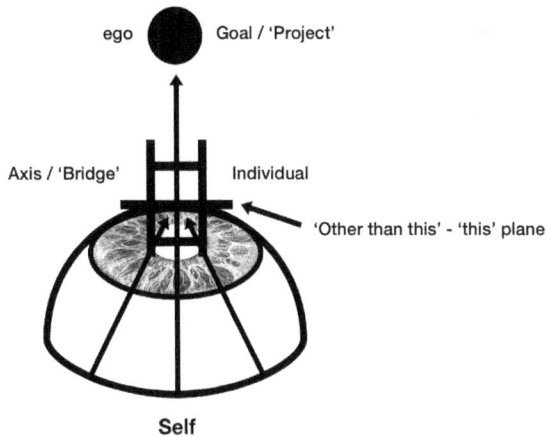

Figure 5 - Limbic resonance and responsibility schematic featuring bottom-up flow of materialization

Remember the direct experience and its value. Remember where the source of that experience actually comes from. Remember how you felt the last time you had one that resulted in numinosity and how undeniably *true* it was (before you got sold on the idea that it, and therefore the real you, was somehow the Lie). Remember when things "used to be so much simpler" and how the only thing that ever really changed was what you were paying attention to, not all "those other people". All I have done here, as in this book and everything leading up to this point, is to begin reminding you of something that "you already know perfectly well". You know it so well, in fact, that all of 'this' is nothing more than an illusion to get you to forget it, which is necessary, for a while. But at some point, if you do not come back, then the entire thing was for nothing. One cannot know what life as limbic resonance is until they know what it is not, i.e., life as limbic dissonance. And now that you know, it might be helpful to go one step further to make sure that you never forget. Although, for those who are paying close attention, we have done this twice already, but you know what they say, "third time is a charm", and I love providing people with options.

Harnessing the Projection

"If we deny the existence of the autonomous systems, imagining that we have got rid of them by a mere critique of the name, then the effect which they still continue to exert can no longer be understood, nor can they be assimilated to consciousness. They become an inexplicable source of disturbance which we finally assume must exist somewhere outside ourselves. The resultant projection creates a dangerous situation in that the disturbing effects are now attributed to a wicked will outside ourselves, which is naturally not to be found anywhere but with our neighbors *de l'autre cote de la riviere*. This leads to collective delusions, 'incidents', revolutions, war – in a word, to destructive mass psychosis" – Jung, *Alchemical Studies*

We have now arrived at the entire heart of the matter: Projection. The entirety of this book was aimed at phenomenologically arriving at this final perspectival point. And just like so many other things in this book that have been 'flipped on their head', Projection itself is not the problem, it is the solution – Projection _IS_ the Organizing Idea. One only enters the realm of functional, existential, or otherwise 'problems', mental illness, or other forms of misery, when one insists on enforcing top-down thinking and being, which is synonymous with enforcing nothing other than 'this', which is synonymous with any other form of delusion and the resulting individual or mass psychosis. I will even go so far as to say that the non-recognition of Projection is the non-recognition of reality itself as well as how reality actually works.

As usual, Herd psychologists only exacerbate the problem by telling people that they should stop projecting when they recognize Projection, when in fact the solution is and always has been to harness it, which requires a complete and total reversal of every major abstract idea that we have of human existence, which results in the invalidation of all societal core values since every last one of these values is *necessarily* top-down. Furthermore, this reversal into bottom-up thinking and being leaves one in a situation in which there is simply nothing in 'this' to contradict, effectively overcoming contradiction (the original problem with which this book started). Again, one only runs into problems with all of that if they assume nothing other than 'this' and/or that there *should* be a conceptual value system in 'this' that *can* be contradicted – something that George Kelly never considered: the possibility that all psychosis and malfunction ultimately comes down to there being any kind of top-down system *to begin with*.

The simple reversal of viewing things from what works into its opposite, which is identical to saying a reversal of reality (bottom-up) into anti-reality (top-down), which has been a theme throughout this book, is the absolute root explanation of the current actual mass psychosis that we see before us today. However, 'psychosis', as Herd psychologists use it, is nothing more than a projection of this societal-wide phenomenon onto convenient scapegoats – "It's not me, it's *them!...*" – which is extremely ironic because these Herd psychologists never considered that everything that they were witnessing was a *message*... The very thing that they had been looking for, and the reason that they had gravitated toward psychology in the first place, was right in front of their face, and, like a good little Herd animal, this message and the responsibility that came with it was twisted into its opposite and projected onto those who cannot defend themselves as *their* responsibility, as is customary in a post-totalitarian world of nothing other than 'this'. Since the most important thing in this situation was the message, they then look to anyone else who reports hearing or seeing the same message (but are too freaked out to properly process or articulate it) and tell them that they are delusional if they think that anything like a message is present – only schizophrenics receive messages from 'things' or 'unrelated' events; therefore, if one believes there is a message, then they have a clinically categorized disease and that's that. Literally the only difference here between what results in schizophrenia and being a prophet is whether one looks at what is happing from the top-down or bottom-up, respectively.

I started by diving into a grounded, observable problem: everyone seems to be contradicting themselves – people are doing the exact opposite of everything that they claim to believe in (which tends, in this day and age, to all be rooted in the assumption that there is nothing other than 'this'). And, since it is likely that everything that they are *saying* is the simple reversal of reality, well, it should be no surprise that they would actually be *doing* the opposite (i.e., reality), would it?! Once again, as I pointed out in Part 1 and Part 2, no matter how many layers of this problem are peeled back it always seems as if people are protecting themselves against a far more horrific and terrifying realization than something as simple as identity or value invalidation or even any other highly debated concept like 'God' and whether one is or is not this concept (however that would work). The realization is simply this idea of a bottom-up versus a top-down reality, which invalidates *all* concepts as 'true'…

I then explained how throughout history people have entered into a certain type of misery by denying some form of reality or another, after which they and their culture are inevitably and ultimately obliterated. Due to this, some person or another steps up and speaks the actual truth of Good and Evil, to which many people happily hop on board out of sheer relief. However, the responsibility side of this at some point sinks in, and, for one reason or another – perhaps because the actual problem and solution were never clearly articulated – they forget about what works and attempt, once again, to keep out reality by coming up with some new cleverly crafted top-down concept to replace the lived reality of their bottom-up revolution and to assume all responsibility that came with it, after which they are once again in a state of unconscious projection and the cycle repeats itself all over again and again and again.

And is it not a bit too much of a coincidence that many of the world's major religions (consider Buddhism against the above point) all seem to be getting at something that almost nobody takes seriously and yet remains the core of the religion, and that this has been going on for the entire history of our species? What else would explain this? What, people just keep doing it because it is fun? Or could it be that the same process that has been driving the history of the Universe is still happening, will continue to happen, and humans with their supposed magical nature are just doing a whole lot of sophisticated squawking? Just because there is an argument for actuation, individuation, and even decision, this in no way shape or form *necessitates* top-down *anything*, and this single idea is something that even our most 'intelligent' and level-headed simply cannot seem to get through their thick skulls. If they did, then they would actually become what they are rather than talking about it until the end of time (unless their defensive systems fail and they go insane).

I then outlined some of the most popular semantics and conversations that have served as nothing but a distraction in order to keep people so busy with 'this' that they would increasingly never question it and would also increasingly put up with more and more misery before they crack – i.e., they have more and more opportunities to unconsciously project onto external objects and people, in the form of concepts, the very thing that they should be paying attention to, i.e., their-Self. Almost nobody wants to confront any of this, and so we end up with people willingly asking for and enforcing the post-totalitarian system and its assumption of nothing other than 'this' simply because people want certainty and an easy existence, and, in our post-totalitarian world, this only comes in the form of a top-down concept or system that alleviates the individual not only of all responsibility but also their having to deal with any form of reality – they can simply live a lie from birth to grave.

However, as I have attempted to explain, nothing about living this lie makes any sense whatsoever with respect to reality, so some people get fed up and are more or less forced into individuality as a means of reality fighting for itself. This mismatch between reality and top-down thinking is the source of every argument between those who buy into the top-down fad of the time and those that see it as completely at odds with reality, and this is because no human being seems to be able to function without certainty in some form, they simply have no idea of what it is that they should be certain about. Therefore, based on a saner model of how things work from pragmatic observations of several thousand years of what works and what does not, I provided a definition of Good and Evil with exemplars so that people have something certain to go by (not a concept, but a general way of life that seems to be in harmony with nature). I explained that if one follows this way of life, which is to say following the way of nature, as well as who and what they actually are, then that means almost certain and total ostracization and alienation (in every imaginable way), and the way out of this is, first of all, not being afraid to go it alone, then focusing like a lazer on one's parallel structures. "The way out" is simply a perspective on how reality works. The pay-off is the alleviation of a life-long, socially induced "chronic muscular tension" (see Watts). However, I have also alluded to the fact that this perspective is just as powerful as the perspective that was gotten when the first monkey grabbed a bone, started breaking things with it, and had an epiphany that led to the first human beings. Hence, this perspective will be met by the Herd with the same hostility and real-life threat that is completely warranted by any species that is under threat of total invalidation or annihilation. Just because one is aware of some transition in which they might be a part of, and therefore also aware of exactly what should or should not be done, does not mean that they will not be killed or imprisoned in the process, since this is often the rule rather than the exception.

This combined with the very real suffocating power of the post-totalitarian system, along with the inability to directly fight it, led to the discussion of parallel structures, where parallel structures are basically any individual activity that focuses on the actual aims of an individual's life, removes the "bridge of excuses between the system and the individual", and whose domain of operation is outside that of the approval of the post-totalitarian system, whose purpose is to "rise out of the ashes" and take over the moment that part or all of the post-totalitarian system cracks or fails. I then discussed how the focus on parallel structures and the aims of life, because of their necessarily individual nature, leads one to consider the idea of limbic resonance since it would be the only way to discern what these aims of life actually are and what parallel structures could or should come out of them.

I then explained that the only effective way of viewing limbic resonance is by viewing it as a bottom-up phenomenon, and that the reason that it is effective is because, well, it is the only thing that can be observed over a long period as actually effective... because that is how reality appears to work. Anything else is, therefore, quite simply an *illusion*. Although, there is nothing to say that an illusion cannot be highly useful, so long as it is recognized *as* an illusion. The idea of not setting, but discovering, a Goal (fighting Evil, when to say "Yes!", parallel structures, etc.) via options is how one ends up overcoming contradiction because then 'values' are nothing but options! Again, the difference in a value or an option is simply a matter of viewing reality as top-down or bottom-up, however, the result of this simple shift in perspective means everything. And, finally, I pointed out that if anyone were to return to an age somewhere before that of their 25th birthday or so that they would have absolutely no problem with this idea at all! In fact, they would *assume* it!

That leads us to one of the most contentious topics that I can think of: "becoming something". One's 25th birthday is precisely the cutoff date, so to speak, where everyone on top-down Earth has an opinion on this matter. As with everything else, everyone seems to be looking at this through a top-down lens, and, on top of that, nobody ever considers other highly relevant phenomena that we already know about such as the observer effect, which is something else I, as well as Nietzsche and Jung, have been alluding to all along. I.e., "How One Becomes What One Is". Not only is Projection showing you what needs to be done, it is providing you with options around how to realize it in the literal meaning of that word. Not only is Projection showing you who and what you are, it is also showing you how reality itself works. More importantly, Projection is yet another pointer in sea of pointers that is signaling the existence of *something* 'other than this', an idea that gets around the "give us one miracle and we'll explain the rest" logic flaw of existence. No matter how sophisticated the argument, there is not a single argument for nothing other than 'this' that has ever not relied on this miracle (I'm looking at you Bloom – your rule had to come from *somewhere*). And yet, what I am saying does not rely on a miracle at all! (Apparently, 'other than this' is not testable but a miracle... is???) It does, however, rely on a bottom-up perspective, which can roughly be translated into: "YOU DON'T KNOW...", something that the *Herd* has *never* been able to accept, regardless of epoch, topic, or whatever.

Therefore, from the beginning up to this point, I have provided a theory of existence – a theory about how all of this actually works

– as well as a schematic of the dynamics of existence that explain why a theory of this type must necessarily be fought in order to be knowable at all. Neither the theory nor the person who understands it would be possible without the opposite of either.

No matter what the topic at hand, there will always be "two types of people". A problem only arises when those who understand attempt to dominate through force or coercion because NOTHING will EVER function in the long-run if it is top-down, understand? And just because something is bottom-up does not mean that whatever it is has some kind of privileged status in terms of being correct, workable, or realistic *just because* it is bottom-up – this 'something' is always a concept, and therefore is nothing more than a placeholder. This can be clearly seen in the idea of democracy, where it is obvious that *something* is indeed trying to be communicated (the value of bottom-up versus top-down), however, the actual lesson is ignored and, instead, projected onto a socio-economic system, i.e., a concept. As if the Herd has any fucking clue as to what is 'best' or how to properly handle things in any given situation. Democracies only work in the *beginning* because the beginning of any democratic system has *always* consisted of people who were both smart and brave enough to break out of the system that they were in, which is simply not the case anymore once a society is established and the Herd is allowed to breed again, obviously. Then, what is forced from the top-down is the concept of democracy itself! Proponents of either democratic or monarchical systems always point at the times when their favorite system succeeded and conveniently throw out when it did not, when the reality is that both have failed 100% of the time throughout history, fact, because they are all ultimately top-down systems on a timeline of more than a few decades. And every top-down system fails because it fails to recognize the nature of Projection and that Projection applies to *everything*, including one's own death..............

All of this leads the alluded-to-just-now person having the perspective, and thereby weaponry, to consciously harness and steer the Projection rather than letting it continue to unconsciously run every aspect of their being or, worse yet, fighting it. Still confused? Let us go through this step by step and outline the process of harnessing the Projection.

Step 1: Become fully immersed in the Projection

This is arguably the easiest of all steps because the only thing that is required is to be born. However, this necessitates a complete and utter lack of awareness of anything, anywhere, regardless of anything else that one may or may not buy into. To say that someone is 'merely' born, or to say "of course, pffft!" is missing the point – it *is* a *requirement* – do not forget the various philosophical and/or political points and counter-points that let to us talking about all of this in the first place.

At some point one is floating around in a certain type of universe where there is apparently nothing other than 'this' (just after a similar situation before 'one' got in 'this' situation), one gets their nutrition and environment from somewhere (who cares where, right? Must be a miracle.), then they begin forming organs and body parts and finally they start using those body parts by kicking and moving around until they can barely stand it anymore. And for what? Stupid fetus! Don't you know that there is nothing other than 'this'? What started out as a nice womb ends up becoming a

360

suffocating prison in which one's movements are completely and totally restricted, and so then one makes what could be considered the ultimate decision – in the literal usage of that term – in that situation, which is to cut themselves totally off from 'this'. In this decision was it the fetus or was it the environment? Again, don't fall for it, nobody, ever, in the history of biology or obstetrics, has shown anything other than the *necessitation* of *both*. Don't split something and then pretend it wasn't you that did the splitting! Oh wait, yes, do those things at first when you become fully immersed otherwise you could not be fully immersed…

So, in an instant, one is literally transported from one reality to another, where the definition of reality in this situation has not a *single shred of difference* to the definition that the Herd gives to reality once you cross over into the new 'this', which is to say: if you cannot validate it with the senses, it does not exist, and this is the lesson that you will be taught for the rest of your life, even though just seconds ago that definition of reality did not hold and would have been a complete and total contradiction. But hey, these giant things walking around in this new place seem to know how things are done here and they say they have it all figured out, and just because you thought that 'that' was the only 'this' and now there is a new 'this' but supposedly it is the only 'this', you are the one who is wrong and confused because you just don't know anything about 'this', so let's just go with whatever they say for now and completely forget what just happened (something you will make a habit of). 'This' is all there is now. On a positive note, you will be the most important thing around, for a while.

Step 2: Learn that you are not it

After you fully immerse yourself in 'this', all you have to do is scream really loudly or try a variety of tricks, and that should get you mostly whatever you want. You are not 'conscious' at this point, so you will have no idea why you are doing what you are doing. The big things walking around will eventually tell you that you are doing this because of a combination of 'instinct' and DNA. At some point these big things get really tired of you screaming, yelling, and manipulating them, at which point they will shout something that resembles: "you aren't the center of the Universe, you stupid little shit!" At this point you will become very confused because everything that these big things have done since day 1 would have suggested otherwise. Now, they are suddenly angry at you for just going along with the reality that they constructed for you. "You were too young to be *able* to do anything on your own", they will tell you, and, as it turns out, they were correct. You were too possessed and unconscious of your personal projections to have any say-so about anything, and this entire process considered as a projection, even at this early stage, holds, regardless of whatever baseless story you end up buying into regarding why. In other words, there is something, coming from somewhere, that drives all of your behavior, and you could care less what or why because there is nothing other than... "HEY!!! What did I say? You little know-nothing. You are not the center of the Universe; you are nothing more than a child."

Whether these notions are true or not makes no difference because what ultimately happens is that these big things will not allow you to keep making unlimited demands on them, so they assign you a social role and if they do not like what you are doing then they reserve the right to walk away. And what you ultimately realize is the same thing as when your mother was teaching you the difference between a ball and an apple. What you realize is that while you were told that there is nothing other than 'this', there actually was – they are called other people, inanimate objects, etc. "YOU are not IT, WE are IT => 'THIS' is IT. And how dare you for not knowing what we know." You will naturally see this, as every other child does, as completely ridiculous. However, at the same time you will experience a certain kind of embarrassment and shame. But don't worry, you will easily forget this moment of your life and the accompanying contradiction just like every other important moment up to now, just like every other child, even though you are perfectly conscious enough to remember it, just like every other child. You will not, however, be able to stop the very thing that started it all in the first place (Projection). You will be taught that that 'thing' is basically the source of all Evil and should be silenced. And you will learn to replace it with whatever we tell you to. If you ask "why" too many times and we cannot or will not answer you, you will be met by anger. You will learn that asking "why" beyond one or two levels deep is supposedly the stupidest thing one can do in 'this'. Why? Because we have the answer to everything, except that we obviously do not, so stop being so annoying you useless thing.

Step 3: Become indoctrinated into the world of schizophrenic thinking

Just about the time that you start to realize what is really meant by 'this', so to do these other people that look and sound approximately like you, and, as it turns out, you are now placed in a big group of them so that you can all start learning about 'this' and how it works. These much larger people called "teachers" are also hanging around, ready to enforce what is right and wrong, including what 'this' 'is' and 'is not', what you are allowed to do and not do in your waking hours, what language you can or cannot use, and so on. Again, if you dare to question why you will simply be punished. And not only will you be punished, we will do it in a way as to maximize embarrassment. See, we know that since your parents are not around all of the time anymore that you have taken to this whole social acceptance thing as a way to soothe yourself. Therefore, if you break a rule, we will send you into the hallway where no one exists to make you feel ostracized, or perhaps we will stick a giant dumb-looking hat on your head and make you sit in a corner with your face in it. You have to learn something:

> "We have these rules so that we can have a functioning society, ok?! If something, anything, leads to a more dysfunctional society, then that is an utterly selfish thing to do! Have you gotten that through your thick skull or do you need to sit in the corner some more?"

Thus, a powerful lesson is learned: Anything that leads to a dysfunctional society is bad...

This is your first moment of being a 'real' human being – your first encounter with Projection proper as well as irony, even though you do not realize that right now. Although, don't worry, you will soon forget about this important moment just like every other important moment in your life.

For the time being, however, you and all of your newly made friends and acquaintances take the first step in being future members of society: you start enforcing the standards on each other in order to not "get in trouble". The answer to any "why" is simply "because we say so". But, again, this is because you actually are incapable of doing anything 'higher-level'.

Some time passes and you now find yourself being taught things that are far more complex than drawing or playing nice with others. There are weird symbols being thrown at you, rules around how you speak and write, and so on. At about this same time, the teachers seem to be hinting at things you will one day do in "the real world". Uh oh, it turns out that your view of 'this' is somehow wrong again and that there is something 'other than this' and they call it "the real world". And in this "real world" there are a couple of fundamental things that are required to be successful: you need to be able to "think for yourself" and "question everything". And with these fundamental requirements to be successful there is a single message: "anything is possible and you can be whatever you want to be". So, you then think to yourself, "hey, I really would like to be a part of this society!", and so you reach really far down and deep and say to one of these teachers:

> "Is this school thing really the best way for us to learn and have a functioning society? How are teachers picked? Who makes these rules? Why are mommy and daddy not allowed to play with other mommies and daddies? If doing things that make a society dysfunctional is selfish and against the rules then why are there so many bad things happening, especially by those that make and enforce the rules? Why is showing your private parts bad? I don't think that it should be – why is that different than hands or eyes? I also don't understand why certain words are bad

and nobody can explain to me why, so I think that I will make up my own mind and just use them on occasion. If anything is possible then I would like to grow up to be the first person to escape the Universe! It sounds like those people in those buildings with crosses or domes with spikes have some ideas on that, although I think maybe those particular ideas don't really make a lot of sense, but then again I think in some way that they do – maybe I'll come up with my own way of looking at it and write a book about it one day. Or maybe I will grow up to be someone who changes the way that everything in society is done to be better – maybe I could be a teacher, like you! Maybe I could teach people how to think for themselves and question everything! I'm so excited I can barely stand it!!!"

"GET THE FUCK OUT OF MY CLASSROOM RIGHT NOW, YOU SMART ASS LITTLE SHIT!!!"

"But I, I don't under..."

"GO TO THE PRINCIPLE'S OFFICE, RIGHT NOW!!!!!!!!!! Just wait until I get a hold of your parents, you little smart ass. Who the fuck do you think you are? Oh, I got something for you, just wait. You have to be here every, single, day. Oh, we'll see. We'll just see..."

Regardless of what is actually going on here, you will, again, learn a very important lesson: that you need a balance between 'this' and 'other than this', so that is exactly what you do, but in a very particular way... However, this is also exactly the same time that you will learn to act just like an adult, which is to say that you take a fundamental truth and apply it to a completely inappropriate object or situation, i.e., unconscious Projection. Since you are not yet aware of the many layers still left to peel back in the "real world", what you have effectively also just been taught is to silence your-Self – to silence a very specific type of 'other than this'. Although it is true that you do need a balance between 'this' and 'other than this', the adults don't know anything more (really) than you do, other than how to, sort of, do things in this "real world" – I mean, they get you food and shelter and all that, right? And that was supposed to be the aim of this 'functioning society' and the definition of success that hinges on… Oh, you look very, very confused – I'm sorry, that is because "you are just too young to understand". And thus, the seeds for lifelong psychological projection and contradiction are planted with a nice socially sanctioned role model to follow. You eventually give in and project all that perfectly reasonable sense you *were* making as something Evil, outside of yourself, onto someone or something else, in order to make yourself feel better and signal that you are indeed a 'functioning' member of society. Welcome.

Step 4: Become extremely skeptical of 'this'

As the years go by you get really good at this whole 'functioning society' thing and being a part of it, i.e., being a 'good' member of society. You develop your language abilities so that you can dig deeper into the rules, get clarification on certain aspects of the rules, and thereby also understand what exactly makes a 'bad' member of society. This, of course, will be completely dependent on where you are geographically! That is correct – there are different rules that define what makes a good and bad member of society, depending on where one is located in the society, however, the rules apply to *all* of society, apparently. Your parents might make you go to church so that you can listen to all the reasons 'your' religion is good and all the others are bad. Then you go with one of your friend's family to the other side of town to hear about why one of these other religions is good and why the one that your parents made you subscribe to is bad.

You learn more and more about the history of different countries and how hundreds of millions (that we know about) people have been killed throughout history so that some group or another could enforce its *rituals*.

There is also a rather, how should we say, interesting, game that the adults play with you as well during this time. They will invent all kinds of stories to get you to believe in along the way, along with inventing all sorts of even higher-level utter bullshit stories for why those stories continue to exist. Some of these in the West include Santa Claus, the Easter Bunny, the Tooth Fairy, and so on. Then one day, because you are not a total idiot, you start to question these things, especially since you hear conflicting information on these matters from other people your age. Perhaps you conduct an experiment where you let a tooth fall out on its own, do not tell your parents, and then stick it under your pillow to find out the next morning that the Tooth Fairy never came. You then ask your parents if anything else is real or was it all made up. "Oh, yes, sorry, Santa Claus, Easter Bunny, etc., yes, they are also all made up." And your parents may or may not tell you that this is a lesson in how 'this' works. To which you might respond, "ok, well, what about everything else?" To which the parents will look very surprised indeed. "What do you mean?", they say, "we are just talking about entities at holidays". "No", you say, "I mean *everything else.........*". To which they simply stare back at you, dumbfounded and speechless. In any other situation in life the person or group would be labeled as liars, forever. But don't worry, eventually you will forget this moment just like every other important moment in your life.

In the meantime, you are taught that certain drugs are absolutely horrible while the same person spewing this information is sucking down a Coke (which you then ask your science teacher about and it has the same chemical structure and effect on the brain as cocaine, after which the teacher recoils because they realize what they have just done), and in their non-working hours mixes this with whiskey or bourbon. In another class you are told about the affect alcohol has on society, and then you ask why it appears that alcohol seems to be doing the most damage but is also quite legal and abundant. You say that that makes absolutely no sense. The teacher rolls their eyes at you.

Therefore, what you have learned up to this point is that 1) the things that adults seem to get the most excited about and focus on are lies, and 2) there is absolutely *zero* consistency between *anything* that you were taught between now and when you were first taught that you are not IT.

As the unreal number of contradictions mount, you begin to see 'this' for exactly what it is: a giant pile of *RELATIVIZED* bullshit. After which all kinds of people will jump in to give their opinion on 'relativization', completely forgetting where, how, and why, *exactly*, this idea of 'relativization' started and was reinforced! Simultaneously, they will absolutely insist that this relativization only applies to such and such, but not '*this*' (whatever 'this' happens to be…). When it comes to 'this', you will do what you are told or what is expected or you can be ostracized or go to prison. And the real kicker: anything that *actually* could not be relativized, anything that has held for thousands of years (i.e., anything that is consistent), or anything that would in any way get everyone on the same page is precisely the most Evil thing one can subscribe to. Welcome to the "real world"!

Obviously, no sane individual can stand this level of contradiction, bullshit, and general insanity, therefore, you will do what 99.99% of all people at your age do: rebel, hard, and without concern. Indeed, why *would* you do anything else?

Step 6: Rebel

The first time that you really rebel everyone around you will make you feel like you are the most horrible human being to have ever walked the Earth (especially if you are doing it correctly). However, because you are now hip to this bullshit game you ask: "and I suppose that you were an angel at my age, no? That's what I thought…". You suddenly feel like you "know everything" *because you do* (everything that actually matters anyway). However, "there is a difference between knowing the Path and walking the Path", so don't worry, you will eventually forget this just like every other important moment in your life.

After you have initially shocked everyone by standing up for your-Self and proclaimed that you will explore whatever you want, however you want, especially if you are not hurting anyone, eventually people (including parents) start backing off. You begin to notice a pattern: the more rules you break, especially if you can be militant about it, the more people back off, up to a point anyway. And this is especially so if you decide to go to a university, where suddenly even the police start to back off! You have now found yourself in a world where you can do almost anything as long as you are not hurting anyone, and so you start really pushing the boundaries, during which you hear some older Herd members muttering "there is a time and a place", to which you do not pay any attention at all because you are actually living your life and there is a good chance you are completely "off your face".

It is during this time that you have all sorts of encounters with 'other than this'. If you are in America, psychedelics can be found at almost any time, parties will be thrown that would make Roman hedonists blush, and generally every social taboo that can be broken will be. At the same time, you best get your act together when it's called for or you can't graduate, and in some instances, this might mean just camping out at your respective building on campus because some projects mean working from 6am to midnight (I knew a guy in Industrial Arts who would leave on Monday morning and not come back until Friday night). So, in a sense, you are balancing hedonism and hard work; chaos and order. Although there are probably a hundred thousand variations of this, you will feel as though you really have found 'the secret', again, because you have... However, not everyone will make it this far. Many people will be casualties to all of this because, well, you can't actually pass your courses if all you do is drink and don't study; you can't do acid every day for 6 months and ever come back to 'this'; and, no, you cannot fly from the 20th story balcony of your hotel. Thus, you again learn something about having a balance between 'this' and 'other than this' if you want to keep playing the game.

And for those that do, this equates to a very specific kind of thriving that rarely exists in any other environment on Earth.

You feel good. Actually, for the first time in your life you feel confident. Somehow all of the contradiction and bullshit you had experienced in your life seems to make sense, as though it was all somehow necessary. You suddenly see everything as a unified whole. But don't worry, you will very soon forget this just like you will forget every other important moment in your life, because not long after that you will go out and preach what you have learned to anyone that will listen as well as anyone that will not, *demanding* that they see this answer and start replacing broken systems with ones that work. The problem, just like every fan of The Hitchhikers Guide to the Galaxy or every Ph.D. student ends up finding out, is that an answer is, quite literally, worthless to anyone or anything else if you do not have the right question. Thus, your ideas of how to replace the broken systems are worthless.

But, not to worry, you have university professors to help you come up with the 'right' question, except that you will only be allowed to ask certain questions. And do you know why?

> "We have these rules so that we can have a functioning society, ok?! If something, anything, leads to a more dysfunctional society, then that is an utterly selfish thing to do! Have you gotten that through your thick skull or do you need to repeat this course?"

I know, you did a fair amount of psychedelics, including DMT, so you will probably experience a certain sense of Déjà vu. But it is almost as if you might have heard this somewhere before... Wait! It was just about the time when you first...

"OK, congrats, you made it, thanks for the money and/or your indentured servitude, time to go to the real world!"

A deeply disturbing and sinking feeling hits you in the stomach. And for good reason.

Step 7: Experience the quarter-life Encounter

This is the time of your life when you will arguably be the stupidest you have ever been in your whole life, and this is when most people will get their first 'real' job. On one hand you will more or less have a perspective that probably actually is the answer to the world's problems, on the other hand you know so little about the details of those problems (especially *why* they are problems) that every time you present the answer to anything everyone just rolls their eyes because your answer is in fact just that stupid (or perhaps I should say "uninformed"). Why? Because there is something 'other than this'. Uh oh, here we go again.

As I have already pointed out earlier in the book, after working for a few years and proving that you can 'hack it', this is when all sorts of competing parties will step in and attempt to recruit you to their version of 'this'. You will, of course, be rather overwhelmed, and the entire thing will become the central focus of discussion between you, your friends, and everyone else in your life. Furthermore, you will be told by each party that everything you were taught up to that point was a lie and that it is time you now faced the "real world" – yes, that is correct, the "real world" we kept talking about before you graduated wasn't *actually* the "real world", 'this' is, silly child. It is time for you to "grow up". And by "grow up" what we mean is to choose a socially constructed identity. We do not really care which one. You can be "anything", such as a teacher, a solider, an activist, an artist, a drug dealer, or other sort of criminal, whatever, as long as there is a label for it then it is fine.

And just like 99.99% of people in the world (exceptions are extremely rare and likely *not* you), including the extremely talented, you will have no idea how to survive on your own and will at least briefly, if not extensively, panic about the possibility of having to do so. So, what do you do? You pick a socially constructed identity, because you more or less have to, and it will tell you exactly what to do, how to look, how to think, who to associate with, or any other question you have about life. And when you do finally choose, you will really not have the slightest clue as to why exactly you made the choice. It will be very fuzzy, not at all well thought out, but, over time, you will slowly convince yourself that it was well thought out and that it was all 'you' that made the choice, especially as you start to see the chaos of individual existence and the responsibility that would come with it slowly fade off into I-don't-care-that's-for-those-other-people-look-at-my-big-house-and-car-and-model-partner-and-social-circle land.

You will start to get so comfortable in your newly found 'identity', whatever it is, along with all of your newly found 'friends' and comrades, that you will begin fighting for it and enforcing whatever standards that these people tell you are important. And you will definitely act as though there is nothing other than 'this'. And, pretty soon, in order to improve your ranking in whatever hierarchy you became a part of (because make no mistake, anything with ranking is a hierarchy), you will become obsessed with the idea of power – as such, you might go to grad school!

I am pretty sure…yeah…I'm positive that something like this has happened before… I can see that you supposedly 'can't remember' at this point. You sure do look uncertain for someone who seems so certain.

SOLD!!!

Anyway, what you will inevitably end up doing, just like everyone else, is to start *saying* one thing about your identity and *doing* something else. It is almost as if you have a set of values and you are contradicting them. And it is always in the most fucked up of ways. The person that picked the identity of family person can't stop their affair with another person which involves all kinds of sadistic and weird sex things, yet they will be the first to accuse everyone on Earth who cheats as being complete scum. The person who chose to be a cop, judge, soldier, or any other enforcer of 'this' can't stop doing deviant things, yet they are happy to put all those "assholes" in jail who choose to deviate. A priest that chose celibacy can't stop fucking little boys, yet they are happy to tell entire congregations how they are going to Hell for doing far less. You might even… wait, we have been here before too, haven't we? It is almost as if we are back at the very first chapter of the book.

And you think that at this point you and everyone your age does not know the absolute and utter lie that you are all living? Look around. What do the faces on the train, bus, or in a car in traffic tell you? Why is it so different than what any form of traditional or social media tells you? Why does doing the 'right' thing always seem to result in a miserable and/or dysfunctional life?

Well, it is mostly irrelevant because what you are going to do is *not* to have some kind of introspective life-changing revelation in the face of this utterly nonsensical set of mounting contradictions. No. What you are going to do is to double down and then subconsciously project as hard as you possibly can. You are going to take the subconscious projection to a never-before-seen level. You are going to target all of those "other people" and take all of them down if it is the last thing you do, goddamnit! If all of those other people would just buy into 'your' identity then things would be fine!

Call it whatever you like, Anima/Animus possession, ego inflation, whatever, but you are now officially and totally possessed, and this behavior will define you for at least another decade or so, if not for the rest of your life.

In other words, you will hate the Projection with all of your might. And to reinforce this hate is the fact that, while you may indeed be miserable, this way of being provides you with more certainty than you have ever had in your life. So, the hell with anything or anyone else.

> "Here comes Santa Claus, here comes Santa Claus, right down Santa Claus Lane..."

Step 7: Recognize projection as Projection

As Jung and Heidegger both pointed out over and over, eventually this way of doing the 'right' thing – which is to say: living in the most unnatural, unreal, and contradictory of ways, stops working. What had initially provided you with a bit of balance and a way to thrive has now become the source of all of your problems. Suddenly, the more determined you become the more things seem to break down; the more you aim to "change the World" the more the World tries to change you. And is this at all surprising? When you first started this new way of being around the age of 25, a huge "win" would have been to simply get a decent job and be able to house, clothe, and feed yourself. Now, with all of your experience and climbing of hierarchies, to get a similar "win", you need to start changing how all of 'this' works. You will look around to others who *appear* to have done this and listen to their words:

> "When you grow up you tend to get told that the world is the way it is and your life is just to live your life inside the world. Try not to bash into the walls too much. Try to have a nice family life, have fun, save a little money. That's a very limited life. Life can be much broader once you discover one simple fact: Everything around you that you call life was made up by people that were no smarter than you. And you can change it, you can influence it... Once you learn that, you'll never be the same again." – Steve Jobs

Except that there are hundreds of thousands of people that do understand this, sacrifice their entire being toward a very sensible project, and nothing happens. In fact, the vast majority of people who go down this route end up in financial and relational ruin. But they are continuously told that it was simply because they did not work hard enough, they did not believe enough, they were not able to articulate their vision enough, or whatever, because remember, "anything is possible and you can be whatever you want to be – just look at <insert highly influential person here>".

Now, there are both truth and lies mixed in with these messages, but you do not know that yet. All that you are able to process at this point is that something is 'off' and nothing seems to be working in the same way as it once did. You naturally have no idea what to do since you are so far removed from... well, what word should I use here? ... anyway, you have no idea what to do... And in that exact moment of not having any idea what to do, "IT" strikes. This can manifest in all kinds of monstrous forms and but is *always tailored to the person*... Again, if the person sees themselves primarily as a "family person" their family might break down and/or dissolve, then, depending on even more individual-specific things, the reasons for this could be professional, sexual, or whatever, then depending on which one of those, and you get the point... The person could see themselves as an "entrepreneur", "businessperson", whatever; the pattern is always the same.

Regardless of how this materializes, there will always be a very specific point in the person's life where things stop working and there is a decision that needs to be made, one could even say THE Decision, which comes down to two options:

1) Get to the bottom of 'this', or
2) Run/submit

And this really is the worst kind of trap. As Jordan Peterson has rightfully pointed out, no matter what you do you are a sacrificial being – you simply cannot get away from it. If you choose to get to the bottom of 'this', whatever that might mean, you will experience such a profound sense of isolation and possibly psychosis that you might never come back. If you choose to run/submit, then you will sacrifice quite literally everything you are or ever could be and you will teach others to be just like you, where your message will always be "*this* is the real world, everyone else just needs to grow up" (that one never seems to stop working, does it?). In either case, it really and truly is a matter of "the ringing of the Division Bell had begun". There really are only two types of people. However, both, contrary to almost any belief, will experience 'the Fall' – it is simply a matter of which fall, something no philosopher (other than perhaps Jung, who is not considered a philosopher) would admit to. In either case, you will somehow find yourself again at the point of being a child! If you try to get to the bottom of things, you will encounter the World as a child; if you run/submit you will simply revert back to acting like a child. In the case of getting to the bottom of 'this', and this might be the most important point here, you will start anew by *simply wanting to do a good job*... Furthermore, the completely rhetorical question is: what do you think would be the assumption beginning to form and/or crystalize in either of these scenarios?

Your friends choose to run, projecting the archetypal idea of a messiah onto *something*. Some do it with Jesus, others with Mohammed, others with a concept, others with politics, job, government, or some social role. In any case, your friends project this idea onto anything and everything other than them-Selves – someone or something *else* in 'this' is the answer, not one's Self.

They buy into the idea that the only thing that will ever work is a top-down approach of *some* kind, because by the very nature of what they are doing (which can be extremely ironic in the case of religion) they are saying that they can only be saved by something *in* 'this' while simultaneously espousing that there is *nothing* other than 'this'. And so, they truly believe in nothing... How else would that work?

You choose to get to the bottom of 'this', which then inevitably leads to deconstruction even of those that deconstruct. You realize that probably almost everything that has been told you is a lie, and you cannot really trust your own thoughts on things because they have been tied up with these lies for several decades since you were a child. Now you need a way to get to the bottom of *something* because as it turns out you are now in a situation where you have no grounding anymore, and if you do not find something then you are basically fucked. So, you choose your particular form of "hitting the self-destruct button" and simply blow it all away (again, this can be fueled and manifest in many forms), because you know and can feel it in every fiber of your being that there is something 'other than this'.

In both cases, assumptions quite literally become everything, and:
"You become what you believe." – Oprah Winfrey

It then only takes a few years of functional psychosis for you to become so paralyzed with fear that all you *can* do is listen and watch since, once again, you have run into the problem of other systems but now there is nowhere left to go! Not only that, there is suddenly the sensation that you are being *pushed around*. Your ego then starts to learn something about *necessity* in all of this, and you begin to wonder what part of your being was ever truly you, which then might lead you to Jung, or Watts, or this book, or just the obvious realization that you have been contradicting your-Self for a very, very long time (although the details are foggy at this point). You realize you have absolutely no clue what the hell you mean by 'you' in the first place, but there is *something* (obviously) going on here.

After a few years of experiencing this and being completely lost, things suddenly start to work here and there. When they do, you attempt to seize 'it' (whatever it is) so that 'this' will stop, however, it always leads back to failure. After enough times of going through all of this you finally "give up", and scream out to the sky (who or what you're screaming at you still do not really know):

> "FINE, ASSHOLE! I have literally done every fucking thing I could to be a good person! And all you ever do is punish me! Well, I'm not playing anymore! You hear me?! I don't give a shit whether you kill me, destroy the world, or destroy the Universe itself and everyone and everything in it, YOU PIECE OF FUCKING SHIT!!! From now on, I am going to live the aims of life, MY own life, because there is literally nothing else that I *can* do!"

And you storm off feeling both terrified but also relieved for some reason. Then, after some time of *truly* giving up, suddenly things start working (I'm looking at you Watts). Like, *actually working*, and in a way that you cannot explain and most of the time do not really even understand why these particular things are working for you that previously you would have considered a signal of failure or life-disaster, you might have even written and spoken militant things about them.

You then step back and look at the totality of everything that happened up to this point. You see that the *entire* thing was Projection. You also see that you never, ever would have remotely gotten to something that works if you had not gone down the path, as hard as you could, of things that do *not* and *never would* work. If someone would have simply given you the answer (and they did, many times) it would have never meant anything until now (and it didn't) because you never asked the question: what the hell *IS* 'this'?! Which then somehow leads you to the answer of what 'you' are because you have just officially understood what Projection actually is.

In a flash, the entirety of your life and all that ever was or ever will be is somehow experienced and felt in the most numinous of moments – "complete and total knowledge", Jung called it. It suddenly dawns on you that not only has 'this thing' been telling you what to do the entire time (that's why you have ideas such as a messiah, or definitions of good leaders, or whatever), but that is precisely what you have *already been doing* the entire time! You realize that this thing has been the answer all along and all you had to do was to first acknowledge its existence and then ask what it is. You also realize that all of this has already happened; you have been here before. The problem you have now is: what are you supposed to do with this information? What do you do with Projection?

Step 8: Observe the Projection

Except that you kind of already know what to do: observe it. After all, that's what you have been doing all along, right? But this time feels different. It is almost as if you are aware that the *way* that you observe it has something to do with how it materializes...

This is absolutely the most difficult step. If you have made it this far you will be at a certain rock bottom or low point in your life. You are in a state of mind that is in-between unconsciously projecting and observing, where the latter is the goal. And make no mistake, this is where the real tests will happen, of which there is a single type: how much can you take and still maintain a state of observation and the ability to pay attention? Because make no mistake, this is the major league, and the things that will come at you at this point will be the epitome of _**your**_ worst fears. Your mission is to stare them down and not flinch, even if it kills you.

A great way of doing this, as it manifests in people, are encounters with narcissists. However, you now know beyond a shadow of a doubt (based on your direct experience) that there is no such 'thing' as a 'narcissist', there are simply varying degrees of being possessed. Someone who is highly possessed is also highly unconscious, and so, in the same way as the fact that for this person no other person exists, *'they' also do not exist*, yet *something* (obviously) comes through. Therefore, who or what do you think that you are actually talking to?!.............. If you look at it this way, because that is the way it actually is, then my guess is something very, very interesting will happen at this point if you have the nerve to stare them down and counter all of their attacks or points since you know exactly what they all are based on. But again, who or what exactly in this situation are you sparring with? The concept is worthless, but the realization via direct experience is priceless.

Furthermore, while we are on the topic of observation, the entire world, whether they love or hate Jung, seems to have forgotten the collaboration between Jung and Wolfgang Pauli, the latter being one of the founders of quantum physics. For the more astute Jungian scholars, it has never escaped them that there is a link between synchronicity and how reality actually works. We know that things materialize based on how they are observed, period, and no one has ever been able to explain, even remotely, how, or why this would be any different at our level, AND why this level is even here, in this particular way......... You see, it works both ways or it doesn't work at all, the point of this entire book....... I will repeat that, things behave and materialize in a certain way when they are observed or they do not. And this is why I went to all of the trouble of picking apart the idea of 'you' or 'not you' or whatever other irrelevant way you want to look at 'you' that one can come up with as well as simultaneously preaching about the importance and sanctity of the individual. The observed only comes into being when observed, and where that starts or where that ends is anyone's guess, and, is basically irrelevant. What is relevant is that:

1) There is only one answer that makes any sense as to why you are here and we have known it for 100 years: you are being observed. Black holes? Or any of the other thousands of ways one could look at it? It really does not have to be a judgmental man in the sky, so get the fuck over it and actually understand what an archetype is and

how that has nothing to do with people's stories about it, i.e., unconscious Projection.

2) Whatever ultimately ends up materializing in 'this' is all about expectations, period. In the lab a researcher conducts a quantum experiment and expects to see such and such when they apply such and such method, so that is exactly what happens, independently of other methods that measure or observe the exact same thing. Reality, therefore, is simply about the most popular 'method' or RITUAL.......... This is what I mean when I say that assumptions are quite literally *everything* because they ARE, and this is backed by science.

3) The Mother/Father – Child archetype, as such, and as the oldest one in all of history, is irrefutable. The only time it supposedly breaks down is when children try to pretend that their parents do not exist.

And remember, every single thing you have been through in your life up to this point has been the same repeating pattern, with Projection always right at the center of it all. You suddenly realize exactly how and why all of this talk about 'you' or 'not you', 'free will' or 'determinism', and any of the rest of that masturbatory drivel, really and truly is complete and utter nonsense. "You suddenly see through the sham of it all." At this point you know beyond a shadow of a doubt that there is something 'other than this', it is interconnected with 'this', and you start to form an idea of what Good and Evil actually are, as well as having any kind of clue as to what you mean when you say "deontology" or "ethics". And at this point, no one will sway you – you'd rather die than

EVER be sold again. You even have to completely revise your definition of being sold, and up to this point you never would have guessed. Projection *IS* the Organizing Idea. People *ARE* a contradiction (compensatory mirror image / what is going on outside is reflecting something going on inside and vice versa). The individual *IS* the Axis).

Step 9: Harness the Projection

Now that you understand the nature of reality, you also understand that the key to harnessing the Projection lies in bottom-up thinking and being. You understand the necessity of it all, not only what has happened to you and the sequence in which it happened, but the necessity of others and the same – i.e., the value of the Individual and the idea of the Individual in general, but also the value of 'other than this' and 'this' as well.

You start to consider this idea of what you expect to see, *where* that might be coming from, and linking that with synchronicity. You consider something like injuring yourself in a fit of rage where you unconsciously did something that resulted in the injury. If you did NOT become injured in this fit of rage where you might have remembered slamming a concrete countertop with your hand as hard as you can, for example, or especially in more extreme cases (whatever that might be – psychedelics often can come into play here), then 'this' would simply *break down*... Do you understand? Because you would always be able to point at it if it started to be too nonsensical. What happens is what you expect to see because it *has* to be. And what you expect to see is, once again, completely, and totally dependent on assumptions.

It is also just about at this point that the idea of complementarity is no longer something that can be ignored. There is something about all of this that feeds perfectly into the entire idea, where the idea of complementarity is that there is a known schematic for how things work together (that many of the Herd insist on fighting). Light and dark; Man and Woman and what each other does for the other regarding the Anima and Animus when the people actually are complimentary, INTJ and ENFP, dudes and tools combined with women and babies, pick whatever you like; complementarity works because it is the basis for literally everything that exists or ever will. In other words, something can only exist in relation to something *else*... remember? Yes! You do!

This is where the idea of Projection begins to completely illude my ability to keep trying to explain it with words. And it is at this point that, just like a musician, you completely 'forget the notes' – you just *play* and let the music come *through* you. Suddenly, everything, all of it, comes back into view.

Step 10: Remember what you forgot

Now we're getting easier. Basically, all you have to do is remember your life, as it proceeded through these steps – it's that simple, "but the simplest things are often the most difficult". It is only now that you are *able* to remember, or re-member.

Furthermore, 'other than this' and the reality shift that came with it has happened so many times and was forgotten so many times, in the same life, that you suddenly realize that this could have indeed happened a trillion times before and possibly after.

You know perfectly well what Good and Evil are, you always did.

It then dawns on you what the "aims of life" actually are and just how blatantly obvious they always were – yes, it really was that simple. But, again, how else could you have been sure? And, what, you think that this idea only applies to 'this'? Of course not. There are probably plenty of other things you forgot out of necessity and plenty of other opportunities to re-member...

Step 11: Have 'children'

Remember, just because an archetype shows up in a form that we can recognize does not make that form equivalent to the archetype; however, the *effect* is always the same. Furthermore, the exact same hardships, struggles, uncertainty, and so on, apply. And just as with every other lie in 'this', there is no reason that you must choose to do one or the other, and you know perfectly well what I mean. As always, the answer is probably "both". Remember the perils of nothing other than 'this' at the expense of 'other than this', and the thriving that comes with the balance of both, no matter what 'this' or 'other than this' is. Got it?

Step 12: Live YOUR life and die

It is only at this point that you will have any clue as to what *your* life actually is or should be – the point where individuation stops being a concept and becomes lived being.

When we look at Jung's life, this was everything that came after the Red Book, for example. It was all the years he spent looking into the things that *he* cared about, such as alchemical texts, travelling the world including Africa in order to find ancient commonalities among cultures that had never met, and so on. It is no coincidence that so many people, particularly creatives, often say that "life begins at 40". I also once heard Elon Musk say something along the lines of the tutorial for life takes way too long, however, unlike him, I'm not sure that it can be any shorter, and even if it could be, is that really the answer? Would individuation have the sweetness and numinosity that it does without experiencing its opposite? It is highly unlikely.

When I look at my own life, I simply cannot deny that my ownmost potential would have never been reached if it was not for the utter schizophrenic nature of the Herd and everything else that comes with it; if I had no enemy, nothing to alienate me, nothing to fight, then I would be exactly that, nothing. Again, how else would it work? I would have no idea what my life is, who I am, or anything else, if had not had the opportunity to know what all of it is definitely not. And again, how can anyone know anything without direct experience? Direct experience with all of the limitations that would allow one to phenomenologically investigate something in a way that makes that particular something intelligible by backgrounding *everything else* – the only definition of "life" that will ever make sense to me.

If Projection was not there, the whole time, conscious or unconscious, none of this would have worked – at some points you would not have had what was necessary to do some of the more unpleasant things, for example, and therefore nothing would have ever materialized. You think any "birth" is pleasant? And why should it be?

And after many years of finally learning to harness the Projection and live your own individuated life, you look to the final chapter with open arms. You realize that this whole thing was simply practice for death. However, if there is anything that this book should have taught you, it is that you have absolutely no idea what death is. No matter what assumption you take, it will always be a black hole – a complete and total unknown – and none of this would have been possible if you did have any idea. In fact, the *way* that you die (and, no, I am *not* talking about *after* you are dead), might not be anything even *remotely* resembling what you think is going to happen – the *only* requirement is that 'this' is gone... Maybe it happens because of something external, but it is just now occurring to you that maybe it happens because of something internal – something bottom-up. Maybe you will only *achieve* death at the point that you dare to actually think, or assume, the impossible, and then assume complete and total responsibility for it.

The voice of God

Something in this life is not what it seems,
The only things that really make sense are in my dreams.

But when the dreams become real, I tremble and quake,
Because everyone that 'loves' me acts as if it is fake.

Sometimes the loneliness is too much to bear,
So I shut out the World and pretend not to care.

When I've been gone long enough, I feel overwhelming dread,
Everyone forgets me and proclaims that I am dead.

"Where is he now?", they continue to ask,
I'm right beside you, undercover, wearing a mask.

I hate you and you hate me,
At least on that point we can all agree.

All I ever wanted was to create something new,
All you ever wanted was what you already knew.
So I am leaving you behind to find peace of mind,

Maybe one of these days you'll be so inclined,
To pick up your sword and fight for what's real,
Instead of doing what you're told and fighting what you feel.

My heart felt too much for your way of life,
So I gave it all up for another kind of strife,
And when it all crumbled and there was nowhere to turn,
I found myself 'there', where I learned how to learn.

Fought for what I am, fought for what I am not,
And now, in death, maybe we'll both remember what we forgot.

ENANTIANDROMIA

The End?